PASTORAL LETTERS
of the United States Catholic Bishops

Hugh J. Nolan, Editor

VOLUME II
1941-1961

National Conference of Catholic Bishops
United States Catholic Conference

The bishops of the United States have provided religious and moral guidance and leadership to American Catholics since the establishment of the Church in the United States. *Pastoral Letters of the U.S. Catholic Bishops, 1792-1983*, published in a four-volume set, is a collection of statements issued by the Catholic hierarchy of the United States over the past two centuries. This publication was initiated by the Office of Publishing Services and is authorized for publication by the undersigned.

	Monsignor Daniel F. Hoye
October 25, 1983	General Secretary, NCCB/USCC

I am the good shepherd.
I know my sheep
and my sheep know me
in the same way that the Father knows me
and I know the Father;
for these sheep I will give my life.
I have other sheep
that do not belong to the fold.
I must lead them, too,
and they shall hear my voice.

John 10:14-16

Acknowledgements
The Office of Publishing Services, United States Catholic Conference, is deeply grateful to all those who assisted in the compilation and production of this volume of *Pastoral Letters of the United States Catholic Bishops*. Special thanks must be given to Rev. Hugh J. Nolan for his unstinting cooperation and editorial expertise and to Russell B. Shaw, Secretary of Public Affairs of the NCCB/USCC, who suggested this undertaking.

Contents

6

Appendix

Foreword

The volume opens as the clouds of war were gathering over the world, a world shortly to be torn apart in the devastation of World War II. Amid the tensions and threats of that period, the bishops addressed a theme attuned to the times. In their judgment Christianity was facing "the most serious crisis since the Church came out of the catacombs." This was the central theme of the Statement that bore the title *The Crisis of Christianity*.

Declaring that both Nazism and Communism were bent on world dominance, the bishops pointed out that neither system permits freedom in its true Christian sense. "Their dictators assume a power which belongs to God alone." After citing Pius XII's *Five Points for Peace*, the prelates pledged themselves and their people to the "adequate defense of our country" and asked prayers for unity and guidance.

After the United States entrance into World War II in December 1941, the bishops pledged to President Roosevelt personally their total support "for the common security in a world in which individual human rights shall be safeguarded and the will to live on the part of all nations great or small shall be respected." The following year in *Victory and Peace* the bishops reminded all that only the spirit of Christianity can sustain a real and lasting peace for all nations. They asked for moral safeguards for youth in the military service and for the protection of women in war work. Denouncing the persecution of the Jews especially under the Nazis, the bishops again stressed the importance of prayer.

One of the more remarkable documents to come out of this period was the *Essentials of a Good Peace* in 1943. Its tone is caught in the final sentence: "A first principle must be the recognition of the sovereignty of God and of the moral law in our national life and in the right ordering of a new world born of the sacrifices and hardships of war."

In their 1944 *International Order* Statement, the bishops sponsored without reservation the principles of the Atlantic Charter, stated that strong nations should help the weak, proclaimed the rights of man, and insisted on fitting authority for the world court.

As the war drew to a close, the concern of the bishops focused sharply on issues of peace. The 1945 Statement *Between War and Peace* proposed a peace program and lamented: "What is happening behind the blackout of eastern and southeastern Europe is a stark contradiction to the high ideals which inspired our fighting to save the world from totalitarian aggression." In this same document the bishops pleaded for mercy to the enemies.

The bishops in their 1946 Statement *Man and the Peace* expatiated further on the conflict between Russia and the West, denounced the ruthless herding of uprooted peoples, and further developed their teaching on the dignity of every human person. They were trying desperately to contain the ruthlessness of Russian leaders.

The two statements that followed addressed a common theme. In the 1947 *Statement on Secularism* they explained that such a philosophy of life limits itself to the human here and now to the exclusion of man's relationship to God here and hereafter. They developed the sad impact this has on the individual, blinding him to his responsibilities to God and to God's love for him. They noted how secularism has wrought havoc in the family and lamented that in no field of social activity has secularism done more harm than in education. After discussing its impact on the world of work, they mentioned its disastrous effects in the international community. To combat secularism they issued in 1948 *The Christian in Action* in which systematically they traced the helpful influence that religion is in the home, in education, and economic life. They also asserted that religion can make one a more responsible citizen.

Their next statement, *The Christian Family*, developed the teaching that the family is a divine institution with a need for permanence. Family life is essential to the state and religion is indispensable to the family. Continuing this trend of thought, in 1950 the bishops published *The Child: Citizen of Two Worlds* which taught that the child will find his completion only in life with God; and that that life must begin here upon earth. "The child must *know* God. There is a vast difference between *knowing about God* and *knowing God*." These bishops also taught the child to learn he is accountable to God for the use of his time and talents. Thus, the child will acquire not only a sense of responsibility, but a sense of mission as well.

God's Law: The Measure of Man's Conduct stressed the need for sound morality and that God's will is man's measure in the moral order. The statement touched upon morality in education, economics and politics, and taught that the moral standard applies universally. It concluded that to live morally a man must have God's help which he can find only in the faithful discharge of his religious duties. For their next statement the bishops developed the theme *Religion, Our Most Vital National Asset*. In it they insisted on the need of religion for man and for society and warned against the onslaught of secularism and irreligion. They concluded this Statement by declaring that denial of supernatural truth tends finally to the denial of all truth.

In their next four statements, *Persecution behind the Iron Curtain*, *Communist Persecution, Particularly in China*, and *Persecution in Poland* and *Peter's Chains*, the bishops denounced the rising religious persecution that raged from Korea to China and to Indochina from Russia to the Baltic lands, from Poland and Lithuania to Yugoslavia; from the Ukraine to Albania; from Czechoslovakia to Hungary, to Rumania and Bulgaria to the eastern parts of Austria and Germany. They begged in these statements for prayers for the Church in silence. At the autumn meeting of 1953, they published *Man's Dignity*, in which they traced the roots of man's dignity individually in society and economics, labor, and education, and explained that in all these areas man should enjoy liberty, an inviolable right.

For 1954 they published *Victory . . . Our Faith*, a strictly spiritual statement that warned all men against a growing materialistic outlook on life, proclaiming faith as a first essential of life and that to serve Christ is to reign. At that same meeting, the bishops felt compelled to issue *A Plea for Justice*, lamenting that the people of Vietnam and its neighbor nations have recently been added to the lengthening list of nations experiencing oppression.

In the November meeting of 1955, the bishops issued a *Statement on Private and Church-Related Schools in American Education*, which stressed that schools must teach freedom and offer a positive training to the pupils. They recalled that private schools produced the first leaders of the nation and while stressing the accomplishments of public schools they emphasized the right of parents to choose the schools they wished for their children. They taught that the private and church-related schools are part of the American system, and expressed the hope that there would be a cordial appreciation of what the private and church-related schools have done for America, and that they will be upheld so long as this is a nation of free men. Again in 1955 and 1956 the bishops returned in their statements *Religious Persecution and Prayer Plan* and also *Persecuted Peoples* to the denunciation of Communist oppression, and a renewed plea for prayer.

Between these two statements the bishops issued *Peace, Unity: The Hope of Mankind*; praised the heroic people of Hungary; and warned that the world is on the brink of disaster. In their conclusion, the prelates begged for a crusade of prayer. Again, the following November, 1957, the bishops returned to a denunciation of the persecution of the Hungarians, and called upon our people and all who love justice and hate iniquity to make December 29th a day of prayer. At the same 1957 meeting, the prelates took up two domestic issues, *Censorship*, out of a concern for the moral tone of the nation especially as it affects the well-being of children; and *Traffic Safety*, in which they stated that in far too many situations where death or injury occurs in automobile accidents, the driver is at fault. "On the basis of both justice and Christian love, we appeal to our fellow American citizens to join in a crusade to keep our highways safe."

In their November 1958 meeting, the bishops issued a *Statement on the Teaching Mission of the Catholic Church*, to clarify for all men of good will the objects embraced by this right of teaching and the nature of obedience which the Church demands of those who know that hearing her they hear Christ Himself. This was followed at the same meeting by *Discrimination and Christian Conscience*, which stated bluntly

the heart of the racial question is moral and religious. In this Statement the bishops rejected any form of segregation and begged for
equal economic and educational opportunities for all men. They urged
our leaders to act on this matter immediately.

At the 1959 meeting the bishops insisted in their *Freedom and Peace
Statement* that the choice "men and nations must make today is between
freedom and coercion." They outlined the foundations of peace and
cited the present serious obstacles to peace and freedom abroad and
at home. Ending on a positive note they pointed out to their readers
the road to peace and freedom. At that same meeting in *Explosion or
Backfire?*, the bishops exposed the propagandist campaign which promoted birth prevention programs and alleged that there was an
unmanageable population explosion. "In a chronic condition where
we have more people than food," the bishops argued, "the logical
answer would be not to decrease the number of people but to increase
the good supply which is almost unlimited in potential. ". . . and
they warned that the adoption of the morally objectionable means
advocated to forestall the so-called "population explosion" may backfire on the human race.

The 1959 *World Refugee Year and Migration* Statement explained
the Christian attitude toward this very serious problem by declaring
that migration is a right due in justice to the individual, and that it
is an absolute need for many refugees. The bishops then addressed
at length the manner in which the United States is involved and
encouraged the country's leaders to help these needy peoples. The
prelates noted that our sacrifices are relatively minor in comparison
to those of the great portion of the world's population that goes to
bed hungry each night, often with no roof over their heads.

In January of 1960 the bishops issued a strong *Protest against Bigotry*, citing first the rise of anti-Semitism in so many countries and
then went on to denounce religious and racial hatred of any type. In
1960 the bishops published *Personal Responsibility* which they felt was
declining very much in parents' failing to fulfill their responsibilities,
the increasing number of broken homes, and the rising delinquency
of youth—then considered our greatest national domestic problem.
They affirmed that religion fosters both individual responsibility and
social responsibility. They warned that before it is too late we must
revive in our midst and present to the world the ideals that have
been the real source of national greatness.

At the 1961 autumn meeting, they continued with this same theme,
in their *Statement on Unchanging Duty in a Changing World*. In their rejection of moral laxity they taught that many modern men find themselves without God and religion. Left to create their own moral values, these religionless people determine for themselves what is good
or evil, right or wrong according to their own convenience. The bish-

ops urged that morality be inculcated on all levels of education. They declared:

> As God-fearing people we must not only bear witness to those principles governing personal and family life; we must also give testimony to the reality and importance of those moral principles which govern man's wider social relationship. . . . Above all, the Christian today must have a profound sense of mission which will cause him to bear witness to his religious faith and his moral conviction as the early Christians did, by deed and affirmation, even by death. . . . Like Paul, we face a world largely paganized.

The bishops' statements issued over the years covered by this volume are wide-ranging in their themes. Responding to the signs of the times, the bishops have covered domestic as well as international topics. Some are truly prophetic in character. All are clearly pastoral. They express a continuing call to the Christian community to live out its faith-convictions in a society hostile to many of its values. The bishops' statements are a living expression of their desire to be "constantly teaching and never losing patience" (2 Tm 4:2).

John Cardinal Dearden
Former Archbishop of Detroit
May 1, 1984

Preface

This is the second volume of a four volume series of the *Pastoral Letters of the United States Catholic Bishops* 1792-1983. This volume (1941-1961) includes both pastorals and statements receiving the approval of the American hierarchy at their plenary meetings. Our aim has been to be as complete as possible. Occasionally, when a particularly urgent question arises and the next scheduled general meeting of the hierarchy is some months removed, the administrative committee or the NCCB/USCC president prepares a pertinent statement.

Distinguishing a pastoral letter from a statement is sometimes difficult, so the terms are used almost synonymously. To facilitate references, paragraphs are numbered here, although they were not in the original.

From the Catholic Church's viewpoint the historic period (1941-1961) treated in this volume stands as one of the most interesting of all American history. It has been called "The Golden Age of American Catholicism" by several church leaders. The Catholics of that era were a joyous group, positive of their identity, proud of their Church, of their priests and of their schools. Attendance at the Latin Sunday Mass was excellent. Every Saturday there were long lines of parishioners awaiting confession. Novenas of all types were never better attended. The Holy Name Society and the Sodality of the Blessed Virgin Mary flourished in all established parishes.

Parish spirit was truly vibrant. Most Catholics in the parish knew one another; the parochial school pulled the parishioners even closer together as the children played and competed together on the various parish teams; parishioners often socialized together and, in many instances, their children intermarried. Church authority then was unquestioned. In those days an ordinary could declare a boycott of all movies which would be respected by nearly all his subjects.

Novitiates and seminaries boomed in enrollment across the nation. The number of seminarians doubled to total more than 41,000. This twenty year period also witnessed an increase of nearly 20,000,000 Catholics, bringing their total to over 42,000,000. They were ministered to by more than 54,000 priests, a numerical growth of 18,000 since 1941. With post-World War II prosperity, ecclesiastical building forged ahead at a rate never since matched.

There was a broadening of charity projects, national and international. By 1955 the Catholic Relief Services, in its first twenty years of existence, had distributed more than $1.25 billion in relief supplies throughout the world. The Church in the United States became much more active in those two decades in implementing social justice teachings, principally through its labor priests.

This period of American history was enriched by many new Catholic periodicals and newspapers. The solid periodical, *Worship*, formerly *Orate Fratres*, promoted sane liturgical advances. A multiplicity of Catholic books, some of them as definitive as Ellis' *Cardinal Gibbons*, and a few internationally famous authors such as Thomas Merton also made significant contributions to Catholicism. The eloquence of Fulton Sheen and the worldwide leadership of Cardinal Spellman helped make the Church more favorably known. Through the World War II *G.I. Bill of Rights*, thousands of Catholic youth, who otherwise could not economically afford college education, were able to undertake advanced study, most frequently choosing Catholic colleges and universities, a boon to Catholic education.

Constitutional history was made with the 1947 Supreme Court decision allowing free busing for nonpublic school children. Often anticipating civil legislation and court decisions, Catholic ordinaries pioneered in racial integration and, in at least one instance, excommunicated the resisting political boss. American Catholics and their outspoken leaders were in the forefront of the battle against Communism.

In 1960 the Catholic presence, which was making itself felt more on both the local and national levels of government, peaked with the election of the first Catholic president of the United States, John F. Kennedy.

As their number grew to nearly 200, the American bishops became even more articulate and active on the international as well as the national level. With their statements widening in scope, the bishops put the Church on record in many important issues. Some of their statements are timeless and worthy of present day study. Without them, the history of religion in the United States and of a significant segment of its people cannot be known.

The author must express his gratitude to His Eminence, John Cardinal Dearden, for his foreword and his encouragement of this work. I would not only be remiss, but also ungrateful, if I did not acknowledge my debts of gratitude to many others, especially the Office of Publishing Services of the United States Catholic Conference.

Hugh J. Nolan

I. War and Its Aftermath
1941-1950

Introduction

From 1940 to the present there has been at least one pastoral letter or one general statement from the hierarchy annually, with the exception of 1965 because of the publication of the documents of Vatican Council II.

Hitler's aggressions in Europe and Japan's attack on Pearl Harbor in 1941 changed the course of world history, affecting both the Church and the state in this country.

All the pastorals of this period are preoccupied with two problems: peace and secularism. In their 1941 *Statement on the Crisis of Christianity*, less than a month before the United States entered World War II, the bishops reiterated Pope Pius XII's five points for a just and honorable peace: the triumph over hate, mistrust, ruthless selfishness, conflict in world economy, and the false principle that might makes right.

At their meeting in Washington, November 1941, the bishops took the positive step of appointing a Bishops' Committee on the Pope's Peace Points. The purpose was to study the peace principles enunciated by Pius XII, and to make them better and more widely known. Archbishop Samuel A. Stritch of Chicago was named chairman of this committee. The committee announced in December 1941, that it would issue statements at opportune times to foster and encourage research and studies on peace in the light of papal proposals, to give the public scholarly and popular literature "on the peace of our ambitions and prayers," and to inspire lectures on the papal proposals. The committee in a statement issued January 3, 1942, advocated sincere, honest, earnest acceptance by all nations of the principle that international law is the prime necessity for righteous peace. In 1943 the committee issued *Principles of Peace*, compiled by Harry C. Koenig and containing all discourses dealing with the nature and conditions of peace issued by the last five popes. This was the most comprehensive collection of peace documents made up to that date. In 1944 the committee arranged publication of Dr. Guido Gonella's *A World to Reconstruct*, and subsequently prepared a digest of the book in popular language.

In the 1941 Pastoral the bishops declared: "We find two subversive forces, both in control of powerful governments, both bent on world dominance. They are Nazism and Communism." The American prelates then reviewed the Holy See's condemnations of atheistic Communism back to Pope Pius IX's *Quanta Cura* (December 8, 1864) and added their own forceful denunciation:

At no time can there be any possibility of compromising with an ideology that proclaims and acts upon the denial of a personal and omnipotent God, rejects contemptuously the divine Saviour of the world, all Christian principles and Christian culture, ruthlessly persecutes religion, and brutally murders its ministers.

That the status of the American Church had improved in the forty years following *Testem Benevolentiae* (1899), the papal letter on so-called Americanism, was evident in an encyclical from Pius XII (*Sertum Laetitae Sanctae*) to the American hierarchy on the occasion of the 150th anniversary of the establishment of the ecclesiastical hierarchy in the United States. In that November 1, 1939, letter Pius observed:

What a proud vaunt it will be for the American people, by nature inclined to grandiose undertakings and to liberality, if they untie the knotty and difficult social question by following the sure paths illuminated by the light of the Gospel and thus lay the basis of a happier age.

Mindful of that wish of the Holy Father the American bishops, while noting that 1941 marked the fiftieth anniversary of the Magna Charta of labor, the *Rerum Novarum* of Leo XIII, quoted Pius XII on three fundamental values necessary for the reconstruction of the world after the present devastating war: (1) material goods should "flow equitably to all, according to the principles of justice and charity; (2) the duty and the corresponding right to work are imposed on, and conceded to, the individual by nature not by society. Pope Pius XII proclaimed the right of labor to organize and the right of the State to intervene in the field of labor only in the measure "that the common good properly understood demands" for the State must respect labor's "personal character"; (3) the family has a right to possess private property.

At this point of American history there was great unrest in industrial relations principally because of a rapidly mounting inflation. The bishops, expressing again their sympathy for labor, begged priests and leaders among the laity to show "an ever increasing interest in the cause of the multitudes who, in order to eke out a mere existence, are so largely taken up with the material things of life." The prelates quoted Pope Leo XIII's and Pope Pius XI's approval of labor unions, expressing the hope that the leaders of labor would come forth from the emergency of national defense united in closer cooperation with all right-minded employers "and deserving the commendation of the general public." With Pius XII the American bishops were hopeful that when the horrors of war were over a new social order would be reconstructed that would infuse new courage and new prosperity and growth "in the garden of human culture."

The American prelates promised: "We shall pray that the Holy Spirit may enlighten, guide and strengthen our chief Executive, the

Congress, and all who bear the gravest responsibilities of government in these difficult days." In little more than three weeks the United States was in the worst military conflict the world had ever witnessed.

After the disaster of Pearl Harbor on December 7, 1941, the Congress of the United States declared a state of war with Japan the following day; and on December 11, 1941, Germany and Italy declared war on the United States. President Roosevelt, in his war message following that declaration, proclaimed, "Never before has there been a greater challenge to life, liberty and civilization." Because of its historical significance the letter of Archbishop Edward Mooney of Detroit, chairman of the executive board of the NCWC, in the name of the bishops of the United States, to Franklin D. Roosevelt, President of the United States, on December 22, 1941, pledging their "whole-hearted cooperation" is included in this collection as is the President's response which concludes with an interesting sentence.

> We shall win this war and in victory we shall seek not vengeance but the establishment of an international order in which the spirit of Christ shall rule the hearts of men and of nations.

The following year (1942) in a Pastoral entitled *Victory and Peace* the American hierarchy declared without qualification that the United States was right in waging war in the defense of life and liberty against nations united "to bring about a slave world." The bishops, after quoting President Roosevelt in his solemn assurance that this country had no design of permanent conquest, expressed their confidence in the pledge of the Chief Executive. In supporting the war the bishops called on their people to make all the sacrifices necessary for the successful termination of the military effort.

American Catholics responded wholeheartedly. Approximately 25 to 35 percent of the members of the armed services in World War II were Catholics. According to a report of August 31, 1943, the religious preference of 31 percent of the American soldiers was Catholic. The distribution of Catholics was probably higher in the Navy and Marine Corps than in the Army, for early in 1943 the Catholic chaplains estimated that 50 percent of the Navy and over 50 percent of the Marine Corps were Catholics.

Catholic chaplains serving the armed forces between Pearl Harbor and VJ Day numbered 3,036; 83 of these died during the war, 32 were battle deaths and 2 were listed as missing in action. Forty-one percent of the deceased priests received a total of 57 decorations from the government. On July 31, 1945, the Chief of Army chaplains, Brigadier General William R. Arnold, reported the largest number of Army chaplains on duty at any time of the war, 2,270 Catholic priests among the Army total. The first Congressional Medal of Honor ever given to a chaplain of the U.S. armed forces was awarded to Father Joseph

T. O'Callahan, SJ, for service aboard the flaming U.S.S. Franklin. Father Robert White was the first chaplain in active service with the rank of commodore. All Catholic military chaplains were under the jurisdiction of the Military Vicar for the Armed Forces of the United States, then Archbishop Francis J. Spellman of New York. For the duration of World War II, Bishop John F. O'Hara, CSC, formerly president of the University of Notre Dame, was Military Delegate of the Armed Forces and conducted the Military Ordinariate with its far-flung duties.

The bishops asked in their Pastoral for special moral safeguards for young men drafted into the armed forces especially since the draft age had been lowered to eighteen years. Also recognizing that the war effort made it necessary for mothers to work outside their homes, these spiritual leaders expressed their concern not only for the health and moral welfare of these employed mothers, but especially for their children. They pleaded for a wholesome moral atmosphere wherever women were employed.

The American bishops expressed their deepest sympathy in *Victory and Peace* for persecuted peoples of the world, citing specifically the murderous assault on Poland and the systematic extermination of that nation by the Nazis. With "a deep sense of revulsion" the bishops reacted to the cruel indignities being heaped on the Jews and other defenseless peoples not of our faith. They condemned in unmistakable language the brutal reprisals in subjugated countries and the horrors of the concentration camp for thousands of innocent victims.

Moving from the persecutions abroad to the denial of human rights at home, the American bishops in 1942 asked that the fullest measure of economic opportunities and advantages be given to their black fellow citizens. This request applied especially to a growing number of Catholic employers since studies based on information gathered in 1939-40 and in 1948 indicate that Catholics moved up the economic ladder much faster than had been generally assumed.[1] The prelates quoted Pope Pius XII's encyclical to the American bishops on the 150th anniversary of the establishment of the American hierarchy stating the Negro people are entitled to special care and comfort in the fields of religion and education.

The American prelates also apologized to the Latin American bishops for mistakes in past international relations that had been offensive to the religion and culture of Latin Americans. While regretting American efforts to rob the Latin Americans of their Catholic faith, the American hierarchy hoped for a strong bond of friendship among all the countries of the Western hemisphere to help the shattered postwar world.

---

[1]Cf. Appendix in Herbert Wallace Schneider, *Religion in Twentieth Century America* (Cambridge, Mass., 1952).

Although the United States had not yet been engaged a year in World War II and the scales of military success were far from being weighted in favor of the allies, the bishops in 1942, looking to a lasting peace, exhorted their leaders to study carefully the peace plan of Pius XII. Almost prophetically they proclaimed that without a Christian peace, mankind would have only an armistice, and would prepare for a Third World conflict.

Accordingly, the American hierarchy dedicated its 1943 Pastoral to *The Essentials of a Good Peace*.[2] Disclaiming any desire to venture into the domain of statesmanship, but rather speaking as pastors of souls and teachers of religion, the bishops blamed the maladies of modern society on social forgetfulness and the rejection of the sovereignty of God and the moral law. They said that recognition of God and the moral law is basic to the right ordering of international relations. Where God and the moral law are not given social recognition, human laws and agreements lose their stability and binding force. The prelates stated that the United States must be as determined to reap the full fruits of victory in a just peace as to win the war. Every nation and every people must recognize and satisfy its obligations in the family of nations. Adverting to the recent declarations of the Moscow Conference, the bishops perceptively stated that while they represent a definite step in the right direction, "some things these documents imply by statement and more significantly by omission leave an uneasiness in minds intent on peace with justice to all."

The bishops observed that it would be inconsistent to promote a world reconstruction unless in national life men would recognize equality of opportunity for all citizens and willingly extend to them the full benefits of democratic institutions. In 1943 the bishops proclaimed that history imposes a special obligation of justice towards the Negro that he might in fact enjoy all the rights given him in the constitution. The bishops protested that this meant not only political equality, but also fair economic and educational opportunities, a just share of public welfare projects without exploitation and a full chance for the social advancement of the Negro.

The bishops evidently wished to alert American leaders to anticipate the problems of a permanent peace, but they were far more specific in elaborating the guidelines of a true peace in their next three Pastoral Letters.

---

[2] At the 1943 meeting Bishop John Mark Gannon, chairman of the Press Department, reported that the NCWC Press Department was during the past year the only source of complete information on Vatican wartime thought and activities. Through Vatican sources much material was obtained concerning the occupied countries of Europe and war prisoners. The NCWC News Service greatly aided the Catholic press in providing numerous authentic dispatches and interpretative articles to offset erroneous information from secular sources concerning Catholic happenings. This department handled six worldwide papal messages, five of which dealt directly with the war; the sixth was the encyclical on the *Mystical Body of Christ*.

The 1944, 1945, and 1946 Pastorals dealt almost completely with the question of peace and postwar problems. In 1944 the Pastoral, *On International Order* proposed the question most pointedly in the opening words: "We have met the challenge of war. Shall we meet the challenge of peace?" This letter was dedicated almost entirely to the formation and structure of the organization known as the United Nations. This was real positive leadership on the part of the hierarchy. At the time the United Nations was only in embryo. A meeting of representatives of Great Britain, the United States, Russia, and China at Washington in the autumn of 1944 drafted a preliminary outline, but the charter was not issued from a plenary conference of fifty different nations at San Francisco until April 1945. The Charter of the United Nations established an international body considerably stronger than the old League of Nations. But it had the same basic defect, about which the American bishops would complain in their 1945 Letter, of giving each of the "big five" on the Security Council (the United States, Britain, Russia, China, and France) a veto on every decision of this body. Contrary to what is generally thought, this veto was not proposed by Russia, although she has exercised it more than any other nation. It was insisted upon by Britain and America because their respective governments knew that the people would never consent to ratification without such protection to their sovereignty. Russia wanted but was refused a veto also on discussions in the Security Council. Each member nation had one vote in the General Assembly, and complete freedom of discussion there. The area in which the United Nations went beyond the old League, and which the American bishops would praise, was a provision for the use of various pressures against aggression. The Security Council could recommend to the General Assembly the severance of diplomatic relations, or the application of economic sanctions, or ultimately military action against an aggressor. It could even maintain a permanent international military force; but owing to Russian opposition, this never came about. It had the right to appoint a commission (UNESCO) to help backward or impoverished nations, and to draw up an international Bill of Rights. Both were done, and UNESCO accomplished a great deal of good, considering its limited budget; but the Bill of Rights has remained a dead letter to many of the members of the new league. The bishops would point out this failure in their 1946 Letter.

The Senate ratified the United Nations charter by a vote of 89 to 2 on July 28, 1945; and on January 10, 1946, the first session of the Assembly of 51 nations met in London. After investigating various sites, the U.N. settled on New York City as its capital.

In their advice to the international leaders the bishops declared in 1944 that they had no confidence in any peace not unreservedly carrying into effect the principles of the Atlantic Charter, which guaranteed the Four Freedoms, a renunciation of territorial aggrandizement, a promise of the restoration of self-government to those deprived of it, and for all equal access to trade and raw materials. The prelates observed that God Himself has made nations interdependent for their full life and growth; so there was not a question of creating an international community but rather of organizing it. They warned that an international peace organization must be universal and must subordinate power to law, showing regard for the basic rights of all nations strong and weak. As realists the bishops foresaw that such an international organization for peace would require a world court with strictly judicial and not merely advisory authority. Then obligatory arbitration of international disputes would be a major step forward in international relations.

Examining the subject of peace more deeply, the prelates proclaimed, notwithstanding the situation in the Soviet Union, that free nations necessitated free men; civil authority does not confer these God-given rights of freedom and thus may not violate them. The bishops further stipulated that if there is to be a lasting peace, the international peace organization should demand as a condition of membership that every nation guarantee in law and respect in fact the innate rights of men, families, and minority groups in their civil and religious life.

As a rather subtle reminder to American leaders, the prelates concluded their 1944 Letter by quoting President Roosevelt: "In victory we shall seek not vengeance but the establishment of an international order in which the spirit of Christ shall rule the hearts of men and of nations."

One year later in the 1945 Pastoral, *Between War and Peace*, the American hierarchy affirmed that although the war was over there was no peace or proper peace plan. Peace conferences, the bishops complained, thus far had been disappointing in the extreme. "We are perhaps in the gravest crisis of human history." The concerned prelates protested that the results of these negotiations so far did not align with the peace principles previously announced by the United States. The renowned historian, Samuel Eliot Morison, points out that Prime Minister Winston Churchill and President Franklin D. Roosevelt made several basic errors in their relations with the Soviets after World War II. "First, they believed that if they were 'nice to Russia' and helped her to the extent of their ability, Russia would cooperate to support a free world—in the Western sense—after the war. Nothing could have been more mistaken. Actually, Stalin never abandoned the Communist party's objective of revolutionizing the world."[3] Wherever Russian armies penetrated—excepting Austria and Czechoslovakia—they set up Communist regimes, and the local Com-

---

[3]Samuel Eliot Morison, *The Oxford History of the American People* (New York, 1965), p. 1046.

munist party saw to it that the elections, if held at all, would be a farce. Russia proved to be even more troublesome in Asia. Even after the Japanese cease-fire of August 16, 1945, exactly one week after Russia declared war, the Soviet army pushed through Manchuria into Jehol province and forced the Japanese there to surrender to them rather than to China's Generalissimo Chiang Kaishek, as Stalin had agreed. History records few treaties broken more quickly than the Russo-Chinese Treaty of August 14, 1945, when Stalin formed an alliance with Chiang. A few days later when Stalin became convinced that the Reds had a chance to win in China, he began to help them overthrow the Nationalist Chinese government. Fearlessly the bishops stated that Russia had acted unilaterally, that its Asiatic policy, so important for peace, was an enigma; and that its ultimate aim was world domination.

Pursuing the problem of preparing a lasting peace, the prelates warned the United States of the injustice of being an accomplice to the violation of the rights of individuals anywhere in the world. Instead of open and honest discussion in the peace conferences, the bishops noted a return to power politics and balance of power arrangements. They expressed dissatisfaction with the type of Security Council in the United Nations as nothing more than an alliance of great powers for the maintenance of peace.

Equally pointedly, the bishops asked whether or not the victors intended to keep the pledge made at Yalta that the Polish people would be unhampered in establishing their own independent government. As a fact of history Poland, on whom Russia had inflicted two of the most treacherous deeds of the war (the Katyn massacre of captured Polish officers, and the halt of Russian armies ten miles from Warsaw to enable the Nazi massacre of Polish patriots) was sold out at Yalta. Stalin had already set up his own puppet Polish government and absolutely refused to recognize the Polish government exiled in London for six years. His only concession was a weak promise to add a few democratic leaders to that government. Stalin also allowed the establishment of interim governments, "representative of all democratic elements," in the rest of liberated Europe, Austria, Hungary, Czechoslovakia, Bulgaria and Romania, to be followed by free elections. Unfortunately for the future of Europe and the world, these agreements were merely oral rather than definitely written in treaty form. In the so-called "spirit of Yalta" Roosevelt and Churchill trusted the Soviet leader would keep his word. Within a month after Hitler's death, Moscow ordered all Communists everywhere to return to the "hard line." The Potsdam agreements and their collapses if anything were worse than those of Yalta. Again the agreements were based on the false assumption that Russia was sincere, e.g., the Allied Control Council authorized at Potsdam was hindered in each effort to revive German industry by the Russian plundering of German factories under the pretense of reparations but with the actual hope of reducing the Germans to such economic despair they would turn to Communism. In September, 1946, the new American Secretary of State, James Byrnes, declared the United States would no longer be responsible for the "needless aggravation of economic distress" caused by the Allied Control Council's failure to agree on anything because of Russia's constant *niet*. It is now known the Russian government confidently expected capitalist society to collapse as a result of the war, for had not Karl Marx so prophesied? Then the Western Allies would not be able to prevent Communism from taking over one country after another. The U.N. had already been formed, but Stalin was determined to neutralize it if he could not control it.

Winston Churchill, speaking before President Truman in March 1946 at Westminister College in Fulton, Missouri, summarized the European situation well: "From Stettin in the Baltic to Trieste in the Adriatic an iron curtain has descended across the Continent." Soon another iron curtain would shut out most of the Asiatic continent.

The American prelates wondered what apology could be offered for the failure to protest the absorption by force of the Baltic countries into the Union of Soviet Republics. In vain they protested their shock about the oppression of Slovakia, Croatia, Slovenia, and the south-eastern countries and were horrified at the brutal and cunning religious persecution raging in many countries while declaring that "no reason of policy justifies our silence."

The American hierarchy begged for mercy towards former enemies of the United States and declared it imperative for Congress to make adequate appropriations to alleviate postwar suffering and starvation. They encouraged private relief agencies to increase their generous efforts in this same charity, remarking that citizens and leaders of the United States were called upon in a way unique in the annals of mankind to show that democracy which proved itself in war would show itself capable of solving the admittedly difficult problem of peace. "On bended knee let us ask God to help us to be the vigorous champion of democratic freedom and the generous friend of the needy and oppressed throughout the world."

Since 1934 the bishops of the United States at the request of the German hierarchy had been aiding refugees from Nazi persecution through an agency they established for that purpose, the Catholic Committee for Refugees and Refugee Children. After the outbreak of the war, the bishops attempted to meet the rapidly increasing and urgent appeals for help from ecclesiastical authorities in war-afflicted areas by establishing committees of national groups. In 1940, as the number of such agencies increased, all were united into a single committee, the Bishops' War Emergency and Relief Committee, and a special collection was instituted in all churches for its support. The first so-called Laetare Sunday Collection, taken up in 1941, was used to help war victims among the nationals of some fifteen countries, and to assist refugees who had fled to Portugal, Spain, Switzerland, Italy, France, and Iran.

When in 1942 Community Chests throughout the United States established a single, annual fundraising campaign, later known as the National War Fund, to finance private voluntary organizations, carrying on relief activities overseas, the bishops formed War Relief Services of the National Catholic Welfare Conference for promoting and administering their direct relief activities. This new Catholic organization was certified for admission to the National War Fund by the President's War Relief Control Board on April 28, 1943. The bishops, however, continued the Laetare Sunday Collection to provide funds for strictly religious purposes, including special appeals from the Holy See and from numerous bishops and Catholic organizations overseas. When the National War Fund was discontinued in 1947, the bishops broadened their annual fundraising appeal to provide continued support for the wide program of overseas relief, rehabilitation, and resettlement that War Relief Services of NCWC had been administering.

In establishing War Relief Services, the American hierarchy hoped to bring aid to refugees, prisoners, and other victims of war and to strengthen and re-establish local Catholic agencies and institutions that had been weakened or damaged or destroyed by the ravages of war. During the war years, the efforts and resources of War Relief Services were directed chiefly toward aiding four categories of war victims: (1) religious and political persecutees from Germany and the Axis countries; (2) Polish refugees dispersed in twenty-three countries; (3) stateless persons in Spain and Portugal; (4) needy persons in unoccupied Allied countries. In addition, War Relief Services provided welfare and religious services and supplies for merchant seamen and for prisoners of war in prisoner-of-war camps in the United States, Canada, and other countries. The agency also cooperated with groups providing help for students whose educational pursuits had been disrupted by the war.

As countries were successively liberated from Axis control, even before the cessation of hostilities, War Relief Services extended prompt assistance to the inhabitants of the war-torn lands, establishing relief programs in France, Belgium, Holland, Poland, the Philippines and Czechoslovakia. Urgently needed supplies of food, clothing, and medicine were sent to Greece, India, Luxembourg, Madagascar, the Dutch East Indies, Yugloslavia, Rumania, and Korea. Soon after the war ended, extensive relief programs were launched in former enemy countries (e.g., Germany, Italy, Austria, Hungary, and Japan). Where governmental and nongovernmental agencies, such as the United Nations Relief and Rehabilitation Administration, assumed responsibility for basic maintenance of the peoples in the war-devastated countries, War Relief Services, in cooperation with other American voluntary agencies, supplemented government programs by caring for the most hopeless of the victims of war—undernourished children, orphans, the sick, the aged, and the infirm. As Soviet control spread and tightened over Eastern Europe, however, the assistance programs of War Relief Services were suppressed in Poland, Hungary, Czechoslovakia, Rumania, and Yugoslavia.

In 1955, when it became clear that War Relief Services, which had been set up on an emergency and temporary basis, was permanently needed, its name was changed to Catholic Relief Services-NCWC. Because of its far-flung agencies Catholic Relief Services was able to take full advantage of U.S. surplus foods that first became available for overseas relief operations in the 1950s. In addition to these foodstuffs supplied by the United States government, to clothing donated by Catholics in the annual Thanksgiving Clothing Collection, and to funds realized from the Bishops' Relief Fund Appeal, Catholic Relief Services received financial support for its aid programs from a variety of sources including the United States Escapee Program, the Intergovernmental Committee for European Migration, the United Nations High Commissioner for Refugees, local governments, and private groups.

By the end of 1963, Catholic Relief Services had shipped overseas and distributed to needy persons food, clothing, medicines, and other relief supplies having a gross weight of 5,600,000 tons and a total value of $1.25 billion. From 1945 to 1963 it helped more than 425,000 refugees to resettle in the United States and other countries of asylum. An important byproduct of the program carried on by NCWC Relief Services has been the impetus for the hierarchies of other countries to establish Catholic charities organizations on a diocesan and parish level as well as organizations comparable to the National Catholic Welfare Conference of the American Bishops. Nearly all the countries of Asia and the Far East, and notably those in Latin America, took action.

In recent years, Catholic Relief Services has been expanding its programs in the newly independent, emergent nations of Africa and in the underdeveloped countries of Asia and Latin America, giving increased emphasis to assistance and self-help projects designed to eliminate social injustice, economic deprivation, disease and ignorance. Operating in more than seventy countries, the NCWC Relief Services is the nation's largest private voluntary overseas aid agency. All supplies are allocated and assistance rendered to those in need without regard to race, religion, or color. The sole criterion is need.

The initial activities of Catholic Relief Services were, of a necessity, confined to rendering emergency, on-the-spot aid to victims of war. However, the long-range policy of the agency is aimed at improving and eventually eradicating the shocking destitution, disease, and unrest afflicting and degrading more than one-third of mankind.

Despite their prayerful hopes and aspirations, the bishops saw in 1946 little improvement in the world situation. Actually, delay in writing a peace had aggravated many problems. In the opening sentence of *Man and the Peace* the bishops identified the central difficulty in the formulation of a peace as the problem of man. The menace to man as man loomed large in the conflict between Russia and the West. The bishops noted that eighteen months had passed since the German surrender and fifteen months since the defeat of Japan and yet there was no sign of a successful peace. In fact the peace negotiations caused grave doubts for anything like a permanent cessation of international hostilities. Agreements previously made to safeguard basic human rights had been repudiated unilaterally and these repudiations were accepted or tolerated by other nations who had been parties to the previous agreements. Fatal compromises had been made either explicitly or implicitly by toleration of shocking aggressions. Soviet totalitarianism persecuted the citizen who dared assert his native rights, and imposed on peoples its philosophy of life in which there is no authority above the state. But there could be no compromise on the basic issue concerning the treatment of man as man. After citing that the signatories of the charter of the United Nations contracted to promote and encourage respect for human rights and for fundamental freedoms for all, the bishops asked the nations in the making of peace to secure men everywhere the enjoyment of their God-given rights.

The American hierarchy praised the policy of the United States to bring about the repatriation of prisoners of war as soon as possible, even though the peace had not been concluded. Denouncing the use of prisoners of war as slave labor, the American prelates reminded offending nations of their strict obligation to treat these prisoners as humanely as they wanted their own captured soldiers treated. The bishops requested proper treatment of displaced persons and regretted the ruthless herding of uprooted peoples into areas unable to support them or for the purposes of enslaved labor. They observed that man is his brother's keeper and that he cannot be truly Christian and complacent while any of his brothers in the human family groans under tyranny and is denied the free exercise of his human rights. The prelates praised the generosity of the people of the United States in their relief work for war-torn countries and begged that it might continue since the delay in making peace had prevented many nations from becoming economically self-sustaining.

The dislocation of normal economic relationships and the devastation of vast areas during World War II demonstrated the need for concerted efforts in relief, rehabilitation, and reconstruction. To meet these needs in part the United Nations Relief and Rehabilitation Administration (UNRRA) was established in 1943. Under the leadership of Governor Herbert H. Lehman and later Mayor Fiorello H. La Guardia, UNRRA spent about a billion dollars a year, of which the United States contributed 68 percent, for relief in continental Europe. In addition to this the United States Congress on April 3, 1948, voted $5.3 billion for the Marshall Plan, allowing the European countries to formulate their own reconstruction programs "to permit the emergence of political and social conditions in which free institutions can exist" and the United States would provide the cash to get started. On the same day Congress voted an additional $275 million for Greece and Turkey. This was only the beginning of foreign aid by the United States, which came to $80 billion by July 1, 1961. So successful was this aid that in little more than a decade the balance of trade with the United States had turned in Europe's favor.

At the 1947 meeting of the American hierarchy, attended by three cardinals, sixteen archbishops, and one hundred and thirteen bishops, the Most Rev. John T. McNicholas, OP, Archbishop of Cincinnati, Chairman of the Administrative Board of the NCWC, reported that during the past year "the lines of cleavage between the East and the West became more sharply and, at the same time, more clearly drawn" and "totalitarian materialsm emerged more plainly than ever before as the force engaged in a mortal struggle with Western civilization."

The needs of domestic welfare, and "the growing importance of the United States and of Washington in the political and economic life of the world," had given the Church in the United States and the NCWC, in particular, responsibilities of vast proportions and significance. "These responsibilities and the efforts required to meet them," the Archbishop pointed out, "are reflected in some measure in the reports of the various departments and bureaus of the NCWC, which experienced a year of tense activity."

Calling "the care and settlement of displaced persons" one of the "most distressing problems" facing the postwar world, the Archbishop said that the Catholic War Relief Services would assist the Vatican Migration Office, and that related problems had brought into sharp focus the need of a strong and effective international organization of Catholic charity to act as a contact between charity groups of various nations. The report indicated other matters of concern for the Church in the United States such as the U.N., the "iron curtain" in Europe, the Church in Latin America, the school-law difficulties and other proposals on national, regional, and local levels.

The 1947 Pastoral, *On Secularism*, is a classical statement among documents from the Catholic hierarchies of the world. It identified the errors of this insidious philosophy of life which became widespread in the 1940s, and then offered the proper antidotes. Criticizing this view of life that limits itself not to the material in exclusion of the spiritual, but to the human here and now in exclusion of man's relation to God here and hereafter, the bishops declared: "No man can disregard God—and play a man's part in God's world." They warned that secularism blinds the individual to his responsibility to God and removes account-ability to God as a practical consideration in the life of man, thus taking from him the sense of personal guilt of sin before God. Apprehensive for the world's situation, the bishops affirmed that the moral regener-ation which is recognized as absolutely necessary for the building of a better world must begin by bringing the individual back to God and to an awareness of his responsibility to God. "This, secularism, of its very nature cannot do."

The bishops affirmed: "In no field of social activity has secularism done more harm than in education." They showed how secularists had exploited for their own purposes the public schools and had positively excluded God from school, relegating Him to the inner chambers of private life. Theirs is a philosophy of education in which God has no place. The prelates, warning that secularism departs from the American tradition, advised that if secularism were not so deeply entrenched in the public educational system, there would be less danger for the future of democratic institutions.

At the end of World War II, the United States had to make the difficult transition to a peace economy, a change causing many minor-ities great hardship. Considering next "The World of Work," the prelates remarked that the Christian viewpoint of the social order rejects inexorable economic laws and blames human failure rather than uncontrollable forces. Economic enterprise is an important social function in which owner, manager, and workman cooperate for the common good. In this area the bishops denounced two extremes: 1) ruthless individualism that brings misery to millions; 2) labor organ-izations disregarding personal and property rights, and so seeking only the victory of one group. Both extremes are founded on the loss of a sense of responsibility to God and fellow man. American bishops alerted all citizens to those exiling God from the factory, the office, the market place, and thus destroying the solid foundation of broth-erhood in ownership, in management, and in work.

On the international scene since the end of World War II the situation had worsened especially in Europe, for Russia pushed to control the eastern half of the continent. The prelates identified athe-istic Communism as the force which, through violence and chicanery, was obstructing the establishment of a right juridical order in the international community. They were somewhat encouraged by the Truman Doctrine initiated in 1947 for

> the creation of conditions in which we and other nations will be able to work out a way of life free from coercion. . . . I believe that it must be the policy of the United States to support freed peoples who are resisting attempted subjugation by armed minorities or by outside pressures.

Delving deeper, the bishops asserted that secularism, which over the years had weakened the divinely laid foundations of the moral law, was responsible in part for the world situation. In exiling God from life, secularism cleared the way for the acceptance of godless ideologies. Showing the subtlety of this error, the prelates labelled it the solvent of practical religious influence in the everyday life of men and nations and consequently the most insidious hindrance to world reconstruction. There would be no hope for a just and lasting peace, the bishops thought, unless nations were convinced that neither secularism nor atheism offers any sound basis for international agreements. The prelates begged Americans and their leaders to be true to their historic Christian culture, and to reject secularism which offered no valid promise of better things for this country or for the world. Men must not allow secularism to divorce Christian truth from life. Rather, those who believe in God must make that belief evident in their workaday lives and train their children in that belief and in God's way of life.

The 1948 Pastoral, *The Christian in Action*, in many ways continued and developed the 1947 Letter *On Secularism*. In 1948 the bishops in their opening paragraph warned: "The failure to center life in God is secularism . . . the most deadly menace to our Christian and American way of living." Not satisfied with condemning secularist trends, the prelates called for constructive efforts to counteract their corrosive influences in every phase of human life—home, school, office, and government. Pleading with individual Christians to have a full vision of Christian truth, these spiritual leaders realistically admitted:

> The sorry fact is that many, very many Christians see this vision only dimly . . . and miss its impact on reality. . . . By their apathy they actually abet those who work for destruction and chaos. . . . Much of the confusion and chaos about us is attributable more directly to the effectiveness of the feverish effort of the destroyers.

The bishops proposed to every Christian the question: "What am I doing to build a Christian world?"

In their section on "Religion in the Home" they lamented that precisely in modern times came the first experiment in secularizing the home, "an experiment which is at the root of so many of our greatest evils." Mere profession of the Christian truths of the stability and sanctity of the marriage bond is insufficient—"the Christian must make his home holy."

Referring to "Religion in Education" the American hierarchy rejoiced that

> at a time when secularism has captured the minds of very many leaders in education . . . Catholic parents are becoming more insistent . . . for schools . . . integrated in the teaching of religion.

The bishops expressed a special concern about higher education, reflecting that possibly "much of the success of the secularist is due to the fact that the number of excellent Christian scholars is inadequate for the needs of our times." Seven years later Monsignor John Tracy Ellis would develop this theme in a provocative article in *Thought*, "American Catholics and the Intellectual Life."

American Catholic prelates warned that the inroads of secularism in civil life and law challenged the Christian citizen and opposed the American tradition of an essential connection between religion and good citizenship. They explained that the First Amendment to the Constitution regarding the establishment of a religion meant that no particular religion was to receive preferential treatment, but it did not mean that there was to be indifference or opposition to religion, or exclusion of cooperation between religion and government. The Catholic bishops deplored the term "separation of Church and State" as a shibboleth of doctrinaire secularism, noting that this reading of the First Amendment would greatly accelerate the trend toward the secularization of American culture. In particular the prelates cited the McCollum case and showed at length the lack of logic and of historical and accepted interpretation in its majority opinion. In the McCollum v. Board of Education (333 U.S. 203) the Supreme Court of the United States in a narrow decision declared unconstitutional (as an establishment of religion) the Champaign, Illinois "released-time" program of religious education for public school children. The "released-time" movement in the United States had originated among Protestants in Gary, Indiana in 1913. By 1947 it was in operation in one form or another in forty-six states with an enrollment of two million students in approximately 2,200 communities. In the Champaign program a Council on Religious Education composed of Protestants, Catholics, and Jews received permission from the Board of Education to employ at private expense, teachers of the respective faiths to give religious instruction in the regular classrooms one period of the weekly school schedule to pupils who had written parental consent. Those whose parents did not wish them to participate were required to go to another classroom to pursue secular studies. Reports of absences from religious classes were made to the regular school authorities. Vigorous criticism of the McCollum decision came from prominent Protestants and from many of the country's most respected legal scholars. The bishops declared they would not rest until "the novel interpretation of the First Amendment recently adopted by the Supreme Court will in due process be revised." The final and one of the most forceful sentences of the 1948 Pastoral denounced secularism as threatening the religious foundations of national life and preparing the way for the advent of the omnipotent state.

The 1949 and 1950 Pastorals were treatises on the damage secularism was doing to the family and child, respectively, and included the proper steps to be taken to prevent this destruction. Together these letters form one of the clearest and most inspiring statements in this century on the Christian home and its children whose "first and highest allegiance is the kingdom of God."

In this period it is difficult to identify the actual authors of the pastorals, for the bishops had begun to enlist more expert assistance, especially from the faculty of The Catholic University of America and from the NCWC staff. Among the bishops more prominent in the preparation of these statements the Irish-born, former theology professor, Archbishop John T. McNicholas, OP, of Cincinnati ranks first.

The Crisis of Christianity

*A Statement Issued by the
Administrative Board of the National Catholic
Welfare Conference*

November 14, 1941

1. Christianity faces today its most serious crisis since the Church came out of the catacombs.

2. We, the members of the Administrative Board of the National Catholic Welfare Conference, deputed in the annual meeting of the bishops of the United States to express their mind on the crisis of Christianity, declare, as shepherds of souls, that our concern is the supreme interest of religion. Our thoughts, therefore, turn to the two greatest evils of today, which would destroy all spiritual values. We find two subversive forces, both in control of powerful governments, both bent on world dominance. They are Nazism and Communism.

3. However plausible their constitutions and their propaganda, the alarming reality is that neither system understands nor permits freedom in its true Christian sense. Both systems usurp arbitrary power over the lives and destinies of men; their dictators assume a power which belongs to God alone.

4. Our late Holy Father significantly issued his epochal encyclicals on Nazism and atheistic Communism within five days of each other.

Systems and Their Victims

5. His Holiness condemned the aberrations of Nazism, its denial of God in the true Christian sense, its deification of the state, its usurpation of the powers of God, of religion, and of parents, its falsification of Christian terminology, its betrayal of the eternal principles of objective morality, and its rejection of the rights and dignity of every human being. Pope Pius XI, with prophetic vision, declared that "its [Nazism] machinations, from the beginning, had no other aim than war of extermination." He branded the Nazi oppressors of the Church in Germany as "the nullifiers and destroyers of the Christian West."

6. The late Holy Father, while condemning the Nazi system, expressed his love for the German people in these words:

> Before our eyes stands the countless throng of faithful sons and daughters for whom the suffering of the Church in Germany, and

28

their own suffering, has in no way diminished their devotion to the cause of God . . . nor diminished their cheerful readiness to remain true to what they believed and have received from their forefathers as a sacred inheritance. From a heart that is deeply moved, we send them our paternal greeting.

7.   The Holy See has condemned atheistic Communism. Popes Pius IX, Leo XIII, and Pius XI pronounced their solemn condemnations of the system. Exercising their God-given commission, the Roman pontiffs could take no other course than to condemn the errors, the tactics, the satanic designs of Communism. At no time can there be any possibility of compromising with an ideology that proclaims and acts upon the denial of a personal and omnipotent God, rejects contemptuously the divine Savior of the world, all Christian principles and Christian culture, ruthlessly persecutes religion, and brutally murders its ministers. The leaders of atheistic Communism have done this nefarious work. Under them only anti-God and anti-Christian propaganda can have liberty of action.

Pope Pius XI's Condemnation of Communism

8.   Pope Pius XI, who pronounced the most explicit condemnation of atheistic Communism, expressed in the same encyclical his paternal and compassionate benevolence for the people of Russia in these words:

> In making these observations it is no part of our intention to condemn en masse the peoples of the Soviet Union. For them we cherish the warmest paternal affection. We are well aware that not a few of them groan beneath the yoke imposed on them by men who, in very large part, are strangers to the real interests of their country. We recognize that many were deceived by fallacious hopes. We blame only the system, with its authors and abettors who consider Russia the best field for experimenting with a plan elaborated decades ago, and who from there continue to spread it from one end of the world to the other.

Aims for Just Peace

9.   We, the bishops, who here express, at this critical hour, our judgment in these matters of gravest import, while enjoying, as we do, a well-ordered liberty in a free country, declare our devotion to His Holiness, Pope Pius XII, and our loyalty to his leadership as the Vicar of Christ and the Common Father of all nations and peoples. We unite with our Holy Father in praying for the attainment of a peace that will be accepted by all right-thinking governments and individ-

uals as permeated by justice and charity. We earnestly ask our priests and people to continue their prayers that the violence of the war tempest may soon be spent, and that a just peace and an ordered prosperity may be restored to a distracted world.

Pope Pius XII's Five Points

10. In a Christmas message to the world, His Holiness, Pope Pius XII, on December 4, 1939, laid down five points for a just and honorable peace. In our own statement of April 1941, we urged the consideration of these conditions proposed by our Holy Father.

11. Again, in his message delivered on Christmas Eve, 1940, His Holiness reiterated these five indispensable prerequisites for the right kind of a new order in the world. He called them triumphs—the triumph over hate, over mistrust, over the spirit of ruthless selfishness, over the conflict in world economy, over the false principle that might makes right.

Fundamental Values in World Reconstruction

12. Observing the fiftieth anniversary of the Magna Charta of labor, the *Rerum Novarum* of Leo XIII, His Holiness, Pope Pius XII, on June 1, 1941, spoke of "three fundamental values" which must be kept in mind for the reconstruction of the world after the present devastating war.

13. The first of these values has to do with the use of material goods. His Holiness quotes from the letter which he addressed to the American hierarchy, *Sertum Laetitiae*, on November 1, 1939, in which he stated that "the goods which were created by God for all men should flow equitably to all, according to the principles of justice and charity."

Value of Human Labor

14. The second fundamental value considered by His Holiness is human labor. He says:

> The duty and the corresponding right to work are imposed on, and conceded to, the individual in the first instance by nature and not by society. . . . The duty and the right to organize the labor of the people belong above all to . . . the employers and the workers. It devolves upon the state to intervene in the field of labor and in the division and distribution of work according to the form and measure that the common good, properly understood, demands. Every legitimate and beneficial interference of the state in the field of labor should be such as to safeguard and respect its personal character.

15. The third "value" emphasizes the importance of the possession of private property by the family. His Holiness insists that, of all goods which can be held as private property, "none is more comformable to nature than the land." The Holy Father lays stress on the social significance to widespread ownership of land in the form of the family homestead. To him, the function of the family as the root of a nation's greatness and power is bound up with family ownership of "the holding on which it lives, and from which it draws all or part of its subsistence." Without that "stability which is rooted in its own holding," the family cannot be the "cell of society" which nature destined it to be.

16. Domestic progress and peace depend on securing vital space for the rural family, as world progress and peace depend on securing living space for all the nations of the world. Accordingly, an adequate solution of the problems of emigration is of major importance in bringing tranquility to a confused world.

Hope for Tomorrow

17. Our Holy Father, despite the horrors of war which sadden his paternal heart, and the crushing burdens which his pontificate has laid upon him, is full of hope. His Holiness is looking, as he tells us, to that tomorrow

> when the ruin of this world hurricane is cleared, and when the onset
> of a reconstruction of new social order (which is a desire worthy of
> God and of man) will infuse new courage and a new wave of pro-
> fusion and growth in the garden of human culture.

The words of the Pope of Peace regarding the conditions he lays down for peace and the triumphs to be achieved in the reconstruction of a world order in which justice and charity are to prevail deserve our most careful study.

Prayers for Suffering and Oppressed

18. With apostolic liberty and with fraternal charity we send our greetings and sympathy to our suffering brother bishops and their flocks in all countries where subversive forces are persecuting religion and denying freedoms of conscience. Our fervent prayers are offered for their liberation, for their freedom to worship God according to the dictates of their conscience, for their freedom of education, their freedom of assembly, their freedom from the slavery of tyranny, the freedom of the sons of God.

19. Our sympathy goes out again to the peoples of those countries who have been crushed under the heel of the invader, and, indeed, to all upon whom war has imposed so heavy a burden of suffering and sacrifice. We cannot too strongly condemn the inhuman treatment to which the Jewish people have been subjected in many countries.

20. In the hour of cruel torture, we are mindful, daily at God's altar, of all the innocent victims of the war, of the homeless, the exiled, the imprisoned, and all who are suffering because of hunger or disease. We ask the faithful to unite with us in offering daily prayers and sacrifice in their behalf.

Defense of Our Country

21. We support wholeheartedly the adequate defense of our country. Thoughtful statesmen are perplexed, patriotic citizens are divided in their opinions as to the procedure our own country should follow. In these crucial times, when the civil fabric of every country is threatened and when dictators would destroy all religion, we herewith restate the position of the Catholic Church in the language of the immortal Pope Leo XIII:

22. "The Almighty has appointed the charge of the human race between two powers, the ecclesiastical and the civil: the one being set over divine, and the other over human things. Each in its kind is supreme; each has fixed limits within which it is contained, limits which are defined by the nature and special object of the providence of each, so that there is, we may say, an orbit within which the action of each is brought into play by its own native right.

23. "But inasmuch as each of these two powers has authority over the same subjects, and as one and the same thing, under different aspects but still remaining identically the same, might chance to fall under the jurisdiction and determination of both powers, God, who foresees all things and is Author alike of these two powers, has marked out the course of each in correlation to the other, 'For the powers that are, are ordained of God' (Rom 13:1). Were this not so, deplorable contentions and conflicts would often arise, and not infrequently men, like travelers at the meeting of two roads, would hesitate in anxiety and doubt, not knowing what course to follow. Two powers would be commanding contrary things, and it would be a dereliction of duty to disobey either of the two. But to judge thus of the wisdom and goodness of God would be most repugnant. . . . One of the two has for its proximate and chief object the well-being of this mortal life; the other, the joys of Heaven. Whatever, therefore, in things human is of a sacred character, whatever belongs, either of its own nature or by reason of the end to which it is referred, to the salvation of souls, or to the worship of God, is subject to the power and judgment of the Church. Whatever is to be under the civil and political order is rightly subject to the civil authority. Jesus Christ has Himself given command that what is Caesar's is to be rendered to Caesar, and that what belongs to God is to be rendered to God."

Respect for Authority

24. Pondering this solemn teaching of Pope Leo XIII, we must recognize that all lawful authority is from God. "Let everyone be subject to the higher authorities, for there exists no authority except from God" (Rom 13:1). Disrespect for authority, both ecclesiastical and civil, must be condemned. In the confusion of the hour, we deplore the presumption of those who, lacking authority, strive to determine the course of action that the Church should take within her clearly defined field. Recognizing the liberty of discussion, and even of criticism, which our democratic form of government guarantees, we urge and commend respect and reverence for the authority of our civil officials which has its source in God.

Conduct during the War

25. At the present moment, in varying degrees, in every part of the world, the peaceful course of events is disturbed. People are called upon to make sacrifices and to suffer. Comparing our conditions in the United States with those of other lands, we must recognize that our country is singularly blessed. But we cannot avoid the repercussions of a world cataclysm. Our faith in a Divine Providence ruling the universe should inspire us to have confidence in the benevolent designs of a loving God who permits suffering to correct evil and to bring forth the fruits of justice and charity and peace.

Urge Spirit of Restraint

26. In this solemn hour when fateful decisions are to be made, it is evident that a spirit of exemplary restraint should characterize our priests and people. In every national crisis and every danger, our priests have been an inspiration. We are confident that their good example of strong faith and courage, founded on the virtue of fortitude, will not be lacking now. As moral teachers, they show that freedom has its limitations. It is limited, first of all, by the rights of God, and next, by the rights of others and by the interests of the common good.

27. As shepherds of souls, we are gravely concerned about the future of supernatural religion in our country. Here, as elsewhere, it is seriously threatened by growing evils of which our Holy Father has but recently warned the world. These are the evils of "false doctrine, immorality, disbelief, and reborn paganism." The threat is to our youth, above all. Not only must we have a thorough understanding of the thoughts of the youth of our day, of its urge for action, of its fixed purpose to put teaching into practice, but preeminently, we must encourage youth to realize the constructive need of Christian doctrine and Christian discipline.

Hope for Labor Peace

28. We are hopeful that priests and leaders among the laity will show an ever increasing interest in the cause of the multitudes who, in order to eke out a mere existence, are so largely taken up with the material things of life.

29. We express again our sympathy for labor and we appreciate the difficulties of maintaining family life with the mounting cost of living. In union with the Holy See, we have, on many occasions, condemned the evils of unrestrained capitalism. At the same time, in union with the Holy See, we hold that "our first and most fundamental principle, when we undertake to alleviate the condition of the masses, must be the inviolability of private property."

Papal Approval of Union Labor

30. Pope Leo XIII declared:

> Religion teaches the laboring man and the workman to carry out honestly and well all equitable agreements freely made; never to injure capital nor to outrage the person of an employer; never to employ violence in representing his own cause, nor to engage in riot and disorder; and to have nothing to do with men of evil principles, who work upon the people with artful promises, and raise foolish hopes which usually end in disaster and repentance, when too late. Religion teaches the rich man and the employer that their workpeople are not their slaves; that they must respect in every man his dignity as a man and as a Christian.

Popes Leo XIII and Pius XI expressed their approval of unions for the workers. As we think of the present difficulties in labor and trade unionism, we express the hope that the leaders will be well-advised for the welfare of the workers of the nation; that they will keep before them the common good of the country; that they will refrain from doing anything that is harmful to the general welfare, and that they will come forth from the emergency of national defense united in closer cooperation with all right-minded employers and deserving the commendation of the general public.

Prayer for Unity and Guidance

31. If we trust in God we shall be constant in prayer. We shall pray for all the world, but especially for our own country; for the well-being of the Church, and for unity among our citizens. We shall pray that the Holy Spirit may enlighten, guide, and strengthen our Chief Executive, the Congress, and all who bear the grave responsibilities of government in these difficult days.

Administrative Board
National Catholic Welfare
   Conference
Washington, D.C.
November 14, 1941

Most Rev. Edward Mooney, Chairman, Archbishop of Detroit

Most Rev. John T. McNicholas, Archbishop of Cincinnati

Most Rev. Samuel A. Stritch, Archbishop of Chicago

Most Rev. John Gregory Murray, Archbishop of St. Paul

Most Rev. Francis J. Spellman, Archbishop of New York

Most Rev. John Mark Gannon, Bishop of Erie

Most Rev. Hugh C. Boyle, Bishop of Pittsburgh

Most Rev. John F. Noll, Bishop of Fort Wayne

Most Rev. Edwin V. O'Hara, Bishop of Kansas City

Most Rev. John A. Duffy, Bishop of Buffalo

Catholic Support in World War II

*A Letter Written by the Chairman of the
Administrative Board to the President of the
United States*

December 22, 1941

Dear Mr. President:

1. As chief executive of our nation you have called upon the American people for full service and sacrifice in a war of defense against wanton aggression.[1] Congress in grave and inspiring unity has spoken the will of a great nation determined to be free. We, the Catholic bishops of the United States, spiritual leaders of more than twenty million Americans, wish to assure you, Mr. President, that we are keenly conscious of our responsibilities in the hour of our nation's testing. With a patriotism that is guided and sustained by the Christian virtues of faith, hope, and charity, we will marshal the spiritual forces at our command to render secure our God-given blessings of freedom.

2. We will do our full part in the national effort to transmute the impressive material and spiritual resources of our country into effective strength, not for vengeance but for the common good, not for national aggrandizement but for common security in a world in which individual human rights shall be safeguarded, and the will to live on the part of all nations great or small shall be respected—a world in which the eternal principles of justice and charity shall prevail.

3. The ultimate strength of a people is in the things of the spirit. The historic position of the Catholic Church in the United States gives us a tradition of devoted attachment to the ideals and institutions of government we are now called upon to defend. Our predecessors, in the Third Plenary Council of Baltimore, solemnly declared:

> We believe that our country's heroes were the instruments of the God of nations in establishing this home of freedom; to both the Almighty and to His instruments in the work, we look with grateful reverence; and to maintain the inheritance of freedom which they have left us, should it ever—which God forbid—be imperiled, our Catholic citizens will be found to stand forward, as one man, ready to pledge anew 'their lives, their fortunes, and their sacred honor.'

---

[1]This letter was written by the Most Rev. Edward Mooney, Archbishop of Detroit, Chairman of the Administrative Board of the NCWC in the name of the bishops of the United States to President Franklin D. Roosevelt. He pledged the bishops' support in the national crisis of World War II.

4. Today, in the face of the peril they feared, we reaffirm their solemn words. We give you, Mr. President, the pledge of our wholehearted cooperation in the difficult days that lie ahead. We will zealously fulfill our spiritual ministry in the sacred cause of our country's service. We place at your disposal in that service our institutions and their consecrated personnel. We will lead our priests and people in constant prayer that God may bear you up under the heavy burdens that weigh upon you, that He may guide you and all who share with you responsibility for the nation's governance and security, that He may strengthen us all to win a victory that will be a blessing not for our nation alone, but for the whole world.

5. The undersigned, Chairman of the Administrative Board, National Catholic Welfare Conference, authorized to forward this letter in the name of the bishops of the United States, has the honor, Mr. President, to be, with sentiments of high consideration,

Faithfully yours,

Edward Mooney
Archbishop of Detroit
Chairman, Administrative Board

President Roosevelt's Response

Dear Archbishop Mooney:

1. The letter which you forwarded under date of December 22 as Chairman of the Administrative Board, National Catholic Welfare Conference, and in the name of the bishops of the United States, gives me strength and courage because it is a witness to that national unity so necessary in our all-out effort to win the war. Please convey to all of your brethren in the episcopate an assurance of my heartfelt appreciation of the pledge of wholehearted cooperation in the difficult days that lie ahead. In those days we shall be glad to remember your patriotic action in placing your institutions and their consecrated personnel at the disposal of the government.

2. We shall win this war and in victory we shall seek not vengeance but the establishment of an international order in which the spirit of Christ shall rule the hearts of men and of nations.

Very sincerely yours,

Franklin D. Roosevelt

December 24, 1941

Victory and Peace

A Statement Issued by the NCWC
Administrative Board in the Name of the
Bishops of the United States

November 14, 1942

1. Our country has been forced into the most devastating war of all time. This war, which is the absorbing interest of all the world, involves unquestionably the most important moral issue of today. Some nations are united in waging war to bring about a slave world—a world that would deprive man of his divinely conferred dignity, reject human freedom, and permit no religious liberty. We are associated with other powers in a deadly conflict against these nations to maintain a free world. This conflict of principles makes compromise impossible.

Justice of Present War

2. While war is the last means to which a nation should resort, circumstances arise when it is impossible to avoid it. At times it is the positive duty of a nation to wage war in the defense of life and right. Our country now finds itself in such circumstances.

3. Even while we meet here, the exigencies of war have driven our armed forces into unexpected areas of conflict in Africa. Our president, in letters addressed to the rulers of all the friendly nations concerned, has given solemn assurance that the United States has no designs of permanent conquest or sordid interest. Our aim, he pledged, is to guarantee to countries under temporary occupation as well as to our own the right to live in security and peace. We bishops are confident that the pledge of our chief executive, not lightly made, faithfully mirrors the mind and conscience of the American people. That pledge is in full harmony with the expression of high purpose which the president made to the Catholic bishops of the United States when our own country was plunged into war: "We shall win this war and in victory we shall seek not vengeance but the establishment of an international order in which the spirit of Christ shall rule the hearts of men and nations."

4. From the moment that our country declared war we have called upon our people to make the sacrifices which, in Catholic doctrine, the virtues of patriotism, justice, and charity impose. In every section of this nation the voices of our bishops have been heard. Their instructions, their pastorals, their counsels, their appeals for prayers are an encouragement and an inspiration to their flocks. Our priests as chaplains on the war front have inspired confidence in the men whom they so zealously serve. Our men in the armed forces deserve unstinted gratitude for their heroic services to our country and high commendation for the faithful practice of their religion.

Prayers for Victory

5. In every diocese prayers have been incessantly offered, asking God's pardon for the sins of individuals and nations, begging divine mercy for all, pleading for a victory which will have the sanction of infinite justice and for an enduring peace founded on the love of God and the love of all men. Priests and people have earnestly prayed that the Holy Spirit may guide our president and all who share with him the heavy responsibilities of directing the war efforts and of winning the victory from which all peoples will derive a just and lasting peace.
6. In the discharge of our pastoral responsibility, we are gravely concerned about the world peace of tomorrow.
7. Secularism cannot write a real and lasting peace. Its narrow vision does not encompass the whole man, it cannot evaluate the spirituality of the human soul and the supreme good of all mankind.
8. Exploitation cannot write a real and lasting peace. Where greedy might and selfish expediency are made the substitutes of justice there can be no securely ordered world.
9. Totalitarianism, whether Nazi, communist, or fascist, cannot write a real and lasting peace. The state that usurps total powers, by that very fact, becomes a despot to its own people and a menace to the family of nations.

Christian and Peace

10. The spirit of Christianity can write a real and lasting peace in justice and charity to all nations, even to those not Christian.
11. In the epochal revolution through which the world is passing, it is very necessary for us to realize that every man is our brother in Christ. All should be convinced that every man is endowed with the dignity of human personality, and that he is entitled by the laws of nature to the things necessary to sustain life in a way conformable to human dignity. In the postwar world, the profit element of industry and commerce must be made subservient to the common good of communities and nations if we are to have a lasting peace with justice and a sense of true brotherhood of all our neighbors. The inequalities of nations and of individuals can never give to govern-

ments or to the leaders of industry or commerce a right to be unjust. They cannot, if they follow the fixed principles of morality, maintain or encourage conditions under which men cannot live according to standards befitting human personality.

12. Unfortunately, in our day we must wage a global war to secure peace. War is abnormal and necessarily brings on abnormal conditions in the life of a nation.

13. During the war crisis free men must surrender many of their liberties. We ask our people to be united and prepared to make every sacrifice which our government deems necessary for a just and enduring peace through the victory of our armed forces. We are confident that they will perform their wartime duties gladly because they know that our country has been the defender, not the destroyer, of liberties and has in the past always reestablished the full measure of peacetime freedom on the conclusion of hostilities.

Protection of Women in War Work

14. Our government has announced that the war emergency makes it necessary to employ an unprecedented number of women in industry. While we are wholeheartedly cooperating with our government in the prosecution of the war, we must, as shepherds of souls, express our grave concern about the Christian home in our beloved country in these crucial days. When mothers are engaged in industry a serious child-care problem necessarily arises. Every effort must be made to limit, as far as necessity permits, the employment of mothers in industry, particularly young mothers. Due provision in harmony with American traditions should be made for the day care of the children of working mothers. The health and moral welfare of mothers employed in industry should be thoroughly safeguarded. With a full realization of the role which women must play in winning the war and of the extreme measures that our government must take, we ask that all try to realize the dangers involved, especially the moral dangers. We urge that there be a wholesome moral atmosphere wherever women are employed.

Moral Safeguards for Youth in Military Service

15. We know that patriotic mothers are generous in giving their sons to the defense of our country. We express their concern, and ours, about youths of eighteen years of age who are now to be called to the armed forces. We hope that special moral safeguards will shield them, so that they may serve their country without moral blemish.

Denunciation of the Persecutions of the Jews

16. We express our deepest sympathy to our brother bishops in all countries of the world where religion is persecuted, liberty abolished, and the rights of God and of man are violated. Since the murderous assault on Poland, utterly devoid of every semblance of humanity, there has been a premeditated and systematic extermination of the people of this nation. The same satanic technique is being applied to many other peoples. We feel a deep sense of revulsion against the cruel indignities heaped upon the Jews in conquered countries and upon defenseless peoples not of our faith. We join with our brother bishops in subjugated France in a statement attributed to them:

> Deeply moved by the mass arrests and maltreatment of Jews, we cannot stifle the cry of our conscience. In the name of humanity and Christian principles our voice is raised in favor of imprescriptible rights of human nature.

We raise our voice in protest against despotic tyrants who have lost all sense of humanity by condemning thousands of innocent persons to death in subjugated countries as acts of reprisal; by placing other thousands of innocent victims in concentration camps, and by permitting unnumbered persons to die of starvation.

17. The war has brought to the fore conditions that have long been with us. The full benefits of our free institutions and the rights of our minorities must be openly acknowledged and honestly respected. We ask this acknowledgement and respect particularly for our colored fellow citizens. They should enjoy the full measure of economic opportunities and advantages which will enable them to realize their hope and ambition to join with us in preserving and expanding in changed and changing social conditions our national heritage. We fully appreciate their many native gifts and aptitudes, which, ennobled and enriched by a true Christian life, will make them a powerful influence in the establishment of a Christian social order.

Concern for the Black Man

18. We recall the words of Pope Pius XII expressing his paternal solicitude for the colored people of our country. In a letter addressed to the American bishops on the occasion of the 150th anniversary of the establishment of the American hierarchy, His Holiness said:

> We confess that we feel a special paternal affection which is certainly inspired of Heaven for the Negro people dwelling among you; for in the field of religion and education we know that they need special care and comfort and are very deserving of it. We, therefore, invoke an abundance of heavenly blessing and we pray fruitful success for those whose generous zeal is devoted to their welfare (*Sertum Laetitiae*, 1939).

Latin American Relations

19. We send our cordial greetings to our brother bishops of Latin America. We have been consoled by recent events which give a sincere promise of a better understanding by our country of the peoples of Mexico, Central and South America. Citizens of these countries are bound to us by the closest bonds of religion. They are not merely our neighbors; they are our brothers, professing the same faith. Every effort made to rob them of their Catholic religion or to ridicule it or to offer them a substitute for it is deeply resented by the peoples of these countries and by American Catholics. These efforts prove to be a disturbing factor in our international relations. The traditions, the spirit, the background, the culture of these countries are Catholic. We bishops are anxious to foster every worthy movement which will strengthen our amicable relations with the republics of this continent. We express the hope that the mistakes of the past which were offensive to the dignity of our southern brothers, their culture, and their religion, will not continue. A strong bond uniting in true friendship all the countries of the Western Hemisphere will exercise a most potent influence on a shattered postwar world.

Peace Directives

20. We urge the serious study of the peace plans of Pope Pius XII which insist that justice be inspired by love—first, love of God and then, love of every human being. "The command of love among individuals found in the Gospels," said Benedict XV, "differs in no respect from that which should reign among states and peoples" (*Pacem Dei*, Benedict XV, 1920). If we are not to have a Christian peace, then we shall be given only an armistice, and we shall begin to prepare for a Third World conflict.

Importance of Prayer

21. We conclude by urging, again, unceasing prayers: the prayer of all prayers by priests, the Holy Mass; prayers addressed to the Blessed Virgin that she will intercede with her divine Son for mercy on a war-blighted world. We ask that Tuesday, December 8, the feast of the Immaculate Conception of our Blessed Mother, the patroness of our country, be set aside as a special day of prayerful supplication. In its observance, the priests and faithful of every diocese will follow the timely instruction of their bishop. We recommend the recitation of the rosary in common, both in our churches and in our homes. We trust that the children of our country will, in response to the many appeals of our Holy Father, offer their innocent prayers to God for peace. Let us all unite in praying for a victory and for a peace acceptable to God.

Signed by the members of the Administrative Board, NCWC, in the name of the bishops of the United States

Edward Mooney, Archbishop of Detroit

John T. McNicholas, Archbishop of Cincinnati

Samuel A. Stritch, Archbishop of Chicago

John J. Mitty, Archbishop of San Francisco

Joseph A. Rummel, Archbishop of New Orleans

Francis J. Spellman, Archbishop of New York

John Mark Gannon, Bishop of Erie

John F. Noll, Bishop of Fort Wayne

Karl J. Alter, Bishop of Toledo

John A. Duffy, Bishop of Buffalo

The Essentials of a Good Peace

A Statement Issued by the NCWC
Administrative Board in the Name of the
Bishops of the United States

November 11, 1943

1. In the spirit of a free nation, whose rights and security have been wantonly attacked, our country is putting into its war effort the whole weight of our resources, our ingenuity, and our patriotism. We must be as determined to reap the full fruits of victory in a just peace as we are to win the war. We know that the sword cannot make peace. It can remove obstacles to peace, and it can impose its terms. But peace must be made first of all in the minds and wills of the victors. Unless we have the vision of a good peace and the will to demand it, victory can be an empty, even a tragic thing.

2. It is with these thoughts in mind that we deem it timely again to focus attention in the first essentials of a good peace. The responsibility for the postwar social reconstruction will fall on the victors. Many serious men have misgivings that there may be tragic compromises and a fateful repudiation of sound principles. These men are not pessimists or obstructionists, but they know the forces at play in the world about us. The declarations of the Moscow Conference do, indeed, open the way to necessary international cooperation for peace as well as for war. In this they represent a definite step in the right direction. They do not, however, dispel the fear that compromises on the ideals of the Atlantic Charter are in prospect. Some things these documents imply by statement and, more significantly still, by omission leave an uneasiness in minds intent on peace with justice to all.

Fundamental Social Truths

3. Not to enter the domain of statesmanship, but speaking as pastors of souls and teachers of religion, we wish to emphasize some fundamental social truths, deriving from religion, and to plead for their general recognition. It is heartening to note the wide agreement on the moral postulates of a just peace among religious leaders, otherwise divided by the deep cleavage of fundamental doctrinal differences. This significant and hopeful agreement has recently been evidenced in three parallel statements on world peace issued by American religious groups. This pattern for peace, fashioned on the moral law has attracted nationwide attention and will, we hope, be carefully studied by all men of good will. It is our purpose here to go deeper into our Catholic heritage of truth in faith and reason and to indicate the application of primary religious truth to the problems of peace and the planning of a right social order.

4.   Without doubt the root of the maladies which afflict modern society and have brought on the catastrophe of world war is the social forgetfulness and even the rejection of the sovereignty of God and of the moral law. There is written in human reason the law of good and evil, which calls to God for its authority and its sanctions. When this moral law is cast aside in social life, every principle, every right, every virtue rests on the shifting sands of mere human conventions. Human dignity, human solidarity become, then, not endowments from the Creator but mere fictions of man-made systems. In the quest for some principle for social stability, the authority of the state is exaggerated and its function of protecting and defending the rights of the citizens in the pursuits of the common good cedes to a tyrannical violation and invasion of these rights. In the name of realism the rights of the weak and the helpless are sacrificed. A first principle for a sane reconstruction of society is the social recognition of God's sovereignty and of the moral law.

God and His Moral Law

5.   What reason tells us about God and His moral law is complemented and supplemented, is made definite and achievable in the Gospel of Christ. It is significant that when the Western peoples socially ostracized the Savior and put their faith in secularism, they lost a clear vision of the moral law. They found no effective inspiration to civic virtue in materialism and naturalism, which despite signal advances in science, invention, and administrative techniques, closed the avenues of genuine social progress. We shall go back to God and the moral law when we reestablish Christ in our social life.

6.   The recognition of the sovereignty of God and of the moral law, as treasured in the Christian tradition, is basic to the right ordering of international relations. In creation God gave to the human race its essential unity and bound all men together in a brotherhood as comprehensive as humanity itself. In the plan of Divine Providence the human family was divided into nations and races, but this division in no way impaired the essential unity of mankind. When sin broke man's right relation with God and brought disunion between man and man, nation and nation, our blessed Savior restored, perfected, and ennobled human brotherhood. The ideal of human brotherhood must inspire international relations. Only when this ideal is accepted by men and nations will the exploitation of the weak cease and jungle exaltation of might be outlawed.

7. This does not mean that national rights and national sovereignties, rightly interpreted, must be surrendered to a world government. It does mean that every nation and every people must recognize and satisfy its obligations in the family of nations. The discharge of these duties is entirely compatible with national differences which give a happy variety of cultural treasures in human unity. Indeed these differences must be respected and defended, and every effort must be made to assist peoples now in tutelage to a full juridic status among the nations of the world.

8. In the circumstances of our times it is imperative that the nations in satisfaction of their responsibilities unite in setting up international institutions for the preservation of world peace and mutual assistance. Such institutions, rightly conceived, are in full harmony with the divine plan of human solidarity and should be helpful to rightly interpreted sovereignty and independence.

9. The social recognition of the sovereignty of God and of the moral law must be a first norm for the right ordering of the internal life of nations. Circumstances of history, differences of culture, and economic inequalities create differences of political forms. But all nations, if they are to conform to the moral law, must embody in their political structures the guaranty of the free exercise of native human rights, encouragement in the practice of virtue, an honest concern for the common good, and a recognition of the inviolability of the human person. No nation has under God authority to invade family freedom, abrogate private ownership, or impede, to the detriment of the common good, economic enterprise, cooperative undertakings for mutual welfare, and organized works of charity sponsored by groups of citizens. It is only when nations adhere to right principles in their domestic administration that they will cooperate for the common good of the family of nations.

10. Where God and the moral law are not given social recognition, human laws lose their stability and binding force. Ours is a tradition of government under law. In that tradition, law is not the expression of the will even of the majority, but of right reason, which reflects the law of nature and of God. We ourselves have seen in the sorry experiences of other countries the tyranny and injustice which come from government by decree under a dictator or a party. When civil law conforms to the moral law and seeks its greatest sanction in that law, there is social stability, and the common good is promoted. It would be a tragic mistake to forsake our tradition of law even to achieve a greater efficiency in administration. It would be a greater tragedy to forsake our tradition of law for a currently popular philosophy which fails to base law on the eternal maxims of justice and disregards the inalienable rights of the citizen which derive from God.

Lawlessness among Youth

11. It troubles us to see in the publication of crime statistics that there is a widespread disrespect for law, particularly in the youth of our country. No graver indictment of our social behavior could be written. A greater effort to protect the stability and the sanctity of the home and to inculcate moral discipline will contribute much to the solution of this problem. A better supervision of recreational activities in our communities will likewise be helpful. But more than all, we must instill in the soul of youth deeper respect for authority and greater devotion to the common good. How can these things be done unless there is a frank social recognition of God and the moral law? Certainly no system of thought and action based on a materialistic concept of life offers any promise of better things.

Role of the Family

12. In God's plan the family is a social institution with its own rights and dignity. Its stability, unity, and sanctity are as necessary to a right social order as the proper constitution of government itself. If in the family right order prevails, and the children are trained in virtue, there is a guaranty for social well-being. Where the state violates family rights and makes light of family stability and parental responsibility, no amount of welfare work carried on or promoted by public authority will adequately provide for social well-being. The political authority which earnestly seeks the common good of all citizens will not fail to lend itself to the establishment of a just family wage, in order that family income may be commensurate with the discharge of family duties. Nor will the prudent, wise, political authority, for any seeming temporary advantage, fail to recognize the function and dignity of woman in society and to warn her against the false economy of our times, which turns her mind and heart away from the home, thereby depriving the family, state, and Church of her proper contribution to the common welfare.

Neopagan Views on Marriage

13. We voice a grave warning against the propaganda of so-called planned parenthood, which violates the moral law, robs the family of its nobility and high social purpose, and weakens the physical and moral fiber of the nation. We plead for a return to the Christian concept of marriage, in which sex has such a high and noble function. We condemn the prevalent perverted teaching on sex which is

degrading our youth, destroying the sanctity of the home, and pros-
tituting the social function of the family to individual caprice. God is
not mocked with impunity. Neopagan views on marriage which are
being propagated with misguided zeal in our country can lead only
to moral ruin and national decadence.

14. It would be inconsistent to promote a world reconstruction in
which all nations, great and small, powerful and weak, would enjoy
their rights in the family of nations, unless in our own national life
we recognize an equality of opportunity for all our citizens and willingly extend to them the full benefits of our democratic institutions.

Constitutional Rights of the Black Man

15. In the providence of God there are among us millions of fellow
citizens of the Negro race. We owe to these fellow citizens, who have
contributed so largely to the development of our country, and for
whose welfare history imposes on us a special obligation of justice,
to see that they have in fact the rights which are given them in our
Constitution. This means not only political equality, but also fair economic and educational opportunities, a just share in public welfare
projects, good housing without exploitation, and a full chance for the
social advancement of their race. When given their rights in fact as
in law, they will prize with us our national heritage and not lend ear
to agitators whose real objective is not to improve but to destroy our
way of living.

16. In many of our great industrial centers acute racial tensions exist.
It is the duty of every good citizen to do everything in his power to
relieve them. To create a neighborhood spirit of justice and conciliation will be particularly helpful to this end. We hope that our priests
and people will seek opportunity to promote better understanding of
the many factors in this complex problem and strive for its solution
in a genuine Catholic spirit.

17. And we plead as well for a generous interest in the welfare of
our Spanish-speaking population. Many of them go back through a
long line to the first settlers who came into our Southwest, and others
have come in recent years from Mexico. They also have a right to
expect the full enjoyment of our democratic institutions and that help
in social life which is accorded to others. The sincerity of our Good
Neighbor Policy with Latin America, so Christian in its spirit and so
well calculated to foster right international relations, will be attested
by our attitude toward our fellow citizens of Latin-American origin
or descent.

A Sound Peace

18. If the responsibility faced by the victors is great, the opportunity is historical. Now there comes the chance not in hatred or vengeance but in justice and charity to base a social reconstruction on truth and right. The men of our fighting forces, in whose gallantry and heroism we rejoice: their loved ones whose anxiety we share will be satisfied with nothing less. The peoples of the world, the simple peoples, the fathers of families, the toilers and laborers, the people who have the same interests and the same ambitions which we cherish are looking to us, to this great land of freedom. We must not disappoint them. It is our historic opportunity to do our full duty in the family of nations. The causes of war must be removed, the honest needs of people must be met, their rights recognized. This must be a good peace which our victory will achieve. But first let us make ourselves in very truth peacemakers. Let us recognize the problems in our own social life and courageously seek the solution of them. A first principle must be the recognition of the sovereignty of God and of the moral law in our national life and in the right ordering of a new world born of the sacrifices and hardships of war.

Signed by the members of the Administrative Board, NCWC, in the name of the bishops of the United States

Edward Mooney, Chairman, Archbishop of Detroit

Samuel A. Stritch, Archbishop of Chicago

Francis J. Spellman, Archbishop of New York

John T. McNicholas, Archbishop of Cincinnati

Joseph F. Rummel, Archbishop of New Orleans

John J. Mitty, Archbishop of San Francisco

John F. Noll, Bishop of Fort Wayne

John Mark Gannon, Bishop of Erie

Karl J. Altar, Bishop of Toledo

John A. Duffy, Bishop of Buffalo

Statement on Federal Aid to Education

*A Statement Issued by the Administrative
Board of the National Catholic
Welfare Conference*

November 13, 1944

1. Under present economic conditions, areas of certain states of the Union do not provide an education that is defensible on the basis of even minimum standards. We recognize that these states cannot find taxable wealth available to provide adequate educational opportunity for all their children.

2. The Department of Education, National Catholic Welfare Conference, recommends the acceptance of the following basic principles which are a necessary condition for the just granting of federal aid:

(a) The aid given by the federal government for education should be distributed according to a law or plan that will bring this aid only to areas in which it is needed, and will be equitable to all children in that area without regard to color, origin, or creed, and in any school that meets the requirements of compulsory education. If necessary to achieve this purpose because of any state constitutional prohibition, then the federal authority should distribute the funds directly and not through state channels.

(b) The federal aid given should be distributed in all areas where the need is proved.

(c) Where federal funds are distributed for education, they must supplement the state, local, or private funds; they must not entirely supplant them. State, local, and private funds should be used to the utmost before invoking federal assistance.

(d) Federal aid should never impose in our country federal control of education either in law or in practice. The American tradition of local boards in control of education would be more responsive to the parent or to the family that has the primary and imprescriptible right in the education of children.

3. The Department of Education, National Catholic Welfare Conference, has in the past opposed bills which were undemocratic, discriminatory, and wasteful of public funds. It has opposed federal measures which were so worded as to defeat the purpose of equalizing educational opportunity for all children in those areas where such equalization was really needed. It cannot support bills now pending before the United States Senate or the House of Representatives for use of federal funds to equalize educational opportunity because these are objectionable bills.

4. It is un-American to offer as an argument for federal aid, the poverty and need of many children, and at the same time to exclude millions of other children, equally poor and in need, because of religious or racial considerations.

5. All fair-minded citizens, if not misinformed by propaganda, will oppose any bill advocating federal aid which is not fair to all American children regardless of color, origin, or creed.

Resolution on Eastern Europe

*A Resolution Passed by the Administrative
Board of the National Catholic
Welfare Conference*

November 13, 1944

The bishops of the United States, in Christian solidarity, share the sufferings, misery and fears of their brother bishops, the clergy, the religious, and the faithful of all the war-torn countries of Europe. The circumstances of the moment excite in them a particular anxiety for the fate of religion among their fellow-Christians in Poland, the Baltic States, and neighboring Catholic lands. They recall how centuries ago the Western Slav, later joined by the Lithuanians, associated themselves with the peoples of Europe in weaving and embellishing the fabric of Western Christian civilization. History records their heroic exploits in the defense of the West against Tartar and Moslem. Mighty tyrants enslaved them and even in their shackles they fought and bled in the sacred cause of freedom. Never losing their identity, they chose ever to shed martyr blood rather than deny or dilute their Christian faith. Cruel, inhuman aggressors are now heaping upon them frightful atrocities and unprecedented barbarities. The exercise of their religion is either denied them or is so thwarted as to be practically impossible. And dark fear is now in them that when our victory comes their hope for a better day with security in the enjoyment of their civil and religious freedoms will not be realized. To them the bishops of the United States, with their clergy and people, extend deep sympathy with the prayerful hope that the strong, victorious nations in charity and justice will give them succor in their sufferings and the full enjoyment of their indisputable rights. American Catholics would ever resent their country's being made a party to the de-Christianization of historic Catholic peoples.

Statement on the Silver Jubilee
of NCWC

*A Statement Issued by the Administrative
Board of the National Catholic Welfare
Conference*

November 13, 1944

1. Twenty-five years ago under the presidency of His Eminence,
Cardinal Gibbons, ninety-three bishops of the United States assembled in these halls of The Catholic University for the purpose of
planning annual meetings of the bishops of our country. The initiative
for this gathering was taken by Pope Benedict XV, in February 1919,
through his Representative, at the Golden Jubilee of the Episcopate
of Cardinal Gibbons at which seventy-seven Bishops were present.
The Bishops were asked to take common counsel annually in order
to find the best solutions of the many and grave problems facing
them after the first world war. They were told by His Excellency,
Archbishop Cerretti, that His Holiness looked to the bishops of the
United States for that initiative and courageous planning which would
help the Church to overcome the pressing evils of the times and also
enable her to build constructively for the expansion of religion.
2. Five months before the bishops convened in their first annual
meeting, a quarter of a century ago, Pope Benedict XV, in April 1919,
addressed a letter to the American Episcopate in which His Holiness
congratulated its members for taking the opportunity of the Golden
Episcopal Jubilee of Cardinal Gibbons to discuss "matters of the highest import for the welfare of both Church and country." The pope in
this letter also expressed his satisfaction "that a yearly meeting of all
the Bishops shall be held," and also that commissions "appointed
from among the Bishops—will report to their Episcopal brethren."
His Holiness continued: "It is indeed wonderful how greatly the progress of Catholicism is favored by those frequent assemblies of bishops,
which our predecessors have more than once approved." In concluding this memorable letter, the pope charged the American bishops with their tremendous responsibilty in these words:

> Greater efforts are demanded of you than of all others, owing to the
> vast influence which you exercise among your people. Retaining,
> as they do, a most firm hold on the principles of reasonable liberty
> and of Christian civilization, they are destined to have the chief role
> in the restoration of peace and order, and in the reconstruction of
> human society on the basis of these same principles, when the vio-
> lence of these tempestuous days shall have passed.

3.   Twenty-five years ago the words of the pope were an inspiration and a challenge to the bishops of the United States. Many prelates, as well as the first general secretary, who worked untiringly to perfect the organization founded by the American episcopate in 1919, have been called to their eternal reward.

4.   The achievements of twenty-five years, through the departments and episcopal committees of the National Catholic Welfare Conference, have brought to the priests and the faithful a fuller realization that their particular labors however humble are a necessary service to advance the divine mission of the Church. The letters and statements issued either by the administrative board or by the general body of bishops have done much to unify the thought of the Catholic body by making it realize its obligations to the parish, to the diocese, and to the Universal Church, with due regard for the spirit, conditions, and opportunities of our country. The trials and sufferings of the Church in many parts of the world, during the past quarter of a century, especially during the present war, the most cruel ever waged, have made our people suffer with their afflicted brethren in other parts of the world. The spirit of generosity manifested by our people in helping suffering humanity deserves the highest commendation.

5.   While the Conference of the Bishops has passed through trying days which tested its value to the Church and to our country, it is today stronger and better organized because of its trials. The field of Catholic action is clearly defined and many worthy activities are encouraged.

6.   The Conference has brought our bishops, priests, and laity in closer contact with the Holy See and has given them deeper insight into the apostolic and universal mission of the Church. The many commendations given by Popes Benedict XV, Pius XI, and His Holiness, our present Holy Father, to the Conference, express some fulfillment of the hopes of the Supreme Pontiffs for the organized activities of the American Bishops through annual meetings, and also encourage them to continue their indefatigable labors.

7.   The Conference, through its headquarters at the National Capital, has ever sought to render service to all dioceses and religious institutes of our country. It has been at once a clearing house, an exchange for varying judgments and opinions, a source of information, an agency to serve every Catholic cause, a medium of contact with our government, and a unique center of Catholic thought and action which only future generations can fully evaluate.

8.   The national and international activities of the Conference, owing to the present global war, are numberless. Decisions have to be made in fields where there are new applications of principles, where new courses have to be charted, new situations tested in the light of the noonday sun. The sanity of the Catholic faith, of Catholic principles, and of the Catholic position of the Conference so far has merited the praise of all informed and right-thinking men. The achievements of the bishops, of the staff at the national headquarters, of the priests and laity of our country, working in harmonious cooperation, might well be considered impossible if we were not witnesses of their realization.

9.   In prayerful confidence we express the hope that the Conference may be privileged to do much for the peace of our country when the warring nations end their present world conflict. Peace, prosperous and happy times will not come as the direct result of the cessation of hostilities. The best thought of patriotic men and the wisdom which comes only from reliance on prayer, as well as unremitting labors, will be necessary to reconstruct the war-ruined nations and to reestablish our own beloved country in the ways of happy homes, of reasonable prosperity, with love in our hearts for God and for all men. The cessation of war and the beginning of peace will be another serious challenge to the Conference. God grant that it may meet it and thereby render a notable service to Church and country.

A Statement on International Order

A Statement Issued by the NCWC
Administrative Board in the Name of the
Bishops of the United States

November 16, 1944

1.   We have met the challenge of war. Shall we meet the challenge of peace? This is the question uppermost in the minds of men everywhere who in suffering and hardship have stood out against ruthless aggression. The men of our armed forces, the masses of our citizens, our leaders, all want to be true to our heroes who have given so much, some even their lives, in this war for freedom. They want to be true, as well, to future generations on whom we have been forced to place a heavy burden as the price for their freedoms. Honestly, earnestly we want to garner from the sacrifices, hardships, and losses which have gone into this war, the full fruits of victory, in a good peace. The foremost problem in postwar planning is how to secure for ourselves and all the world a just and lasting peace.

2.   Recently representatives of the United States, the United Kingdom, the Soviet Union, and China at Dumbarton Oaks formulated and presented to their governments broad tentative proposals for an international organization for "the maintenance of peace and security and the creation of conditions which make for peace." These proposals have been given to the public for full study and discussion by peoples of all countries. Our own secretary of state has expressed the hope that leaders of our national thought and opinion will discuss them in the spirit of constructive effort.

Freedom from Hatred, Greed

3.   Public opinion in our country can exert a tremendous influence in making the peace and determining the manner of international collaboration for its maintenance. If public opinion is indifferent or uninformed, we shall run the risk of a bad peace and perhaps return to the tragedy of "power politics," which in the past divided nations and sowed the seeds of war. If public opinion is alert and informed, we can have a lasting peace and security. It is imperative that all our citizens recognize their responsibility in the making and maintenance of the peace. They must inform themselves on the issues and form their judgments in the light of sound reason and our Christian democratic traditions. They must free themselves from hatred, from dis-

trust, and from the spirit of mere expediency, from national greed, and from indifference to right in the use of might, and they must form their judgments on the basis of stern objective realities.

4.   This war came largely from bad education. It was not brought on by primitives or unlettered peoples. The contemporary philosophy which asserts the right of aggression is the creation of scholars. Discarding moral principles and crowding God out of human life, scholars produced the monstrous philosophies which, embodied in political and social systems, enslave human reason and destroy the consciousness of innate human rights and duties. In these systems the notion of the common good is utterly distorted; it is no longer conceived as the consequence of the common enjoyment of rights and the common discharge of duties, but the creation of the caprice of a dictator or a group or a party. The gilded dreams of a new era, which these systems heralded, have proved to be a hideous nightmare. If we are to have a just and lasting peace, it must be the creation of a sane realism, which has a clear vision of the moral law, a reverent acknowledgment of God its Author, and a recognition of the oneness of the human race underlying all national distinctions.

Atlantic Charter without Equivocations

5.   We have no confidence in a peace which does not carry into effect, without reservations or equivocations, the principles of the Atlantic Charter. We feel, too, that it should provide assistance for prostrate nations in reconstructing their economic, social, and political institutions. If justice is compromised, if unreasonable concessions are made to might, grievances will rankle in the bosom of aggrieved nations to endanger the peace of the world. If prostrate nations are not assisted in giving to their people fair economic opportunities, they will become the arena of civil strife and turmoil. No international organization will be able to maintain a peace which is unfair and unjust.

6.   There is an international community of nations. God Himself has made the nations interdependent for their full life and growth. It is not, therefore, a question of creating an international community but of organizing it. To do this we must repudiate absolutely the tragic fallacies of "power politics" with its balance of power, spheres of influence in a system of puppet governments, and the resort to war as a means of settling international difficulties.

Might Must Yield to Law

7. After the last world war an attempt was made to organize the international community. It failed not because its objective was mistaken but because of inherent defects in its charter and more especially perhaps because the nations were not disposed to recognize their duty to work together for the common good of the world. International law must govern international relations. Might must be subordinated to law. An international institution, based on the recognition of an objective moral obligation and not on the binding force of convenant alone, is needed for the preservation of a just peace and the promotion of international cooperation for the common good of the international community. The common good of every nation is inseparably connected with the common good of the international community.

8. The international institution must be universal. It must seek to include, with due regard to basic equality of rights, all the nations, large and small, strong and weak. Its constitution must be democratic. While it is reasonable to set up a security council with limited membership, this council must not be an instrument for imperialistic domination by a few powerful nations. Before it every nation must stand on its rights and not on its power. It must not allow any nation to sit in judgment in its own case. Frankly it must recognize that for nations as well as individuals life is not static. It must, therefore, provide in its charter for the revision of treaties in the interest of justice and the common good of international community, as well as for the recognition of a people's coming of age in the family of nations.

Strong Nations Must Help the Weak Ones

9. The function of the international organization must be the maintenance of international peace and security, the promotion of international cooperation, and the adoption of common policies for the solution of common economic, social, and other humanitarian problems. In the maintenance of peace it is reasonable that the organization have at its disposal resources for coercing outlaw nations even by military measures.

10. In fostering and promoting international cooperation it must seek to guarantee to the weak and poor nations economic opportunities which are necessary to give their peoples reasonable standards of living, and it must seek to prevent selfish monopolistic control of raw materials which are needed for the economic stability of other nations. Effective international cooperation lays definite duties on favored nations. No nation may view with unconcern conditions that permit millions of workers in any country to be without the opportunity to secure from their labor adequate family support. Nations rich in natural resources must remember that ownership of property never dispenses from the social obligations of stewardship. Nations gifted with inventive and productive genius are obligated to serve the reasonable needs of other nations. Nations should open, under effective guarantees, world lanes of commerce and world avenues of communication to all law-abiding countries. Protective national legislation for legitimate national economic interests must not impede the flow of international commerce and the right social function of international exchange.

Teeth for World Court

11. In the international organization there should be a world court to which justiciable disputes among nations must be submitted. Its authority should not be merely advisory but strictly judicial. A condition for the right functioning of this court is the proper development and codification of international law. Competent international authority must enact into positive law the principles of the moral law in their international references, and to these will be added positive treaty provisions and the charter and legislation of the international organization.

12. The world court should be empowered to render decisions in cases submitted to it either by any party in interest or by the international organization. It must have authority to refer its decisions to the international organization for execution. It would be useless to set up a world court and either deny it the right to demand the execution of its decisions or make the execution of them subject to the discretion of the international organization. Nations which refuse to submit their international disputes which constitute a threat to the peace or the common good of the international community should be treated by the international organization as outlaw nations. Moreover, obligatory arbitration of international disputes which threaten world peace would mark a signal advance in international relations.

Rights of Man

13. The international organization must never violate the rightful sovereignty of nations. Sovereignty is a right which comes from the juridical personality of a nation and which the international organization must safeguard and defend. However, national sovereignty may not be interpreted as absolving a nation from its obligations in the international community. Moreover, even within the state, national sovereignty is limited by the innate rights of men and families. Since civil authority does not confer these God-given rights, it may not violate them.

14. The ideology of a nation in its internal life is a concern of the international community. To reject this principle is tantamount to maintaining that the violation of the innate rights of men in a country by its own government has no relation to world peace. Just at this moment, in the interest of world peace, our nation is exerting itself to root out some ideologies which violate human rights in the countries we are liberating. We hold that if there is to be a genuine and lasting world peace, the international organization should demand as a condition of membership that every nation guarantee in law and respect in fact the innate rights of men, families, and minority groups in their civil and religious life. Surely our generation should know that tyranny in any nation menaces world peace. A nation which refuses to accord to its own people the full enjoyment of innate human rights cannot be relied upon to cooperate in the international community for the maintenance of a peace which is based on the recognition of national freedom. Such a nation will pursue its own selfish international policies, while paying lip service to international cooperation.

Free Men, Free Nations

15. We have it within our power to introduce a new era, the era for which peoples have been longing through the centuries, the era in which nations will live together in justice and charity. It is a Christian hope we want to realize, the hope of a world at peace, a world of sovereign states cooperating in assuring all men the full enjoyment of their rights, a world of free men and free nations with their freedom secured under law. War may come, but if our hope is realized it will be a war of punishment meted out to outlaw nations. Through all the sufferings and sacrifices of this war we have remembered and we recall today the words of our chief executive, written at its beginning:

> We shall win this war and in victory we shall seek not vengeance but the establishment of an international order in which the spirit of Christ shall rule the hearts of men and of nations.

Signed by the members of the Administrative Board, NCWC, in the name of the bishops of the United States

Edward Mooney, Chairman, Archbishop of Detroit

Samuel A. Stritch, Vice-Chairman, Archbishop of Chicago

Francis J. Spellman, Secretary, Archbishop of New York

John T. McNicholas, Archbishop of Cincinnati

John Gregory Murray, Archbishop of St. Paul

John J. Mitty, Archbishop of San Francisco

Joseph F. Rummel, Archbishop of New Orleans

John F. Noll, Bishop of Fort Wayne

Karl J. Alter, Bishop of Toledo

James H. Ryan, Bishop of Omaha

Between War and Peace

*A Statement Issued by the NCWC
Administrative Board in the Name of the
Bishops of the United States*

November 18, 1945

1.   The war is over, but there is no peace in the world. In the Atlantic Charter we were given the broad outline of the peace for which we fought and bled and, at an incalculable price, won a great martial victory. It was that ideal of peace which sustained us through the war, which inspired the heroic defense of liberty by millions driven underground in enslaved countries. It made small, oppressed nations confide in us as the trustee of their freedoms. It was the broad outline of a good peace. Are we going to give up this ideal of peace? If, under the pretext of a false realism, we do so, then we shall stand face to face with the awful catastrophe of atomic war.

2.   Since the Moscow Conference of 1943, the United States, Great Britain, and Russia have undertaken to shape gradually the peace which they are imposing on the nations. From the conferences of these victorious powers there is emerging slowly their pattern for the peace. It is disappointing in the extreme. Assurances are given us in the announced peace principles of our country but so far results do not square with these principles. We are in perhaps the greatest crisis of human history. Our country has the power, the right, and the responsibility to demand a genuine peace, based on justice which will answer the cry in the hearts of men across the world.

3.   We want to work in unity with other nations for the making of a good peace. During the war perhaps, it may have been necessary for strategic reasons to postpone final decisions on many questions mooted at the conferences of the three great powers. Now we must face the facts. There are profound differences of thought and policy between Russia and the Western democracies. Russia has acted unilaterally on many important settlements. It has sought to establish its sphere of influence in eastern and southeastern Europe, not on the basis of sound regional agreements in which sovereignties and rights are respected, but by the imposition of its sovereignty and by ruthlessly setting up helpless puppet states. Its Asiatic policy, so important for the peace of the world, is an enigma.

4.   The totalitarian dictators promise benefits to the masses through an omnipotent police state which extends its authority to all human relations and recognizes no innate freedom. Their theories, moreover, look to the realization of world well-being as ultimately to be secured by the inclusion of all countries in their system. Sometimes Russia uses our vocabulary and talks of democracy and rights but it attaches distorted meanings to the words. We think in terms of our historic culture. We see God-given, inviolable human rights in every person and we know democracy as the free collaboration under law of citizens in a free country.

5.   There is a clash of ideologies. The frank recognition of these differences is preliminary to any sincere effort in realistic world cooperation for peace. The basis of this cooperation must be mutual adherence to justice. It would be unjust for us to be an accomplice in violating the rights of nations, groups, and individuals anywhere in the world.

6.   A first step toward effective negotiation for peace is to have a plan. A good plan states principles in terms of all the specific questions at issue. Instead, so far we have compromised and sought to make mere piecemeal settlements. Instead of honest, promising discussion even on diverging plans, we are witnessing a return of the tragedy of power politics and the danger of balance of power arrangements which, with the substitution of mere expediency for justice, have begotten war after war. We must indeed aim at collaborating with all of our allies in the making of a good peace. There are, however, concessions which we dare not make because they are immoral and destructive of genuine peace.

Peace Program

7.   Our peace program envisions a world organization of nations. The charter which emerged from the San Francisco Conference, while undoubtedly an improvement on the Dumbarton Oaks proposals, does not provide for a sound, institutional organization of the international society. The security council provisions make it no more than a virtual alliance of the great powers for the maintenance of peace. These nations are given a status above the law. Nevertheless, our country acted wisely in deciding to participate in this world organization. It is better than world chaos. From the provision in the charter for calling a constituent assembly in the future, there comes the hope that in time the defects may be eliminated and we may have a sound institutional organization of the international community which will develop, not through mere voluntary concessions of the nations, but from the recognition of the rights and duties of international society.

8.   While peace is in the making, there are urgent issues which we can no longer evade. At Yalta we gave a pledge to the Polish people and assumed responsibility before the world that they would be unhampered in setting up their own independent democratic government. Are we working to the fulfillment of that pledge in the full measure of our responsibility and our power? What apology can be offered for the failure of the protagonists of democracy to protest the

absorption by force and artifice of the Baltic countries into the Union of Soviet Republic? We are shocked by the news which is leaking out from Slovakia, Croatia, Slovenia, and other southeastern European countries. Religious persecution which is both brutal and cunning rages in many lands. No reason of policy justifies our silence. What is happening behind the blackout of eastern and southeastern Europe is a stark contradiction to the high ideals which inspired our fighting to save the world from totalitarian aggression.

9.   No one can fail to see the importance of a reconstructed, revitalized Europe which is the cradle of Western culture. We deplore the tragic indifference to the plight of the Italian people who threw off the chains of a fascist regime, who fought side by side with us in ardent loyalty. For over two long years of agony the friends of democracy in that country have had to stand by in impotence while we have toyed with the vital problems of relief and rehabilitation and deferred the fulfillment of our own solemn promises.

Mercy to Enemies

10.   Our own national interest, as well as the cause of world peace, and the fate of Christian culture are at stake in Italy. Today it is an outpost of Western civilization. We are fully confident that the Italian people, if we save them from despair by our helpful interest, will stand fast against the deceitful appeal of alien and subversive ideologies and shape their future in the spirit of their own noble tradition.

11.   We cannot be unconcerned about the future of Germany, Austria, and Hungary. Whatever period of probation must be imposed on the vanquished nations, we must help them to take their rightful place in the family of nations. To treat them in a spirit of vengeance is neither right nor politic. Justice demands the punishment of the guilty and reasonable reparations of damage done. But we cannot forget, or allow our representatives to forget, that our traditional system of punitive justice is anchored to the concept of individual responsibility. The inhumanities which now mark the mass transference of populations, the systematized use of slave labor, and the cruel treatment of prisoners of war should have no place in our civilization.

12.   Acute suffering is the daily lot of whole populations in many wartorn lands. Every report indicates that unless heroic measures are taken at once, millions will die from starvation and exposure during the coming winter. The feeding and clothing and sheltering of these suffering people is not a work which can be left to some future convenient date. Our country, because of our greater resources, must do the major part of this work of relief. In it we have the right and duty to insist on the leadership which corresponds to our sacrifices and contributions. It is imperative that Congress make adequate appropriations for this work from the public treasury.

Private Relief

13. It is equally imperative that private relief agencies be given a full opportunity to carry on their beneficent work among all suffering peoples. And relief must envision something larger than merely feeding the starving and sheltering the homeless. Help must be given to peoples whose economies are ruined. They have the right to assistance in getting back to normal economic life. Neither the prosperity of the greater nations nor their might will prevent war unless conditions are removed in which poor, helpless peoples are denied the opportunity of a decent living standard. The world is one only insofar as men live together as brothers under God.

14. Ours is a grave responsibility. The heart and hand of America are called upon in a way that is unique, not only in the history of our country but even in the annals of mankind. We know that democracy is as capable of solving the admittedly difficult problems of peace as it has shown itself in war. We must be true to ourselves. We must hold fast to our own free institutions. We must resolutely oppose the few amongst us who are trying to sabotage them. We may well pity those who in their half-veiled sympathy for totalitarianism are playing with the thought that perhaps in this great emergency its day is at hand. On bended knees let us ask God in His blessed providence to help us to be the vigorous champion of democratic freedom and the generous friend of the needy and oppressed throughout the world.

Signed by the members of the Administrative Board, NCWC, in the name of the bishops of the United States

Samuel A. Stritch, Archbishop of Chicago

John Gregory Murray, Archbishop of St. Paul

Francis J. Spellman, Archbishop of New York

John Mark Gannon, Bishop of Erie

John J. Mitty, Archbishop of San Francisco

Joseph F. Rummel, Archbishop of New Orleans

Richard J. Cushing, Archbishop of Boston

James H. Ryan, Archbishop of Omaha

John F. Noll, Bishop of Fort Wayne

Karl J. Alter, Bishop of Toledo

Statement on Compulsory Peacetime Military Service

*A Statement Issued by the Administrative
Board of the National Catholic Welfare
Conference*

November 1945

1. We recognize the imperative need of preparedness for the adequate defense of our country in all circumstances.

2. In determining what constitutes national defense in our present circumstances, our government, we feel, should explore the possibility of having military conscription abolished in all countries, and, to that end, might well consider how our control of economic assistance to other countries may be used to lend weight to our plea for such abolition.

3. If a wide extension of military training is found necessary for present adequate defense of our nation, we feel that such training should be in keeping with American traditions, and that, specifically:

(a) Voluntary enlistments in the armed forces should be stimulated as much as possible, to provide our first line of defense;

(b) Any period of enforced training should be integrated with normal school life; and,

(c) The War and Navy Departments should work with recognized moral leadership to correct certain policies and attitudes which have wrought grave moral damage to great numbers of young people in the armed services during the past five years.

Man and the Peace!

*A Statement Issued by the NCWC
Administrative Board in the Name of the
Bishops of the United States*

November 17, 1946

1. At the bottom of all problems of the world today is the problem of man. Unless those who bear the responsibility of world leadership are in basic agreement on what man is, there is no way out of the confusion and conflict which block the road to real peace. Clashes on the question of boundaries, national security, minority safeguards, free movement of trade, easy access to raw materials, progressive disarmament, and the control of the atomic bomb, important as these are, take a second place to the need of unity in protecting man in the enjoyment of his God-given native rights. The struggle of the small nations for their indisputable rights and the stalemate among the strong nations in a contest of power would admit of bearable, even though hard, compromise if the fate of man, as man, did not hang in the balance.

2. To be more explicit, it is a question whether national governments are disposed to protect or to hinder the individual in the exercise of rights and in the discharge of duties which are proper to him prior to any action by the state. The words of our own Declaration of Independence express no new doctrine but voice the basic tradition of Christian civilization:

> We hold these truths to be self-evident, that all men are created equal, that they are endowed by their Creator with certain unalienable rights, that among these are life, liberty, and the pursuit of happiness.

Respect for the rights and duties of man as an individual and as a member of civic and domestic society we hold to be the first obligation of any government to its citizens. The state has a just claim on the cooperation of its citizens for the common good, but not to the point of coercion in violation of their personal political, social, and religious rights. What a government cannot do in the exercise of its own sovereignty it cannot approve or abet on the part of another government in the settlement of complicated issues such as confront the nations in making peace and planning for its preservation.

The Conflict between Russia and
the West

3.   The menace to man, as man looms large in the outstanding questions which engage the attention of the victorious allies. It hangs in the background of the conflict between Russia and the West which has so long delayed the making of the peace. Eighteen months have passed since the surrender and occupation of Germany and fifteen months since the capitulation of Japan. There have been continuous negotiations among the three great victors, the United States, Britain, and Russia, for the conclusion of agreements on stable peace and reconstruction. These negotiations have brought out in the clear the tragic lack of unity among the peacemakers on fundamental issues. In some instances agreements which were pointed to the safeguarding of basic human rights, reached in conferences, have been repudiated unilaterally by the action of one of the victors, and these repudiations have been tolerated by the other nations which were parties to the agreements. In an effort to preserve unity, fatal compromises have been made, either explicitly or by tolerance of shocking aggressions. In so difficult a task it is understandable that there should be differences and a clash of interests. Some sort of sacrifice of particular national advantages for the common good of the international community, and therefore for the ultimate good of all nations, must be made. But the tragic fact is that the cleavage touches on issues on which there can be no compromise. While it is stated that the Western democracies and Russia with her satellite governments in the countries of eastern Europe are at a stalemate over questions of security against aggressions, the fact is that underlying these questions there is the question of man, as man. Throughout the war our battle cry was the defense of native freedoms against Nazi and fascist totalitarianism. The aftermath of war has revealed victorious Soviet totalitarianism no less aggressive against these freedoms in the countries it has occupied. Totalitarianism does not acknowledge and respect these freedoms. It persecutes the citizen who dares assert his native rights. It imposes on peoples its philosophy of life, in which there is no authority above the state, and in which all values in life are derived from human conventions. The corollary of such philosophy is the police state, which terrorizes its citizens and dominates them in all fields of human behavior. Before we can hope for a good peace there must come an agreement among the peacemakers on the basic question of man, as man. If this agreement is reached, then secondary, though important, defects in the peace may be tolerable in the hope of their eventual correction. Misrepresentations, deceitful promises, the use of equivocal language, and violation of agreements only widen the cleavage between nations. In the charter of the United Nations, the signatories have contracted to cooperate "in promoting and encouraging respect for human rights and for fundamental freedoms for all without distinction as to race, language, or religion." Let the nations in the making of the peace do even more and in solemn covenants actually secure men everywhere in the enjoyment of their native rights. Then there will be the beginnings of peace, and the fear of war will be banished from men's minds.

Plea for Prisoners of War

4.   Considerations of human dignity are deeply involved in the fate of prisoners of war. The strict observance of international law does not oblige the victorious nations to repatriate prisoners of war until after the conclusion of the peace, but owing to the circumstance of the long delay in making peace, the contention of our country for the speedy repatriation of these prisoners is admirably humane and almost a dictate of justice. There are millions of them separated from their families and kept from their normal occupations, engaged in forced labor, and in many cases underfed. They are needed at home for the work of reconstruction. The use of prisoners of war as slave laborers in alien lands should not be any part of reparations levied by the victors. They are men, and they should be treated as men. So large is their number, estimated as high as seven million, that even with every effort put forth for their speedy repatriation, it will take years to transport them back to their own countries in an orderly way. It is the strict obligation of all nations to treat these prisoners as we demanded that our combatants, who fell into the hands of the enemy, be treated. It is unworthy of the victors to revenge injustices by violating human rights and heaping insults on human dignity. As things are now, future generations may well charge the victors with guilt of inhumanities which are reminiscent of Nazism and Fascism.

Humane Treatment of
Displaced Persons

5.   A serious problem which challenges the nations is finding a way rightly to provide for the hundreds of thousands of refugees from persecution and dire danger now in camps in central Europe. These victims of injustice have the right of refuge, a right that is sacrosanct in our history and culture. To provide for them and to give them an opportunity to begin life anew in useful pursuits without fear is the inescapable responsibility of the nations. All of them, the displaced persons and the persecuted peoples, must be treated humanely without discrimination. A perfect solution of the problem would be to

give them the full guarantee for the enjoyment of their native rights in their countries of origin. Since this solution is not forthcoming, the nations must extend to them the help which their very human rights demand. It is plain that to continue indefinitely to support them in camps is not a solution of the problem and is, in fact, an injury to them. To force them against their will to return to their countries of origin, where, with reason, they fear that grave dangers await them, is stark inhumanity. By agreement among the victors those in the displaced persons camps allegedly guilty of crimes must be returned to their countries of origin. If guilty, they should be punished, but they should not be made the victims of political persecution with the cooperation of the authorities of the military occupation. Before honoring demands for the return of these persons to their countries of origin the military authorities are obligated to give the accused honest juridical preliminary hearings to prevent grave injustice. Tragic indeed was the decision of the United Nations Committee on Refugees that "all measures be taken" to repatriate child refugees to their countries of origin. Nor can we condone with any sense of humanity the alternative of either returning refugees against their will to their countries of origin or throwing them on the economy of any already overcrowded and impoverished Germany. With justice to all these unfortunate men, women, and children, and without discrimination in favor of any group of them, the nations must find a way to resettle them in countries where opportunities to begin life anew await them. It is heartening that the president of the United States has pledged himself publicly to ask our Congress to enact a law which will permit the entry of considerable numbers of them into the United States. If this is done, the generosity of our country will stir other nations to give these unfortunate people a haven and a chance to live in the enjoyment of their God-given rights. The problem is admittedly very difficult, but the difficulty in it should be a challenge to the nations to solve it in a constructive, humane way, in which charity will do even what justice does not compel.

Ruthless Herding of Uprooted People

6. Something has been happening in Europe which is new in the annals of recorded history. By agreement among the victors, millions of Germans who for centuries have lived in eastern Europe are being forced from their homes, without resources, into the heart of Germany. The sufferings of these people in their weary travels, the homelessness of them, and the hopelessness, make a sad story of the inhumanity of their transplantation. Had there prevailed in the councils of the victor nations a right appreciation of the dignity of man, at least arrangements would have been made for transplanting these people in a humane way. We boast of our democracy, but in this transplantation of peoples we have perhaps unwittingly allowed ourselves to be influenced by the herd theory of heartless totalitarian political philosophy.

7.   The reports of the deportation of thousands in areas of Soviet aggression to remote and inhospitable regions just because they cannot subscribe to Communism tell of a cruel violation of human rights. These men are men and have the rights of men. Our sympathy also goes out to the technicians and skilled workers in enemy countries who have been seized and forced to work for the strengthening of the economy of victorious nations. It is not in this way that peace is made and the nations are united in mutual cooperation. No lasting good can ever come from the violation of the dignity of the human person.

Continued Relief Imperative

8.   In many lands, men, women, and children are in dire need of the very necessaries of life. In some large measure this need is the consequence of the stoppage of that normal interchange of goods between the industrial and agricultural areas of Europe, which for centuries has been at the base of European economy. In some places it is the result of political, racial, and religious persecution. For many millions it is the heavy penalty of war. In our charity we must not be insensible to the misery of our fellow men. Human solidarity, as well as Christian brotherhood, dictates the sharing of our substance with our brothers in distress. We may well be proud of the generosity of the people of the United States in their relief work in war-torn lands. The want, however, is so great that, without continued governmental aid, private charity will be inadequate to relieve it. A way must be found for the nations to continue their work of relief until the danger of widespread starvation and disease is gone and peoples are able to provide for at least their own basic needs. The winter before us will be a hard, bitter winter for millions, and the charity of individuals and governments must be very large to prevent an awful catastrophe. But charity is not a substitute for justice. The continuance of widespread want is largely due to the delay of the nations in making the peace. Justice demands that they make promptly a peace in which all men can live as men.

Dignity of Human Person

9. In the aftermath of war, public opinion tends to overlook the sacredness of human life. We have just been through our first experience with mechanized war, in which the manhood of the world has been in battle on fields of combat and in industry, agriculture, and transportation. Our enemies, with utter disregard for the sacredness of human life, committed brutalities that horrified us and unfortunately we used weapons which brought widespread, unspeakable suffering and destruction. Day after day there were the accounts of the killing and the maiming of thousands. Never before did the human family suffer so large a number of casualties. It was hard always to be mindful of the sacredness of the life of the individual. There was the temptation to think only in terms of mass killings and mass murders. Out of it all many have failed to interpret in terms of the human sufferings which they connote, the headlines in our daily press which even now tell of racial and religious persecution, of the transplantation of millions of people from one area to another and of the seizure of political control by the liquidation of opposition. How can there be a beginning of even a tolerable peace unless the peacemakers fully realize that human life is sacred and that all men have rights?

Prayer for Peacemakers

10. And for us who profess the Christian name, human life is even more precious and sacred, because for every man the Savior shed His blood in bitter anguish on Calvary. We know that in His sacred blood all men are called to be brothers. We are our brothers' keepers. It is not possible for us to be complacent and inactive while any of our brothers in the human family groan under tyranny and are denied the free exercise of their human rights. In Christian solidarity, with humble hearts, we confess our sins and the sins of our race, and pleadingly beg, through the merits of Christ, merciful forgiveness from our Father Who is in Heaven. Mindful of the sacred promise of the Savior, we pray for light and strength for those who in our country bear the heavy responsibility of making decisions for us in the peace conferences; and, indeed, for all the peacemakers. May the Savior enlighten and strengthen them to imitate His blessed example and, in sacrifice and unselfishness, in the clear light of reason, secure for all men the enjoyment of their God-given rights, so that they may follow their vocation as sons of God and brothers in Christ.

Signed by the members of the Administrative Board, NCWC, in the name of the bishops of the United States

Samuel Cardinal Stritch, Archbishop of Chicago

Francis Cardinal Spellman, Archbishop of New York

John Gregory Murray, Archbishop of St. Paul

John J. Mitty, Archbishop of San Francisco

Joseph F. Rummel, Archbishop of New Orleans

Richard J. Cushing, Archbishop of Boston

James H. Ryan, Archbishop of Omaha

John Mark Gannon, Bishop of Erie

John F. Noll, Bishop of Fort Wayne

Karl J. Alter, Bishop of Toledo

Statement on Secularism

A Statement Issued by the NCWC
Administrative Board in the Name of the
Bishops of the United States

November 14, 1947

1. No man can disregard God—and play a man's part in God's world. Unfortunately, however, there are many men—and their number is daily increasing—who in practice live their lives without recognizing that this is God's world. For the most part they do not deny God. On formal occasions they may even mention His name. Not all of them would subscribe to the statement that all moral values derive from merely human conventions. But they fail to bring an awareness of their responsibility to God into their thought and action as individuals and members of society.

2. This, in essence, is what we mean by secularism. It is a view of life that limits itself not to the material in exclusion of the spiritual, but to the human here and now in exclusion of man's relation to God here and hereafter. Secularism, or the practical exclusion of God from human thinking and living, is at the root of the world's travail today. It was the fertile soil in which such social monstrosities as Fascism, Nazism, and Communism could germinate and grow. It is doing more than anything else to blight our heritage of Christian culture, which integrates the various aspects of human life and renders to God the things that are God's. Through the centuries, Christian culture has struggled with man's inborn inclination to evil. The ideals of Christianity have never been fully realized—just as the ideals of our Declaration of Independence and of our Constitution have never been fully realized in American political life. But for that reason these ideals can neither be ignored nor discarded. Without doubt, Christians have often failed to meet their responsibilities and by their transgressions have permitted ugly growths to mar the institutions of their culture. But wherever, despite their lapses, they have held steadfastly to their Christian ideals, the way to effective reform and progress has been kept open. The remedy for the shortcomings and sins of Christian peoples is surely not to substitute secularism for godliness, human vagaries for divine truth, man-made expedients for a God-given standard of right and wrong. This is God's world and if we are to play a man's part in it, we must first get down on our knees and with humble hearts acknowledge God's place in His world. This, secularism does not do.

The Individual

3. Secularism, in its impact on the individual, blinds him to his responsibility to God. All the rights, all the freedoms of man derive originally from the fact that he is a human person, created by God after His own image and likeness. In this sense he is "endowed by his Creator with certain unalienable rights." Neither reason nor history offers any other solid ground for man's inalienable rights. It is as God's creature that man generally and most effectively recognizes a personal responsibility to seek his own moral perfection. Only a keen awareness of personal responsibility to God develops in a man's soul the saving sense of sin. Without a deep-felt conviction of what sin is, human law and human conventions can never lead man to virtue. If in the privacy of his personal life the individual does not acknowledge accountability to God for his thought and his action, he lacks the only foundation for stable moral values. Secularism does away with accountability to God as a practical consideration in the life of man, and thus, takes from him the sense of personal guilt of sin before God. It takes account of no law above man-made law. Expediency, decency, and propriety are, in its code, the norms of human behavior. It blurs, if it does not blot out, the ennobling and inspiring picture of man which the Christian Gospel paints. In divine revelation, man is the son of God as well as God's creature. Holiness is his vocation, and life's highest values have to do with things of the soul. "For what does it profit a man, if he gain the whole world, but suffer the loss of his own soul? Or what will a man give in exchange for his soul?" Secularism may quote these words of Christ, but never in their full Christian sense. For that very reason secularism blights the noblest aspirations in man which Christianity has implanted and fostered. Unfortunately, many who still profess to be Christians are touched by this blight. The greatest moral catastrophe of our age is the growing number of Christians who lack a sense of sin because a personal responsibility to God is not a moving force in their lives. They live in God's world, quite unmindful of Him as their Creator and Redeemer. The vague consciousness of God which they may retain is impotent as a motive in daily conduct. The moral regeneration which is recognized as absolutely necessary for the building of a better world must begin by bringing the individual back to God and to an awareness of his responsibility to God. This, secularism, of its very nature, cannot do.

The Family

4. Secularism has wrought havoc in the family. Even the pagans saw something sacred in marriage and the family. In Christian doctrine its holiness is so sublime that it is likened to the mystical union of Christ and His Church. Secularism has debased the marriage contract by robbing it of its relation to God and, therefore, of its sacred character. It has set the will and convenience of husband and wife in the place that Christian thought gives to the will of God and the good of society.

5. A secularized pseudoscience has popularized practices which violate nature itself and rob human procreation of its dignity and nobility. Thus, selfish pursuit of pleasure is substituted for salutary self-discipline in family life.

6. Secularism has completely undermined the stability of the family as a divine institution and has given our country the greatest divorce problem in the Western world. In taking God out of family life, it has deprived society's basic educational institution of its most powerful means in molding the soul of the child. Public authority and the press are constantly emphasizing our grave problem of juvenile delinquency. On all sides is heard the cry that something be done about the problem. Our profound conviction is that nothing much will ever be done about it unless we go to the root of the evil and learn the havoc that secularism has wrought in the family. In vain shall we spend public moneys in vast amounts for educational and recreational activities if we do not give more thought to the divinely ordained stability of the family and the sanctity of the home.

7. God planned the human family and gave it its basic constitution. When secularism discards that plan and constitution it lacerates the whole social fabric. Artificial family planning on the basis of contraceptive immorality, cynical disregard of the noble purposes of sex, a sixtyfold increase in our divorce rate during the past century, and widespread failure of the family to discharge its educational functions are terrible evils which secularism has brought to our country. What hope is there of any effective remedy unless men bring God back into family life and respect the laws He has made for this fundamental unit of human society?

Education

8. In no field of social activity has secularism done more harm than in education. In our own country secularists have been quick to exploit for their own purposes the public policy adopted a century ago of banning the formal teaching of religion from the curriculum of our common schools. With a growing number of thoughtful Americans, we see in this policy a hasty and shortsighted solution of the very difficult educational problem that confronts public authority in a nation of divided religious allegiance. But it should ever be kept in mind that the original proponents of the policy did not intend to minimize the importance of religion in the training of youth. Erroneously, however, secularists take this policy, adopted as a practical expedient in difficult circumstances, and make it the starting point in their philosophy of education. They positively exclude God from the school. Among them are some who smile indulgently at the mention of the name of God and express wonder that inherited illusions last so long. Others are content with keeping God closeted in the inner chambers of private life.

9.   In the rearing of children and the forming of youth, omission is as effective as positive statement. A philosophy of education which omits God, necessarily draws a plan of life in which God either has no place or is a strictly private concern of men. There is a great difference between a practical arrangement which leaves the formal teaching of religion to the family and to the Church, and the educational theory of the secularist, who advisedly and avowedly excludes religion from his program of education. The first, reluctantly tolerated under certain conditions as a practical measure of public policy, may actually serve to emphasize the need of religious instruction and training, and to encourage public school administrators to cooperate with home and Church in making it possible. The other strikes at the very core of our Christian culture and in practice envisions men who have no sense of their personal and social responsibility to God. Secularism breaks with our historical American tradition. When parents build and maintain schools in which their children are trained in the religion of their fathers, they are acting in the full spirit of that tradition. Secularists would invade the rights of parents, and invest the state with supreme powers in the field of education; they refuse to recognize the God-given place that parents have in the education of their children. God is an inescapable fact, and one cannot make a safe plan for life in disregard of inescapable facts. Our youth problems would not be so grave if the place of God in life were emphasized in the rearing of children. There would be less danger for the future of our democratic institutions if secularism were not so deeply entrenched in much of our thinking on education.

The World of Work

10. Economic problems loom large in the social unrest and confusion of our times. Research students of varying shades of opinion are seeking the formula for a sound program of economic reform. Their common objective is a beneficent social order that will establish reasonable prosperity, provide families with an adequate income, and safeguard the public welfare. The Christian view of social order rejects the postulate of inexorable economic laws which fix recurring cycles of prosperity and depression. It lays the blame for instability in our social structure on human failure rather than on blind and uncontrollable economic forces. It faces the plain fact that there is something gravely wrong in our economic life and sees in secularism, with its disregard of God and God's law, a potent factor in creating the moral atmosphere which has favored the growth of this evil. Pointedly, indeed, has an eminent modern economist called attention to the fact that "in one hundred and fifty years economic laws were developed and postulated as iron necessities in a world apart from Christian obligation and sentiment." He adds:

> The early nineteenth century was full of economic doctrine and practice which, grounded in its own necessity and immutability, crossed the dictates of Christian feeling and teaching with only a limited sense of incongruity and still less of indignation.

11. God created man and made him brother to his fellow man. He gave man the earth and all its resources to be used and developed for the good of all. Thus, work of whatever sort is a social function, and personal profit is not the sole purpose of economic activity. In the Christian tradition, the individual has the right to reasonable compensation for his work, the right to acquire private property, and the right to a reasonable income from productive invested capital. Secularism takes God out of economic thinking and thereby minimizes the dignity of the human person endowed by God with inalienable rights and made responsible to Him for corresponding individual and social duties. Thus, to the detriment of man and society, the divinely established balance in economic relations is lost.

12. In Christian thought the work of man is not a commodity to be bought and sold, and economic enterprise is an important social function in which owner, manager, and workman cooperate for the common good. When disregard of his responsibility to God makes the owner forget his stewardship and the social function of private property, there comes that irrational economic individualism which brings misery to millions. Helpless workers are exploited; cutthroat competition and antisocial marketing practices follow. When men in labor organizations lose the right social perspective, which a sense of responsibility to God gives, they are prone to seek merely the victory of their own group, in disregard of personal and property rights. The Christian view of economic life supports the demand for organization of management, labor, agriculture, and professions under government encouragement but not control, in joint effort to avoid social conflict and to promote cooperation for the common good. In default of this free cooperation, public authority is finally invoked to maintain a measure of economic order, but it frequently exceeds the just limits of its power to direct economic activity to the common good. In the extreme case, where Marxian Communism takes over government, it abolishes private ownership and sets up a totalitarian state capitalism, which is even more intolerable than the grave evils it pretends to cure. Surely it ought to be plain today that there is no remedy for our economic evils in a return either to nineteenth century individualism or to experiments in Marxianism. If we abandon secularism and do our economic thinking in the light of Christian truth, we can hopefully work for economic collaboration in the spirit of genuine democracy. Let us be on our guard against all who, in exiling God from the factory and the marketplace, destroy the solid foundation of brotherhood in ownership, in management, and in work.

The International Community

13. In the international community there can be only one real bond of sane common action—the natural law which calls to God, its Author, and derives from Him its sanctions. There is objective right and objective wrong in international life. It is true that positive human law which comes from treaties and international conventions is necessary, but even these covenants must be in accord with God-given natural law. What may seem to be expedient for a nation cannot be tolerated if it contravenes God's law of right and wrong. In the international community that law has been flouted more openly, more widely, and more disastrously in our day than ever before in the Christian centuries. Shocking crimes against weak nations are being perpetrated in the name of national security. Millions of men in many nations are in the thralldom of political slavery. Religion is persecuted because it stands for freedom under God. The most fundamental human rights are violated with utter ruthlessness in a calculated, systematic degradation of man by blind and despotic leaders. Details of the sad and sickening story seep through the wall of censorship which encloses police states. Men long for peace and order, but the world stands on the brink of chaos. It is significant that godless forces have brought it there. Nazism and Fascism and Japanese militarism lie buried in the debris of some of the fairest cities of the world they vowed to rule or to ruin. Atheistic Communism, for a time thrown into alliance with democratic nations through Nazi aggression against Russia, stands out plainly today as the force which, through violence and chicanery, is obstructing the establishment of a right juridical order in the international community. That is plain for all to see. But thoughtful men perceive as well that secularism, which over the years has sapped the divinely laid foundations of the moral law, bears a heavy burden

of responsibility for the plight of the world today.

14. Secularism which exiles God from human life clears the way for the acceptance of godless subversive ideologies—just as religion, which keeps God in human life, has been the one outstanding opponent of totalitarian tyranny. Religion has been its first victim, for tyrants persecute what they fear. Thus, secularism, as the solvent of practical religious influence in the everyday life of men and nations, is not indeed the most patent, but in a very true sense the most insidious hindrance to world reconstruction within the strong framework of God's natural law. There would be more hope for a just and lasting peace if the leaders of the nations were really convinced that secularism which disregards God, as well as militant atheism which utterly denies Him, offer no sound basis for stable international agreements for enduring respect for human rights or for freedom under law.

15. In the dark days ahead we dare not follow the secularist philosophy. We must be true to our historic Christian culture. If all who believe in God would make that belief practical in their workaday lives; if they would see to it that their children are definitely imbued with that belief and trained in the observance of God's way of life; if they would look across the real differences which unfortunately divide them, to the common danger that threatens; if they would steadfastly refuse to let a common enemy capitalize on those differences to the detriment of social unity, we might begin to see a way out of the chaos that impends. Secularism holds out no valid promise of better things for our country or for the world. During our own lives, it has been the bridge between a decaying devotion to Christian culture and the revolutionary forces which have brought on what is perhaps the gravest crisis in all history. The tragic evil is not that our Christian culture is no longer capable of producing peace and reasonable prosperity, but that we are allowing secularism to divorce Christian truth from life. The fact of God and the fact of the responsibility of men and nations to God for their actions are supreme realities, calling insistently for recognition in a truly realistic ordering of life in the individual, in the family, in the school, in economic activity, and in the international community.

Signed by the members of the Administrative Board, NCWC, in the name of the bishops of the United States

Dennis Cardinal Dougherty,
Archbishop of Philadelphia

Edward Cardinal Mooney,
Archbishop of Detroit

Samuel Cardinal Stritch,
Archbishop of Chicago

Francis Cardinal Spellman,
Archbishop of New York

John T. McNicholas, OP,
Archbishop of Cincinnati

Robert E. Lucey, Archbishop of
San Antonio

Richard J. Cushing, Archbishop
of Boston

Joseph E. Ritter, Archbishop of
St. Louis

James H. Ryan, Archbishop of
Omaha

John Mark Gannon, Bishop
of Erie

John F. Noll, Bishop of
Fort Wayne

Emmet M. Walsh, Bishop of
Charleston

Karl J. Alter, Bishop of Toledo

Michael J. Ready, Bishop of
Columbus

The Christian in Action

*A Statement Issued by the NCWC
Administrative Board in the Name of the
Bishops of the United States*

November 21, 1948

1. Human life centers in God. The failure to center life in God is
secularism which, as we pointed out last year, is the most deadly
menace to our Christian and American way of living. We shall not
successfully combat this evil merely by defining and condemning it.
Constructive effort is called for to counteract this corrosive influence
in every phase of life where individual attitudes are a determining
factor—in the home, in the school, at work, and in civil polity. For
as man is, so ultimately are all the institutions of human society.
2. To combat secularism, the individual Christian must get the full
vision of Christian truth. It is not divisible. One cannot pick and
choose from it. Either it is accepted as a whole or it counts for little
in real life. When the Christian does get this full vision, he becomes
enthusiastic in trying to share it with the world about him. It is a
wonderful vision which gives new meaning to human life, and an
impelling urge to selfless action. The sorry fact is that many, very
many Christians see this vision only dimly and vaguely and miss its
impact on reality. They hold themselves to be Christians and are
accepted as Christians, but they have never been thrilled by the glory
of the truth of Christ in action. By their apathy they actually abet
those who work for destruction and chaos. They criticize and even
deplore the decay of morality and the spread of corruption in public
life, but they feel no obligation to do anything about it. They simply
do not realize that the great wonder of Divine Love is that it brings
the divine into human life and that godliness in living is giving self
to God. The great Christian paradox is that to find you must lose, to
get you must give. Much of the confusion and chaos about us is
attributable more directly to the inaction of Christians than to the
effectiveness of the feverish efforts of the destroyers. The destroyers
are definitely a minority, and yet the work of destruction goes on.
The crisis is at hand. Today every Christian must face the full Christian vision and with no thought of compromise must seek vigorously
to live it. Every day he must ask himself: What am I doing to build
a Christian world? No matter what his condition or state, there is
much that he can do. The reconstruction must start with the individual. He must be vigorously Christian in thought and in action—in

the home, in the training of his children, in his office or workshop, and in his community.

Religion in the Home

3.   In the full Christian vision, there is the divine ideal of the home, the basic social institution. It is not enough to profess the Christian truths of the stability and sanctity of the marriage bond and to keep in mind the purposes of marriage. The Christian must make his home holy. It remained for modern history to record the first experiment in secularizing the home, an experiment which is at the root of so many of our greatest social evils. The Christian home must realize the Christian ideal. The whole atmosphere of the home must be impregnated with genuine Christian living. The domestic virtues must be practiced and family prayer made a daily exercise. It is in the home that the children learn their responsibility to God and in this responsibility their duty to others. The home is the child's first school, in which he is taught to make the vision of Christian truth the inspiration of all living. We strongly commend organized effort to make the home more truly Christian. Our Catholic Family Life Bureau plans and offers programs which make for a veritable apostolate of the Catholic home. It is gratifying to see the use that is being made of these programs by our Catholic lay organizations and the spread of this work in our dioceses. These activities serve as a powerful antidote to the venom of secularism and withstand its withering effect on piety and virtue in the American home. All of us are familiar with the problems which the family faces in our complex and maladjusted society. In trying to solve these problems we must not compromise our Christian principles. The solution of these problems is only a part of the solution of the wider social problems of our day. To do their part, our homes must be thoroughly Christian and must let the glory of the full vision of Christian truth illumine them.

Religion in Education

4.   We know the sacrifices made by our people to educate their children in schools in which the "superabundant wisdom" is the Gospel of Christ. Catholic parents closely associate their schools with their Christian homes, because they know that human living must center in God. Year after year we are making wider provisons for the education of our Catholic youth. At a time when secularism has captured the minds of very many leaders in education, it is heartening that Catholic parents are becoming more insistent in their demand for schools in which the best standards of instruction and training are integrated in the teaching of religion. It behooves us to see that we enable our schools to work out fully the Christian educational ideal.

The field of higher education in particular demands a wider and more active interest. Our institutions of higher learning are the natural training grounds for Christian leadership. The ranks of Christian leadership will draw recruits largely from the undergraduate schools, but these ranks will not be filled without the Christian scholars who are formed in graduate schools. Perhaps much of the success of the secularist is due to the fact that the number of excellent Christian scholars is inadequate for the needs of our times. We ask a deeper appreciation of the contribution our institutions of higher learning are making to Christian reconstruction of society, and we urge a more generous support of their work. For if we as Christians are to do our part in restoring order to a chaotic world, Christ must be the Master in our classrooms and lecture halls and the Director of our research projects.

Religion in Economic Life

5.   Christian principles should be put into action in economic life. It is not enough to find fault with the way our economic system is working. Positive, constructive thought and action are needed.

6.   The secularist solutions proposed by eighteenth century individualism or twentieth century statism issue either in perpetual conflict or deadening repression. Christian social principles, rooted in the moral law, call insistently for cooperation, not conflict, for freedom, not repression in the development of economic activity. Cooperation must be organized—organized for the common good; freedom must be ordered—ordered for the common good. Today we have labor partly organized, but chiefly for its own interests. We have capital or management organized, possibly on a larger scale, but again chiefly for its own interests. What we urgently need, in the Christian view of social order, is the free organization of capital and labor in permanent agencies of cooperation for the common good. To ensure that this organization does not lose sight of the common good, government as the responsible custodian of the public interest should have a part in it. But its part should be to stimulate, to guide, to restrain, not to dominate. This is perfectly in line with our federal Constitution which empowers government not only "to establish justice" but also to "promote the general welfare."

7.   Catholic social philosophy has a constructive program for this organic development of economic life. Pope Pius XI, rounding out the social principles formulated by Leo XIII, laid down the broad outlines of this program seventeen years ago. In line with that constructive program we advocate freely organized cooperation between the accredited representatives of capital and labor in each industry and in the economy as a whole under the supervision but not the control of government. The agencies of this freely organized cooperation have been called by various names: occupational groups,

vocational groups, or, more recently, industry councils. American Catholic students of the social encyclicals have expressed their preference for the name *industry councils* to designate the basic organs of a Christian and American type of economic democracy into which they would like to see our economic system progressively evolve. This evolution can come only as the fruit of painstaking study and effort to safeguard in justice and charity, the rightful interests of property and the rightful interests of labor in the pursuit of the dominant interest of all, which is the common good.

8.   Such a constructive program of social order seems to us to be the answer to the questionings of high-minded leaders of industry and to the explicit proposals of sound and responsible leaders of organized labor. We bespeak for it in these critical times dispassionate consideration and calm, open discussion in an atmosphere of good will and in a disposition to seek solutions by agreement rather than by force, whether political or economic. We call upon men of religious faith and principle, both in management and labor, to take the lead in working out and applying, gradually if need be, a constructive social program of this type. For the moral and social ideals which it would realize are their heritage.

Religion and Citizenship

9.   The inroads of secularism in civil life are a challenge to the Christian citizen—and indeed to every citizen with definite religious convictions. The essential connection between religion and good citizenship is deep in our American tradition. Those who took the lead in establishing our independence and framing our Constitution were firm and explicit in the conviction that religion and morality are the strong supports of national well-being, that national morality cannot long prevail in the absence of religious principle, and that impartial encouragement of religious influence on its citizens is a proper and practical function of good government. This American tradition clearly envisioned the school as the meeting place of these helpful interacting influences. The third article of the Northwest Ordinance passed by Congress in 1787, reenacted in 1790, and included in the constitutions of many states enjoins: "Religion, morality and knowledge being necessary to good citizenship and the happiness of mankind, schools and the means of education shall forever be encouraged." This is our authentic American tradition on the philosophy of education for citizenship.

10. In the field of law our history reveals the same fundamental connection between religion and citizenship. It is through law that government exercises control over its citizens for the common good and establishes a balance between their rights and duties. The American concept of government and law started with the recognition that man's inalienable rights, which it is the function of government to protect, derive from God, his Creator. It thus bases human law, which deals with man's rights and their correlative duties in society, on foundations that are definitely religious, on principles that emerge from the definite view of man as a creature of God. This view of man anchors human law to the natural law, which is the moral law of God made clear to us through the judgments of human reason and the dictates of conscience. The natural law, as an outstanding modern legal commentator has written, "is binding over all the globe, in all countries, and at all times; no human laws are of any validity if contrary to this." Thus human law is essentially an ordinance of reason, not merely a dictate of will on the part of the state. In our authentic American tradition this is the accepted philosophy of law.

11. On this basically religious tradition concerning the preparation of the citizen through education and the direction of the citizen through law, secularism has in the past century exercised a corrosive influence. It has banned religion from tax-supported education and is now bent on destroying all cooperation between government and organized religion in the training of our future citizens. It has undermined the religious foundations of law in the minds of many men in the legal profession and has predisposed them to accept the legalistic tyranny of the omnipotent state. It has cleverly exploited, to the detriment of religion and good citizenship, the delicate problem of cooperation between Church and state in a country of divided religious allegiance. That concrete problem, delicate as it is, can, without sacrifice of principle, be solved in a practical way when good will and a spirit of fairness prevail. Authoritative Catholic teaching on the relations between Church and state, as set forth in papal encyclicals and in the treatises of recognized writers on ecclesiastical law, not only states clearly what these relations should normally be under ideal conditions, but also indicates to what extent the Catholic Church can adapt herself to the particular conditions that may obtain in different countries. Examining, in the full perspective of that teaching, the position which those who founded our nation and framed its basic law took on the problem of church-state relations in our own country, we find that the First Amendment to our Constitution solved the problem in a way that was typically American in its practical recognition of existing conditions and its evident desire to be fair to all citizens of whatever religious faith. To one who knows something of history and law, the meaning of the First Amendment is clear enough from its own words: "Congress shall make no laws respecting an establishment of religion or forbidding the free exercise thereof." The meaning is even clearer in the records of the Congress that enacted it. Then, and throughout English and colonial history, an "establishment of religion" meant the setting up by law of an official church which would receive from the government favors not equally accorded to others in the cooperation between government and religion—which was simply taken for granted in our country at that time and has, in many ways, continued to this day. Under the First Amendment, the federal government could not extend this type of preferential treatment to one religion as against another, nor could it compel or forbid any state to do so. If this practical policy be described by the loose metaphor "a wall of separation between church and state," that term must be understood in a definite and typically American sense. It would be an utter distortion of American history and law to make that practical policy involve the indifference to religion and the exclusion of cooperation between religion and government implied in the term "separation of church and state" as it has become the shibboleth of doctrinaire secularism.

12. Within the past two years secularism has scored unprecedented victories in its opposition to governmental encouragement of religious and moral training, even where no preferential treatment of one religion over another is involved. In two recent cases, the Supreme Court of the United States has adopted an entirely novel and ominously extensive interpretation of the "establishment of religion" clause of the First Amendment. This interpretation would bar any cooperation between government and organized religion which would aid religion, even where no discrimination between religious bodies is in question. This reading of the First Amendment, as a group of non-Catholic religious leaders recently noted, will endanger "forms of cooperation between church and state which have been taken for granted by the American people," and "greatly accelerate the trend toward the secularization of our culture."

13. Reluctant as we are to criticize our supreme judicial tribunal, we cannot but observe that when the members of that tribunal write long and varying opinions in handing down a decision, they must expect that intelligent citizens of a democracy will study and appraise these opinions. The *Journal of the American Bar Association*, in a critical analysis of one of the cases in question, pertinently remarks:

> The traditionally religious sanctions of our law, life, and government are challenged by a judicial propensity which deserves the careful thought and study of lawyers and people.

14. Lawyers trained in the American tradition of law will be amazed to find that in the McCollum case the majority opinions pay scant attention to logic, history, or accepted norms of legal interpretation. Logic would demand that what is less clear be defined by what is more clear. In the present instance we find just the reverse. The carefully chiseled phrases of the First Amendment are defined by the misleading metaphor "the wall of separation between church and state." This metaphor of Jefferson specifies nothing except that there shall be no "established church," no state religion. All the rest of its content depends on the letter of the law that sets it up and can in the concrete imply anything from the

impartial cooperation between government and free religious bodies (as in Holland and traditionally in our own country) all the way down to bitter persecution of religion (as in France at the turn of the century). As was pointedly remarked in a dissenting opinion: "A rule of law cannot be drawn from a metaphor."

15. A glance at the history of Jefferson's own life and work would have served as a warning against the broad and devastating application of his "wall of separation" metaphor that we find in this case. The expression first appears in a letter written by Jefferson in 1802, and significantly enough, in a context that makes it refer to the "free exercise of religion" clause rather than to the "establishment of religion" clause of the First Amendment. Twenty years later Jefferson clearly showed in action that his concept of "separation of church and state" was far different from the concept of those who now appeal to his metaphor as a norm of interpretation. As the rector of the State University of Virginia, Jefferson proposed a system of cooperation between the various religious groups and the university which goes far beyond anything under consideration in the case at hand. And Mr. Madison, who had proposed the First Amendment and who led in carrying it through to enactment by Congress, was one of the visitors of the University of Virginia, who approved Jefferson's plan.

16. Even one who is not a lawyer would expect to find in the opinion of the court some discussion of what was in the mind of the members of Congress when they framed and adopted the First Amendment. For it would seem that the intent of the legislator should be of capital importance in interpreting any law when a doubt is raised as to the objective meaning of the words in which it is framed. In regard to the "establishment of religion" clause, there is no doubt of the intent of the legislator. It is clear in the record of the Congress that framed it and of the state legislatures that ratified it. To them it meant no official church for the country as a whole, no preferment of one religion over another by the federal government—and at the same time no interference by the federal government in the church-state relations of the individual states.

17. The opinion of the court advances no reason for disregarding the mind of the legislator. But that reason is discernible in a concurring opinion adhered to by four of the nine judges. There we see clearly the determining influence of secularist theories of public education— and possibly of law. One cannot but remark that if this secularist influence is to prevail in our government and its institutions, such a result should in candor and logic and law be achieved by legislation adopted after full popular discussion, and not by the judicial procedure of an ideological interpretation of our Constitution.

18. We, therefore, hope and pray that the novel interpretation of the First Amendment recently adopted by the Supreme Court will in due process be revised. To that end we shall peacefully, patiently, and

perseveringly work. We feel with deep conviction that for the sake of both good citizenship and religion there should be a reaffirmation of our original American tradition of free cooperation between government and religious bodies—cooperation involving no special privilege to any group and no restriction on the religious liberty of any citizen. We solemnly disclaim any intent or desire to alter this prudent and fair American policy of government in dealing with the delicate problems that have their source in the divided religious allegiance of our citizens. We call upon our Catholic people to seek in their faith an inspiration and a guide in making an informed contribution to good citizenship. We urge members of the legal profession in particular to develop and apply their special competence in this field. We stand ready to cooperate in fairness and charity with all who believe in God and are devoted to freedom under God to avert the impending danger of a judicial "establishment of secularism" that would ban God from public life. For secularism is threatening the religious foundations of our national life and preparing the way for the advent of the omnipotent state.

Signed by the members of the NCWC Administrative Board in the name of the bishops of the United States

Dennis Cardinal Dougherty, Archbishop of Philadelphia

Edward Cardinal Mooney, Archbishop of Detroit

Samuel Cardinal Stritch, Archbishop of Chicago

Francis Cardinal Spellman, Archbishop of New York

Francis P. Keough, Archbishop of Baltimore

John T. McNicholas, Archbishop of Cincinnati

Robert E. Lucey, Archbishop of San Antonio

Richard J. Cushing, Archbishop of Boston

Joseph E. Ritter, Archbishop of St. Louis

John Mark Gannon, Bishop of Erie

John F. Noll, Bishop of Fort Wayne

Emmet M. Walsh, Bishop of Charleston

Karl J. Alter, Bishop of Toledo

Michael J. Ready, Bishop of Columbus

The Christian Family

A Statement Issued by the
Catholic Bishops of the United States

November 21, 1949

1. The world's horizons are those of time, not of eternity. Its interests are material, not spiritual. The world acknowledges God with an occasional word of reference, but it is not truly interested in God, His purposes, or His law. It wishes God to stay in His Heaven; as occasion permits, it is willing to salute Him there. But it resents intervention of God in affairs on earth. It is irritated by any assertion of God's rights here, any demand for service to God, any exaction of reliance upon God's providence.

2. The Western world today still proclaims human dignity. But in the main it treats man, physically, as the product of materialistic and mechanical evolution. It tends more and more to treat man, socially, as the creature of the state or of control groups within the state. Again, the world recognizes a vaguely conceived spiritual institution which it calls the church. Yet, practically, the Church is treated as a collection of welfare centers, a human thing throughout and not divine, which is to be formed into a unified instrument of social action by general concession and compromise. The world makes no quest for divinely revealed truth. It seeks no divine guidance, no divine indication of duty and spiritual allegiance. It ignores ultimates, and restricts its vision to the here and now. In all this, there is inversion and disorder. Out of such disorder it is not reasonable to expect the emergence of human security, prosperity, and peace.

3. For God comes first. God has revealed His purposes regarding man not only through the light of natural reason but also through the gift of supernatural revelation, which we accept by faith. Paradoxically, as a brilliant modern writer observes, if you take away the supernatural, you have left, not the natural, but the unnatural.

Disregard of the Supernatural

4. Perhaps the most evident and devastating effect of the disregard of supernatural faith in human society is to be found in what it has done to family life. The world which discounts supernatural faith in God's revelation, praises family life, declares its place and function essential to human well-being, and speaks with high sentiment of the sacredness of the home. Yet by countless acts and agencies it

moves steadily to disrupt family life and to destroy the home. It approves and facilitates divorce as a cure for domestic ills. It accepts multiple marriages which usually mean a hopeless entanglement of the infelicities of a plurality of broken homes. It sponsors planned parenthood by use of unnatural and morally degrading means, thus infusing poison into the heart of family life by destroying in husband and wife the self-respect and mutual reverence on which alone are built enduring love and patient fidelity. It is unconcerned, for the most part, about its manifest duty of removing the great difficulties that lie in the way of those who wish to marry and establish homes. Its social legislation in point of suitable housing, decent material facilities, security in income and prospects, is slow, fumbling, and inadequate. An unbelieving world professing recognition of the essential value of family life, actually discounts that value and moves to destroy what it claims to cherish.

5. All this amounts to a calculated attack upon family life. To counteract this attack it is urgent to have the clear knowledge which faith gives of what the family is, and of what it means to the individual man and to human society.

The Family: A Divine Institution

6. In the view of faith the family is, first of all, a divine institution. A divine institution is not within man's control to abrogate or alter. It is God's own work. Attack upon it is, even humanly speaking, disastrous. It strikes tragically at the even balance of right human relations, and ends in calamitous disorder.

7. Faith merely confirms reason in holding that husband and wife constitute conjugal society. When their union is blessed with offspring, this society becomes a family. It is a divinely founded natural society. It is prior, in existence and in its nature, to every other human society, to every state or nation. It is the basic social unit. It has its own native rights which no civil power can take away or unduly limit. To serve and protect the family and its life, states are formed and governments established.

8. Social philosophers, as well as the great mass of mankind schooled only in sanity and common human experience, agree upon the importance of the family to individual man. The formative years of life are normally passed in the bosom of the family. Family life encircles the child with no mere casual set of surroundings. It is his constant school; it is his realm, his world. Even through his adolescence he returns to it as to the moorings of his soul. Family life, far beyond any other external influence, molds lastingly the tastes, the temperaments, the attitudes, the personality of the child. No human social influence can

compare with the family in power to form and to direct the individual lives of men.

9. The importance of family life for individuals is discerned in the service it renders to father and mother as well as to the child. Husband and wife find fulfillment in their fruitfulness, and find strength and comfort in the home. Family life gives dignity and peace and security to the mother. It exercises an ennobling and steadying influence upon the father. In both it awakens and develops a sense of responsibility, and fosters their growth in selflessness, sacrifice, and patience.

Family Life Essential to the State

10. The state measures its true strength by the stability of family life among its citizenry. For the family is the social cell. It is the family that produces the citizen. No nation can be greater than its families. In vain does the world that disregards the injunction of God loosen family ties and break up family life and then look to state schools to produce good citizens. At its best the school is only a strong aid to the home. Good citizens must first be good persons. School courses in civics and political science, and inspirational studies of the lives and works of patriotic leaders, meet a practical need. But these alone never make good citizens. Virtue is best developed in a good home where God is held in reverence. And virtue is the basis of good citizenship. The state which weakens the family inflicts deep injury upon itself. Any attack of the state on family life is suicidal.

11. No less important is the role of the family for the Church. The Son of God, when He walked among men, set up His one Church as a kind of family, and its members call that Church their Holy Mother. Only those who know and live the family life of that Church can appreciate the glory and the solace of soul that abide in this earthly home of the human spirit. The Church, through the sacrament of matrimony, constantly channels the essential grace of God to her faithful children in the home. But history proves that it is God's will and providence that the Church should depend for her continuity and growth, as well as for the devotion of the faithful, upon Christian family life.

12. Since family life is thus essential to the individual, to the state, and to the Church, it follows that whatever protects or promotes good family life is to be diligently fostered. It is of paramount concern to all mankind that family life be preserved in full soundness and moral health.

Permanence of Marriage

13. To exist in full effectiveness, family life must have permanence. This permanence depends chiefly upon the permanence of marriage. Strictly requisite is marriage that is monogamous and indissoluble: the marriage of one man with one woman in divorceless union that is broken only by the death of one of the spouses. Such a marriage is requisite, not for the mere begetting of offspring, but for the rearing and training of children until they come to full maturity. Any marriage which looks to dissolution or divorce, even as a possibility, cannot give to children the security they need; cannot surround children with the enduring atmosphere of home; cannot breathe into children the spirit of true family life. Nor can such a marriage give to husband and wife the complete reliance on each other which is requisite for their peace and happiness under the exacting conditions of marital duty.

14. Further, family life must have freedom. There must be no undue intervening of the civil power in the domain of husband and wife. This requirement involves two points of obligation. Freedom implies that rights be respected. The state must respect the rights of the family. It must not therefore fail to provide opportunities for the adequate housing of families, for the requisite schooling of children, for the use of common benefits supplied through the taxing of citizens. On the other hand, the state must not oppress the family. It must not discount parental authority by invading the home and legislating upon matters which are of strictly domestic concern. It must be neither arbitrary nor tyrannous. It must not usurp the right which belongs to parents of educating their children. On this score, the part of the state is to furnish opportunity for schooling, and to see that parents are not recreant in making use of the opportunity on behalf of their children. The state cannot force a child to attend this school or that; it cannot prescribe courses of study that may involve intellectual or moral dangers for pupils. Nor can the state make discrimination among families, distributing common benefits to some and withholding them from others.

The Church and the Child

15. To the Church belongs the preeminent right to guide the child's spiritual and moral formation; to the parents belongs the natural right to govern and supervise the child's nurture and general education; in society is vested the right to transmit, generally by means of schools, the cultural heritage of successive generations.

16. The function of the state is to assist these three agencies to discharge harmoniously their responsibilities in the best interest of the public welfare. The state must ever keep in mind that children belong to their parents before they belong to the state; the resources to develop them into their full stature as human beings destined for eternal union with God are not the property of political government; these constitute the treasury of families and the Church.

17. Again, the family, to exercise its good influence in full effectiveness, needs a just measure of economic security. When, in a wealthy and prospering nation, diligent and willing parents are forced to live in grinding poverty; when parents have no opportunity of owning their own home; when the aid of government is extended to those who raise crops or build machines but not to those who rear children; there exists a condition of inequity and even of injustice. Social legislation and social action must concur to improve man's economic opportunity, to enable him to marry early, to free him from the peril of unnaturally limiting his family, and to afford him some certainty of sufficiently gainful employment and some assurance that death or accident will not reduce his dependents to the status of public charges.

Religion Indispensable to the Family

18. Finally, the family needs religion. It requires the high morality and the unvarying standards of duty which only the spirit of religion can supply to family life. It needs the strong quality of staunch loyalty to God and to His commandments, to His Church and to her precepts. It needs the filial piety which has its source and support in piety toward God. It needs prayer and the example of prayerfulness. We are consoled by the evident growth of pious practices in the home, the enthronement of the Sacred Heart, regular family prayer, and the wide variety of Catholic devotions, which have given to Christian homes the character of sacred sanctuaries.

19. The family needs to gather again around its hearths and rekindle there the fires of religious fervor. The home must again become a shrine of fidelity, a place where God is the unseen host. We commend the program of the Catholic Family Life Conference as one means of meeting the evident present need for better and happier homes. Family retreats, Cana conferences, courses on family life in schools and colleges, and study groups concerned with preparation for family life, should be widely encouraged and zealously promoted throughout our country. The press, radio, motion pictures, and all agencies of public opinion should give constant aid in emphasizing the ideals of worthy family life. These powerful forces should be an unfailing support for the virtues which safeguard the home and give nobility to the nation.

20. These, then, are the requisites for family life if it is to produce its wondrous benefits in full measure and effectiveness: it must be permanent in its establishment and prospects; it must be free from unwarranted interventions; it must have economic security; it must be religious. Yet even when these requisites are not perfectly realized, family life, though hampered, is productive of incalculable good. In the providence of God it is the best of existing human agencies for social benefit. There is grave danger, however, that, if a godless philosophy be still permitted to prevail, family life among us will not only be further hampered but ultimately destroyed.

21. We have, indeed, supernatural knowledge that God's Church will not be destroyed, and while the Church endures family life will still, in some measure, exist and fruitfully function. But viewing our country and the world by and large and noting the growing tendency to ignore God and His rights in society, the lethal danger to the family is neither chimerical nor remote. It is a present danger, more fearsome than the atom bomb.

22. After thirty-five years of war and its effects which have wrought incalculable injury to family life, we call for an intensive effort to restore the virtues and practices guaranteeing family stability and peace.

23. With confidence in the help of God, through Jesus Christ, His Son, and with constant faith in the intercession of His Mother, the Immaculate Mary, we urge all families to strive by their prayers for the restoration of pure family life. Let all recite the family rosary. Let there be a renewal of devotion, a frequency in the reception of the sacraments, a rebirth of all those virtues which make family life a mirror of the Holy Family of Nazareth. Joseph, the honest workman, is still the guardian of families. Mary, the Mother of God, is the blessed Mother of every Catholic home. And Jesus, subject to them, His creatures, is the model of every child. To Jesus, Mary, and Joseph, we commit your hearts, your souls, and your homes.

Statement issued November 21, 1949, by the bishops of the United States and signed in their names by the members of the Administrative Board, NCWC

Dennis Cardinal Dougherty, Archbishop of Philadelphia

Edward Cardinal Mooney, Archbishop of Detroit

Samuel Cardinal Stritch, Archbishop of Chicago

Francis Cardinal Spellman, Archbishop of New York

Francis P. Keough, Archbishop of Baltimore

John T. McNicholas, OP,
Archbishop of Cincinnati

Robert E. Lucey, Archbishop of
San Antonio

Richard J. Cushing, Archbishop
of Boston

Joseph E. Ritter, Archbishop of
St. Louis

Patrick A. O'Boyle, Archbishop
of Washington

John Mark Gannon, Bishop
of Erie

John F. Noll, Bishop of
Fort Wayne

Emmet M. Walsh, Coadjutor
Bishop of Youngstown

Michael J. Ready, Bishop of
Columbus

The Child
Citizen of Two Worlds

A Statement Issued by the
Catholic Bishops of the United States

November 17, 1950

1. In the present grim international struggle, the American people have resolutely championed the cause of human freedom. We have committed ourselves to oppose relentlessly the aggressions of those who deny to man his God-given rights and who aim to enslave all mankind under the rules of godless materialism. The responsibilities which we have thereby assumed are both grave and continuing. They deserve conscientious consideration.

2. It is of primary importance for our people to realize that human freedom derives from the spiritual nature of man and can flourish only when things of the spirit are held in reverence. Our present principles of action need to be evaluated in the light of the truth. But we must go even further. Small comfort to be successful today if tomorrow the world finds us unworthy of the trust reposed in us. We need, therefore, to examine carefully what spiritual direction we are giving to our children to prepare them to fulfill their future moral responsibilities to God and to their fellow man.

3. In recent decades, striking advances have been made in meeting the child's physical, emotional, and social needs; but his moral and religious needs have not been met with the same solicitude and understanding. As a result, many of our children today betray confusion and insecurity because these unmet needs are fundamental to the harmonious development of their whole nature.

4. The child must be seen whole and entire. He must be seen as a citizen of two worlds. He belongs to this world surely, but his first and highest allegiance is to the Kingdom of God. From his earliest years he must be taught that his chief significance comes from the fact that he is created by God and is destined for life with God in eternity.

5. The child's prospects for fulfilling this great hope which God has reposed in him must be viewed realistically. He will come to maturity in a society where social, moral, intellectual, and spiritual values are everywhere disintegrating. In such a society, he will urgently need the integrating force of religion as taught by Christ. Such a force will give him a complete and rational meaning for his existence.

6. First of all, it will arouse in him a consciousness of God and of eternity. His vision will be opened out upon a supernatural world revealed by faith which differs from the world of nature his senses reveal. Thus he will discover a higher life than this daily one and a brighter world than he sees. Second, it will give him a continuing purpose in life, for it will teach him that he was made to know, love, and serve God in this world as the condition for meriting eternal happiness. Third, it will induce in him a deep sense of responsibility for those rights and obligations he possesses by reason of his citizenship in Heaven as well as on earth. Finally, religion will challenge him to sanctify whatever walk of life he chooses and to seek and accept the will of God in whatever way it may be manifested. Thus, as a principle of integration, religion will help the children to develop *a sense of God, a sense of direction, a sense of responsibility, and a sense of mission* in this life.

I. Sense of God

7. The child is not complete in himself. He will find his completion only in life with God; and that life must begin here upon earth. Parents, therefore, should make early provision for their child's growth in God. This is not something to be postponed for nurture by school authorities. It must begin in the home through simple and prayerful practices. Morning and evening prayers, grace before and after meals, the family rosary, the saying of a short prayer each time the striking clock marks the passage of another hour nearer eternity, the reverential making of the sign of the cross, the inculcation of respect for the crucifix and other religious objects—all these practices which should be encouraged in the religious formation of the child. No one can doubt that there is a readiness on his part to receive such formation, and if parents are remiss in giving it they will lose a splendid opportunity to develop in their child that habitual awareness of God which is vital to his full growth.

8. Only two courses are open to the child: either he will be God-centered or self-centered. He is made and destined for God, but he bears in his nature the lingering effects of original sin which incline him to seek the satisfaction of every selfish whim. To correct this bend in his will so that God, rather than self, will occupy the center of his life is one of the most challenging tasks facing parents.

9. In meeting this challenge, let parents make use of the strong, supernatural motivation which can be drawn from the life of Christ. Let them encourage the imitation of Him, particularly in His obedience, patience, and thoughtfulness of others; and let them foster the emulation of that spirit of unselfish giving so characteristic of Christ. This can be done in many practical ways, particularly through providing the child with frequent opportunities for making acts of self-denial in the home. If he is taught to deny his selfish whims for the sake of Christ, he will not only discover a supernatural motive for his actions, but he will learn to give God that central place in his affections which God must occupy if the child is to come to his full spiritual stature.

10. Little point would be served in intensifying the child's awareness of God during his preschool years, if later his schooling were to rob him of that. The child's education during school years should be of a piece with his education at home. Catholic parents, clearly grasping this essential truth, have undergone great sacrifice and enormous expense to establish and maintain schools which will continue and enlarge the spiritual development of the child that was begun at home. In doing this, parents have acted within their competence, because it is they, and not the state, who possess the primary right to educate. This natural right of parents is one which has ever been recognized in our American traditions. As recently as 1944, the highest court in our land confirmed it in these words:

> It is cardinal with us that the custody, care, and nurture of the child *reside first in the parents* whose primary function and freedom include preparation for obligations the state can neither supply nor hinder.

11. In helping parents to exercise this right, the Church stands ready at hand with all her material and spiritual resources. At infancy she initiates the child into the life of grace and for the rest of his days she stands by his side ready to minister to his needs. She recognizes his preeminent need for God and she meets it by providing Catholic schools for each stage of his educational development. She does this in virtue of the sublime teaching office conferred upon her by Jesus Christ.

12. When it is impossible for parents to take advantage of the God-centered education which Catholic schools offer, they have a grave obligation to provide for their child's religious instruction in some other way. At least they must see that their children attend catechism classes and vacation schools and receive the benefit of other activities of the Confraternity of Christian Doctrine.

13. Nor should the state, which has demonstrated a genuine interest in so many aspects of the child's welfare, be indifferent to the inherent value of religious instruction and training for the child attending tax-supported schools. The continuance and well-being of a state based on democratic principles require that it show a lively concern for moral principles and practices which are firmly grounded only in religion. For the child who is not receiving thorough religious education, the state should look with favor on released-time programs for his religious instruction.

14. Many important services have been rendered by the governmental agencies to the child who has been deprived of the care and support of his parents by death, illness, or misfortune. However, it is a source of growing concern to us that in certain parts of our country there is a trend to regard this whole field of foster care as falling within the exclusive province of governmental authorities. It surely lies within their province to set up and enforce legitimate minimum standards of care for the dependent child; but the responsibility for his care should not be entirely assumed by them. There is a definite place in America for the voluntary agencies of mercy—particularly those operating under religious auspices, which are equipped to safeguard and develop the religious life of the dependent child. Certainly the child bereft of the immediate care of his parents is entitled to those opportunities for a religious upbringing which his parents were obligated to give him. These opportunities can be best supplied by an agency operating under religious auspices.

II. Sense of Direction

15. The child whose eyes have been opened to the vision of God must be encouraged to walk by the steady light of that vision; otherwise he will follow wandering fires. He is too young and immature to be left to himself. His impulses and desires, so largely unregulated because of his tender years, need to be given a sure direction by religious training, if he is to achieve that great purpose for which he was made: to know, to love, and to serve God.

16. The child must *know* God. There is a vast difference between *knowing about God* and *knowing God*. The difference is made by personal experience. It is not enough that the child be given the necessary truths about God. They ought to be given in such a way that he will assimilate them and make them a part of himself. God must become as real to him as his own father or mother. God must not remain an abstraction. If He does, He will not be loved; and if He is not loved, then all the child's knowledge about Him will be sterile. Where love is, there too is service. "If you love me, keep my commandments." That is Christ's test and it must be applied to the child. He should be brought to see God's commandments and precepts as guideposts which give an unerring direction to his steps. In this work, the Church, the family, and the school all have a part to play.

17. From the time that the Church pours the waters of baptism over his forehead, until she surrenders him at death to God, there is no period when she does not provide the child, through her sacraments and teachings, with a steady inspiration to serve God. The inculcation of virtues, both natural and supernatural, the repeated warnings against succumbing to the demands of his lower nature, the balm with which she alleviates the wounds caused by sin in his life, and the channels of grace she holds constantly open for him—all these are aids which the Church gives the child in directing his steps toward God.

18. Parents are obligated to see that he makes ample use of these helps; and in addition they must inspire him to love and service of God by their own daily actions. The home will be his first school. He will be quick to imitate what he sees and hears there. Let them turn this impulse to imitate, which can be the source of much mischief and lasting harm, to the child's advantage by giving him at home a good example of Christian living.

19. If this example is not forthcoming, the child will become confused by the contradiction between what he is taught and what he sees practiced. This confusion will be compounded when he goes to a school where religion is taught. There he will be taught to reverence the name of God, but at home he will hear God's name used irreverently in petulance and anger. At school he will learn to cooperate and get along with his fellow pupils, but at home he will be allowed to offend and wrangle with his brothers and sisters. At school he will be taught strict precepts of honesty and justice, while at home he will hear his parents boast of sharp business practices and clever evasions of the truth. Disturbed by these contradictions and torn by conflicting loyalties to home and school, the child will lose confidence in his parents' and teachers' powers to give him effective direction.

20. A close association between home and school should be maintained by parents and school authorities so as to facilitate an exchange of views and confidences regarding the child. In this way, home and school life can be better integrated and there will be a reduction of those conflicts which very often are at work in his life, and which do not receive the understanding and attention they deserve.

21. When we speak of parents' responsibilities, it should be remembered that they do not devolve entirely upon the mother. The father has his responsibilities, too, and he must not shirk them. It is not enough for him to provide the material means of support for the family. He also has the obligation to identify himself with the interests and activities of his child. If the full benefits of parental direction are to be reaped by the child, such direction should include that steadying and stabilizing influence which it is the father's duty to exert.

22. Fathers and mothers have a natural competence to instruct their children with regard to sex. False modesty should not deter them from doing their duty in this regard. Sex is one of God's endowments. It should not be ignored or treated as something bad. If sex education is properly carried on in the home, a deep reverence will be developed in the child and he will be spared the shameful inferences which he often makes when he is left to himself to find out about sex. We protest in the strongest possible terms against the introduction of sex instruction into the schools. To be of benefit such instruction must be far broader than the imparting of information, and must be given individually. Sex is more than a biological function. It is bound up with the sacredness and uniqueness of the human personality. It can be fully and properly appreciated only within a religious and moral context. If treated otherwise, the child will see it apart from the controlling purpose of his life, which is service to God.

23. Many unsalutary influences are at work in modern society which must not be allowed free play upon the personality of the growing child. Parents should carefully regulate the company and the hours which their child keeps. They should not treat him as an adult. He needs to be warned against, even forbidden, certain associations. Particularly during adolescence, this is extremely important. A vigilant watch should be kept over the type of entertainment in which he indulges, the motion pictures he attends, the books he reads, the radio and television programs to which he is exposed in the home.

III. Sense of Responsibility

24. A common complaint registered against the home and the school today is that they do not sharpen the child's sense of responsibility. He is made conscious of his rights, to be sure; but he also has obligations which are correlates of those rights. His education and training are defective in the proportion that those obligations are not impressed on his young mind.

25. No point is urged with greater insistency by religion than the accountability of each individual before God. It is the duty of parents to see to it that their child develops a deep sense of personal responsibility; learning at the earliest possible period that he is accountable to God for his thoughts, his words, and his actions. His home training must reinforce this teaching in every practical way. He should be held to strict account for the performance of chores and tasks which are given to him by his parents. He must be made to see that each member of the family has a part to play in the service of God by carrying out an assigned role. The child, thus enlightened, will be enabled to see in later life how the faithful discharge of his duties as a citizen can be related to the service of God.

26. Part of the boredom affecting our society today is due to the unsound separation which has developed between work and spiritual growth. The concept of work as a means of furthering sanctification has largely been lost. It remains for parents to recover that concept and apply it to the child's daily experience. From the consciousness that even the smallest household task when faithfully carried out draws him closer to God, the child will derive a continuing motivation for relating all that he does to God. And thus every task, no matter how trivial or menial, can take on a significance which will yield rich spiritual returns.

27. In this way the child will have learned at home a great lesson which will make it easier for him to adjust to the demands of school life. As he takes his place in that larger community, he will do so as a responsible individual. He will see his homework, his attention in class, and his participation in school activities as part of the same divine plan learned in the home, whereby each action has its significance in God's eyes. This mindfulness throughout his daily life of the supernatural value of his actions will be a safeguard against the careless performance of any duty. The greater his talent, the more he will be conscious of his obligation to serve God by a rightful exercise of that talent.

28. If the child is constantly aware that his time and his talents belong to God he will want to use them properly and will avoid those harmful associations and pastimes which frequently lead to juvenile delinquency. This implies however that adequate recreational facilities and opportunities for the development of his interest in hobbies, games, and other activities are available so that his abounding energy can find wholesome channels for expression.

29. The spiritual helps which the child has for deepening his sense of responsibility must not be neglected. Parents should encourage the practice of nightly examination of conscience and weekly confession. The child who goes over his thoughts, speech, and actions at the end of each day, seeking out what has been displeasing to God, will gradually develop a sensitivity to God's claims upon his life. The practice of weekly confession will make him conscious of the manner in which he has misused his time and talents. It will heighten in him that sense of accountability to God which is necessary if he is to show proper contrition for his failings and proper amendment of them.

IV. Sense of Mission

30. In learning the valuable lesson that he is accountable to God for the use of his time and talents the child will acquire not only a sense of responsibility, but a sense of mission as well. For his religious training will remind him that his future happiness lies not in the indulgence of selfish desires, but in the complete dedication of his whole personality to God's service. "I am come to do the will of Him who sent me." This must be the keynote of the child's mission in this world. For him the will of God must come to be more important than any personal consideration. Only when he masters this truth will he be given to see how all things, even disappointments and setbacks, can be turned to good account in the service of God.

31. Since everyone is not called to serve God in the same way or in the same capacity, great care should be exercised in the child's vocational guidance. Otherwise, aimlessness in his training will leave him without permanent direction for his talents and aptitudes. Parents and teachers must help him to choose and to follow a calling for which he is fitted and in which he can best serve God. A deeper awareness in the child of his mission in life will do much to reduce the shocking waste of time and energy which in so many instances characterizes his formative years today, and later prevents him from taking his full place in civic life.

32. Among the boys and girls of our land, God has destined some to carry on the work of His Church for the salvation of souls. To these He has given a religious vocation. Here indeed is a challenge to the generosity of American parents. If in all sincerity they have impressed upon their child that he has a mission in life to do God's will, they in turn will want to cooperate with that will and aid in its fulfillment. God's claims are prior to every human consideration. If He calls the child to His special service, parents should not shrink from the sacrifice often entailed by such a call. The pain of severing home ties will be more than offset by the spiritual joy given to those who labor in the vineyard of the Lord.

33. In emphasizing the supreme importance of religion in the spiritual development of the child, we are but applying to the circumstances of today the eternal principle which the Church received from her divine founder. For nineteen centuries, the Church has lingered lovingly over Christ's tribute to the child: "Suffer little children to come unto Me and forbid them not; for of such is the Kingdom of God." The implications of that tribute should be recognized by all who have care of the child. Theirs is the great vocation to show him that he is a citizen, not only of this world, but of that other world which lies beyond with God whose Kingdom is the kingdom of children.

Statement issued November 17, 1950, by the bishops of the United States and signed in their names by the Administrative Board of the National Catholic Welfare Conference, whose members are:

Dennis Cardinal Dougherty, Archbishop of Philadelphia

Edward Cardinal Mooney, Archbishop of Detroit

Samuel Cardinal Stritch, Archbishop of Chicago

Francis Cardinal Spellman, Archbishop of New York

Francis P. Keough, Archbishop of Baltimore

Robert E. Lucey, Archbishop of San Antonio

Richard J. Cushing, Archbishop
of Boston

Joseph E. Ritter, Archbishop of
St. Louis

Patrick A. O'Boyle, Archbishop
of Washington

John M. Gannon, Bishop
of Erie

John F. Noll, Bishop of
Fort Wayne

Michael J. Ready, Bishop of
Columbus

Emmet M. Walsh, Coadjutor
Bishop of Youngstown

Statement on Compulsory Peacetime Military Service

A Statement Issued by the Administrative Board of the National Catholic Welfare Conference

Revised November 13, 1950

1. We recognize the imperative need for the adequate defense of our country in all circumstances.

2. If a wide extension of military training is found necessary for the present adequate defense of our nation, we believe that such training should be in keeping with American tradition, and that, specifically:

(a) any measure providing for universal military training shall have a terminal clause that would prevent such emergency legislation from supplanting our nonmilitary tradition;

(b) that our military services should continue to encourage and promote voluntary enlistments;

(c) insofar as possible, enforced training should be integrated with normal school life, so that no youth shall be called to serve until his secondary education is complete, and that once called, no more than one school year elapse before he is free to pursue his college course;

(d) the Defense Department should work with representatives of recognized religious bodies to protect our youth in the Armed Services from moral dangers considered common to military life.

Statement on Persecution behind the Iron Curtain

*A Statement Issued by the Administrative
Board of the National Catholic Welfare
Conference*

November 1950

1. The bishops of the United States, one in faith and human sympathy, salute with admiration the Christian heroism, the staunch loyalty to freedom, and the unconquered spirit of their brother bishops, the clergy, the religious, and the faithful, who live and suffer in all those countries of Asia and Europe behind the Iron Curtain and under the influence of a godless persecution.

2. With horror in this so-called civilized age, we view the martyrdom, the exile, and imprisonment of their shepherds; the dispersion of religious; the denial and thwarting of divine worship; the closing of schools; the suppression of the press; the imposition of false teaching and the insidious capture of their youth. All is of a pattern that follows stark fear, planned starvation, the displacement and massacre of millions of innocent people. All is on a vast scale to outdo the most violent barbarism in history.

3. These good people have known persecution in other years. Gallantly have they fought against other tyrants—the Tartar and the Moslem—to help defend the freedom of the West. Now in their midst, human rights, human dignity, and human freedom are at their lowest ebb.

4. With dismay we note the apathy of Christian nations and the futility of their feeble protests in the face of a callous indifference to world opinion that is in its mildest expression inhuman. Again, when all human means seem to fail, we turn inevitably to the God of Mercy and united with our clergy and people storm the throne of heaven that the dawn of a new day of peace may brighten the horizon, that out of the blood and misery and tears of our suffering brothers may come hope and strengthened courage, the shattering of the shackles that bind them, and the unhampered enjoyment of all those human rights they so richly and justly deserve.

II. Coming of Age
1951-1961

Introduction

In this decade the American Church was to celebrate its golden jubilee of graduation from missionary status. The American Church was coming of age in many ways and its impact on even American secular thought was beginning to be felt in ever widening circles. Released on November 17, the 1951 Pastoral Letter was printed in its entirety with a covering story in four major dailies: the *New York Times, New York Herald Tribune, Washington Star*, and the *St. Louis Globe Democrat*.[1] *Time* magazine's November 26, 1951 issue gave first place in its lead-off "National Affairs" department to the bishops' Statement, offering lengthy quotes from the body of the message. *Newsweek* in its corresponding issue had coverage of the Pastoral under the lead "Morals and Bishops" but kept it to the "Religion" section. The Associated Press, United Press, and International News Service all promoted the Pastoral as feature news while several small chains picked up the item to shape as a local story.

The *Pittsburgh Press* connected the Statement with a prepared editorial predicting a presidential house-cleaning in the near future. *Pathfinder* magazine, a bi-weekly aimed at rural readers, called the Statement "a blast against the government without precedent in American history" and puzzled that "less than a month after President Truman sought to appoint an ambassador to the Vatican, members of the Church hierarchy roundly condemned the moral atmosphere of the administration he heads." All editors emphasized the "moral corruption in political life" sequence in the Statement as particularly apt in the current series of administration scandals. James E. Warner (*N.Y. Herald Tribune*) thought "there was a passage obviously directed at Senator Joseph R. McCarthy . . . a Roman Catholic, for irresponsible charges." The *Chicago Tribune's* Washington bureau dispatch flanked the editorial page in the Sunday final edition under "Catholics Rip 'Anything Goes' Political Tenet." Follow-up editorials in Washington's *Star* and *Post* praised the words of the bishops highly. Calling the message "a timely warning," the *Star*, addressing its sizable government worker readership, said: "revival of old-fashioned standards of morality for public servants is an indicated need of the times, and the Church can give valuable leadership in bringing about such a revival."

---

[1]The data for press coverage is mostly from the files of the Bureau of Information of the United States Catholic Conference, filed chronologically. The date on which each Statement was issued is given in the text of this Introduction. The dates of newspapers and periodicals cited are given only when remote from the date of the Statement.

In a statement carried by the *New York Times*, November 22, 1951, Dr. Eugene Carson Blake, then the stated clerk of the 2,500,000 member General Assembly of the Presbyterian Church in the United States, remarked: "I know I speak for most Presbyterians as well as for millions of other Protestants when I express . . . my appreciation for the forthright and able contribution made in this Statement at this time of alarming moral slackness in our beloved nation."

The Protestant *Christian Century*, November 28, 1951, commented on the bishops' Statement: "This year's Statement, released November 17, bore mainly on the moral slump which has overtaken American politics; there is cause for reflection (1) in the fact that the hierarchy thinks the moral letdown so general that a warning is needed and (2) in the further fact that these churchmen, whose dioceses contain so many men and women active in politics, consider it necessary to spell out the common requirements of morality for lay guidance.

"Elsewhere in the Statement 'dishonesty, slander, detraction, and defamation of character' are condemned as 'transgressions of God's commandments.' Could 'detraction and defamation of character' have any references to the performances of a certain Roman Catholic senator from Wisconsin? . . . Sophisticates can sneer the bishops' Statement does not rise above the a-b-c's of morality. To be sure, it doesn't. That may be its greatest significance—that the times call for getting back to the a-b-c's."

In 1952 the bishops followed through their concern for the moral degradation of the nation with *Religion, Our Most Vital National Asset*, a Pastoral of far less national impact than its predecessor. They warned in this Letter that history teaches us that it is spiritual losses rather than material reverses that lead to moral bankruptcy and national ruin. "Our national spiritual assets," cautioned the prelates, "must be greater than the national material assets which are so evident everywhere." The American bishops stated that one of the constant dangers to the religious spirit in a country such as ours is the tendency to regard religion itself simply as the fruit of pious sentiment; or to hold, as the doctrinal basis of religion, what may be called the common factor in the religious opinions held by various groups; or to be content with the great religious truths of the natural order which can be known by unaided reason.

Archbishop Francis P. Keough of Baltimore, retiring chairman of the Administrative Board, told the members of the hierarchy at their 1952 meeting that constant attention was needed for vast international problems, including the most widespread attempt to destroy the Church since the Roman persecutions. He said that these problems had to be faced even at the expense of diverting some energies from purely domestic affairs. At its 1952 spring meeting in Washington, D.C., the Administrative Board of the NCWC with the approval of the bishops had released a factual Statement denouncing the Communist persecution, particularly in China. On November 27, 1952, the hierarchy released another Statement praising the faith of "the multitude of contemporary martyrs and confessors" and deploring the continuing persecution of the Church, again especially in China. However, the Communists intensified the persecution of the Church behind the Iron and Bamboo Curtains in 1953, impelling the hierarchy to issue *Peter's Chains*, a moving account of the Church's suffering under Communism. This they published in conjunction with their regular Statement, *Man's Dignity*. The preceding September the bishops had issued a statement denouncing the arrest of Cardinal Stefan Wyszynski and the Communist persecution of the Church in Poland. *Peter's Chains*, a denunciation of the Communistic worldwide persecution of the Church, received far more notice than the philosophical and theological *Man's Dignity* which was, however, highly acclaimed among small circles of intellectuals. *Peter's Chains* had an NCWC printing of 500,000, one of the largest to that date.

The bishops did more than expose the Communist persecutions; they endeavored to alleviate the sufferings of the victims, however possible. The NCWC reported at the 1953 meeting major relief programs in thirty-two countries and an operation for that year valued at $32,000,000; the expenditure for relief extended in ten years totalled $212,364,319. Since December 1945, the Committee for Refugees had placed 1,767 children in new homes. The Office for UN Affairs was an important clearinghouse for UN information and did much to publicize Catholic principles on international affairs, especially the pope's peace program, and thus fought Communism in a positive way.

The cardinals, archbishops, and bishops of the United States held their next annual meeting at The Catholic University of America, Washington, D.C., November 17-19, 1954. A message of greeting was received from His Holiness Pope Pius XII who sent an earnest expression of his "appreciative gratitude" for the assistance American Catholics had given him in answering appeals for charity that poured into Vatican City from all parts of the world. A generous alms had been sent to His Holiness as a donation from the contribution made in the Laetare Sunday collection. The same message affirmed that the reports of the NCWC contained "ample" evidence that the well-known pastoral zeal of the hierarchy of the United States was sensitively alert to the manifold problems confronting the Church in America.

Some idea of the great multiplicity and variety of issues discussed at these meetings might be gained from this sketch of the meetings' minutes: Archbishop Karl Alter, chairman of the Administrative Board, referred briefly to the sponsorship, with the provision of home and job assurances, of refugees coming to this country, projecting services within the coming year for 190,000 refugees, escapees, and expellees under provisions of the omnibus immigration and naturalization law; the NCWC Immigration Department would have the responsibility of aiding 19,000 relatives of American citizens in Italy, Greece, and the Netherlands. From July 1, 1953, to June 30, 1954, the department aided 1,556 prelates, priests, brothers, nuns, and seminarians, to obtain visas, appeal adverse decisions, secure passports, etc. Reports were also made on programs of overseas relief administered by War Relief Services, the adoption of children, particularly refugee children, participation in the Exchange of Persons Program of the U.S. State Department, service to older students coming to the United States from foreign countries, encouragement of Catholic technicians to serve in the United Nations or the United States technical program, aid to Catholic institutions in war-damaged countries, hospital construction and financing in the United States.

Among the problems discussed at the meeting were those arising from agitation for federal aid to education in the United States, the position of seminarians under the Selective Service Act, varied assistance to men and women in the armed forces and in defense work areas, state and national legislation that touched on religious and moral questions, attacks upon the Church, and the effect of changing tax legislation upon religious, charitable, and educational institutions.

In their 1954 Pastoral, *Victory . . . Our Faith*, the bishops decried the advance of materialism in America and declared that unless the "invasion" was pushed back outside, enemies could not be withstood. "The enemy," they maintained, must be considered as more than a political state, a group of states, or an economic system. That enemy is atheistic materialism. "Whether it be entrenched in the organs of a foreign state, or in one of our own domestic institutions, it is atheistic materialism that seeks to destroy us." The members of the Administrative Board of the National Catholic Welfare Conference, in signing the Statement, asserted that their "greeting" was issued with "mixed hope and concern"—hope in the "blessing of Christ and His Church," and concern from "tyranny already imposed upon a billion souls" over the world. Several passages of the Pastoral were strikingly similar to Pius XII's 1951 Christmas address, *The Church and the Peace*.[2]

This Pastoral was praised highly in some scholarly and religious circles, but seemed to have had little or no impact on the general public and certainly did not have the political significance of *A Plea for Justice*, an appended Statement protesting continued persecution in Communist countries with particular emphasis on the sufferings in Vietnam. This Statement, concluding on an especially strong note, asked for prayers for the alleviation of suffering, then begged the United States that "by action (as far as action lies within our power) we may give comfort to those who are tortured in body or spirit."

---

[2]Cf., Vincent A. Yzermans, ed., *The Major Addresses of Pope Pius XII* (St. Paul, Minn., 1961) II, 149-158.

Pursuing the point further on November 19, 1954, at the close of the meeting, the bishops sent letters to President Dwight Eisenhower, Secretary of State John F. Dulles, Henry Cabot Lodge, Jr., then permanent representative of the United States to the United Nations, and Henri Bonnet, France's ambassador to the United States, to alert them to the Statement: "In the event that it may have escaped your notice, I beg to bring to your kind attention the enclosed news release (*A Plea for Justice*) telling of the concern of the Catholic bishops of the United States over the present situation in Vietnam, with our confident hope that it will receive your most earnest consideration." This brief Statement received far more secular notice than the Pastoral and would be often quoted for the next decade.

Not until the 1968 Pastoral supporting *Humanae Vitae*, the papal teaching on birth limitation, did any American Catholic pastoral get the instant public reaction that the November 19, 1955 Letter, *Private and Church-Related Schools in American Education*, received. By comparison the question of an ambassador at the Vatican was a remote if not ignored issue. The Statement, widely distributed to national and international communications media, received a most generous amount of space in news columns, especially in principal newspapers. Editorials, more so than news stories, interpreted the bishops' request for auxiliary aids to pupils in Catholic schools as a request for aid to the schools. The attack on the Statement by Protestants and Other Americans United for the Separation of Church and State got an early and extensive printing and helped befog the issue.

Fifteen newspapers carried the story on page one; the maximum length of the one hundred eight stories examined ran up to an impressive thirty-two inches for the *Baltimore Sun* and *Chicago Tribune*. Newspapers running both a story and the text devoted the most space to the Statement, of course (e.g., *New York Times* coverage amounted to about one hundred inches). In addition to carrying the complete text of the Statement, the *U.S. News and World Report* carried an eight-column illustrated story about tax aid to private schools (Catholic and southern[3]) as well as the critical statement of Glenn L. Archer, executive director of POAU. Seventy-two of the one hundred eight papers surveyed headlined the bishops' defense of "the Catholic school children's right to benefit from those measures, grants, or aids, which are manifestly designed for the health, safety, and welfare of American youth." Other lead writers, however, had the bishops demanding rights, opposing discriminations to education, or hitting critics. The Associated Press story began: "The nation's Roman Catholic bishops said today that private and parochial schools 'exist by right' in

---

[3]In some Southern states segregation-minded citizens had started private all-white schools.

this country and 'discriminating' treatment of them is unfair." Then in paragraph 9: "The Supreme Court has held that public tax funds may not be used to benefit any sectarian institution, including the parochial school. But it had held also that there is nothing in the Constitution to prevent using public money for services for children in parochial schools. . . . The key decision in a series of Supreme Court rulings came in the Everson Case of 1947 when the high court ruled that it was constitutional for the state of New Jersey to provide public tax money for children to ride buses to parochial schools."

The dispatch enumerated the states giving children of parochial schools bus, health, and textbook grants, and alluded to the timeliness of the Statement in connection with the White House Conference on Education. A second study by AP stressed the issue on the right to grants, clearly pointing out the bishops had asked aid for pupils, not schools.

The United Press dispatch started with the bishops' defending private education and claiming equal rights to aid for Catholic schools. The aid to children distinction appeared clearly in paragraph 9 of this dispatch: "Catholic schools can, and do, participate in the federal school lunch program but are barred from federal aid in school construction."

The International News Service dispatch had the bishops striking hard at critics of private schools, and waited until the ninth paragraph to distinguish between aid to schools and pupils. The *New York Times* also waited until it got deep into its story to bring out the distinction between aid to schools and to pupils. On November 28, Drew Pearson in his column and Fred Hechinger in the New York *Herald Tribune*, discussing the White House Conference, claimed the bishops had asked for aid to schools. However, Washington correspondents Richard L. Strout and Josephine Ripley of the *Christian Science Monitor* on November 21 and 23 very clearly made the distinction in education stories between aid to pupils of Catholic schools and to the schools themselves.

An unusual feature of the *New York Times* story (picked up later by the *Monitor* and *U.S. News and World Report*) was the following: "The stand that private schools have the right to benefit from government aid assumed particular significance today because some Southern states are considering ways to establish a 'private' school system with public funds in the wake of the Supreme Court decision against segregation in the public schools."

Oddly, the December 4 issue of the *New York Times* which included John Morris' clear reference to state tuition grants to parents in connection with the proposed segregated private school system of Virginia, had Benjamin Fine on another page asserting that the bishops' Statement has asked "funds" for Catholic schools.

A one-column story in the *Cincinnati Times-Star* made no mention of the bishops' auxiliary aids request. The *Chicago Tribune* dispatch buried the aids request. The *Washington Star* and *Washington Post* headlined the aids request but marked it clearly for the students. The *Baltimore Sun* headwriter went to the second paragraph of his correspondent's dispatch to stress the aid point; the story properly distinguished the two types of aid.

Glenn Archer of POAU blasted the bishops' Statement. POAU took its usual line: The Catholic Church "teaches the negation of freedom" and, therefore, should not receive subsidies from the American government. Archer labeled the bishops' request for auxiliary aids "very elastic," implying their endorsement of an April 1955 editorial in the *Catholic World*, which had suggested the feasibility of using public funds for private school construction. On auxiliary aids, Archer conceded Catholic pupils the right to benefit only from health and lunch programs.

Starting with the assumption that the bishops had asked aid to Catholic schools, the National Council of Churches argued on December 1, 1955, that such schools should be supported entirely by their church, maintaining that church schools are no more entitled to government help than the churches themselves. The accepted report did not directly mention the Catholic Church or the bishops' Statement.

Nine editorials revealed an impact from the eloquence and cogency of the Statement, but were virtually unanimous in citing "separation of church and state" with reference to aid for pupils attending private schools.

The most dramatic clash came in the *St. Louis Post-Dispatch* which ran editorials on the Monday and Friday following issuance of the Statement. The *Post-Dispatch's* Monday editorial began: "In the strongest statement on the subject of aid for church schools they have yet issued, two hundred eight prelates comprising the Roman Catholic hierarchy in the United States have called for equal church-school rights to financial grants and aids now accorded public schools." The editorial (1) cited the Constitution and the Everson Case as insuring separation of church and state, and forbidding use of public taxes for religious purposes; (2) pointed out that our country because of separation has not been plagued by religious controversy as have Argentina, Belgium, Hungary, Spain, Italy, and Colombia; (3) concluded by citing Blanshard as an example of the "increased opposition" that will "inevitably" follow from increased "agitation" for aid to private schools. A flood of letters from Catholics prompted a second *Post-Dispatch* editorial. Not a retreat from the first, it took cover behind additional apologetical material from the McCollum decision and the Jewish Synagogue Council's opposition to teaching "moral and ethical values" in public schools.

Along similar lines, the *Washington Post* editorial on November 21 said in part: "Everything that is done in private schools is presumably for the 'welfare of American youth.' The use of that phrase in the bishops' statement would seem to argue for the use of tax funds for private and church-related school buildings, for athletic programs, and perhaps for teachers' salaries. We do not think that such aid could be reconciled with the doctrine of separation of church and state that is deeply embedded in the Constitution. Indeed, it is impossible to give even a little public aid to religious schools without encroaching upon that principle. And if the principle should be broken down, every religious group would be clamoring for public funds to support denominational schools. In that event, we do not see how a chaotic situation could be avoided."

The *Christian Science Monitor*, apparently unaware of the clear distinction made by their Washington correspondent, Richard Strout on November 21, claimed on November 22, that the bishops had cited the Oregon School Case to claim "full right to receive government aid" for parochial schools. "This [right to private education] is quite a different proposition from the claim that parochial schools should benefit from tax-supported aids to education, which could lead to the sharing of direct school expenses. . . ."

The editorial also brought up the Southern states' private school situation, comparing Catholic schools unfavorably on the point of maintaining national unity. The *Christian Century*, December 7, 1955, accused the bishops of verbal trickery: ". . . what the bishops are really asserting is not the 'right' of their schools to exist, but their alleged 'right' to exist at public expense.

"This, of course, is not a 'right' but a great wrong, according to the principle enunciated by Thomas Jefferson long ago—that 'to compel a man to furnish contributions of money for the propagation of opinions which he disbelieves, is sinful and tyrannical.' The bishops themselves refer to Jefferson, but without any regard to his real view on this point, just as they misleadingly cite the Supreme Court's opinion in the Oregon School Case of 1925, in which the Court upheld the right of parents to send their children to nonpublic schools but said nothing about any right to do so at public expense."

The *Baltimore Sun* (November 22) editorialized: "There is a large gap between the right to exist and asking the taxpayer for direct subsidy." The *Washington Star* (November 23) urged a "wait and see" policy because of its doubts regarding the bishops' meaning on the request for auxiliary aids. In a long editorial of November 22, the Rutland (Vt.) *Herald* said in part: ". . . the Roman Catholic prelates are, in our opinion, on strong ground in suggesting that programs designed for the 'health, safety, and welfare of American youth'— regardless of the school attended—deserve tax support provided they accept the corollary: that those tax-supported programs must remain in control of the governmental agency (federal, state, or local, or some combination thereof) which is providing the money."

The bulk of the Catholic letters to the *Post-Dispatch, Washington Star, Washington Post,* and *Baltimore Sun* pointed out, rather forcefully in some cases, the distinction between auxiliary aids to taxpayers' children and direct subsidies to parochial schools, as not distinguished by news and editorial writers. Anti-Statement letters followed the POAU line to a great extent with references to the policy of separation of church and state and the "horrors" arising from nonseparation in Spain, Argentina, etc.

The 1955 meeting also included discussion of two other matters related to Catholic schools. The legal department of NCWC again reported that trends in zoning ordinances in many sections of the country posed a threat to parochial schools. "Many ordinances recently enacted exclude nonpublic schools from residential areas. One example involved the action of a Brighton, New York, planning board denying construction permits for a Catholic church and school in a residential area. Lower courts upheld the propriety of the action, but the Court of Appeals finally ruled: "The paramount authority of this state has declared a policy that churches and schools are more important than taxes." Also the House of Representatives received from a subcommittee a recommendation that nonpublic schools be given the benefit of excise tax exemption already enjoyed by the public schools. Congress adjourned before action could be taken on the recommendation. Although the question concerning aid to nonpublic school students raised by the 1955 Pastoral is far from settled, in recent times the Catholic position has been gaining strength.

At the meeting it was agreed by the American hierarchy to release later a Statement on *Religious Persecution and Prayer Plan* for the fifth Catholic national day of prayer since 1952. The accompanying NCWC news release showed the shocking extent of the persecution of the Church, particularly in Red China and Argentina.

Chinese Catholics bore the brunt of the Communist attack now that less than thirty of the five thousand foreign missionaries who once served China still remain there. A bishop, twenty-three priests, and three hundred laymen were arrested and seventeen laymen killed on a single day in September 1954, at Shanghai. Two thousand Chinese laymen had been jailed. Canton, Hankow, and Hanyang, as well as the provinces of Hehol, Fukien, Shantung, and Chekiang, were the scenes of stepped-up persecution. In Chekiang province Communist officials used bribes in an unsuccessful attempt to set up a so-called "Independent Church."

Despite the fact that Peron's power had been broken in Argentina, the country's bishops felt obliged to warn against the de-Christianization of many people following the Peron regime.

In India the national government was hard pressed to ensure religious freedom. Hindu fanatics and misguided municipal officials had been harassing missionaries, but the Indian Parliament successfully beat down a bill which would have banned conversions to Catholicism.

North Vietnam had imprisoned twenty priests; and in North Korea, according to reliable reports, there was not a single priest free to serve the country's forty thousand Catholics.

Tito continued his war with Catholics in Yugoslavia by heavy taxation, closing seminaries, and discouraging vocations to the priesthood. Neither Cardinal Mindszenty nor Archbishop Groesz enjoyed real liberty despite the Hungarian government's claim of their "release." Priests continued to be arrested or removed from their posts. Night raids against the homes of priests and leading laymen highlighted the Czechoslovakian persecution earlier in the year. More nuns were being forced into mining and factory work. Young people were the special targets of the East German campaign. Youths refusing to participate in pagan "initiation" rites had been penalized. "Progressive" Catholics, led by Boleslaw Piasecki, were Moscow's most effective tool against the Catholic Church in Poland. Piasecki's followers urged Catholics to compromise with the Reds who had so far avoided open persecution.

The Catholic Church had been almost wholly destroyed in Albania, Bulgaria, Estonia, Latvia, Lithuania, and Rumania, as well as in the Soviet Union itself. Almost two hundred bishops had been killed, imprisoned, or exiled since the Kremlin's campaign against the Catholic Church began and approximately 60 million Catholics were under Communist control.

The noncontroversial nature of the 1956 Letter, with a circulation of only 82,000, failed to evoke the sharp newspaper editorials which met the 1955 Statement. In 1955 the repercussions of the bishops' Statement in the form of editorials, letters to the editor, etc., lasted for weeks. Of the ninety-one newspapers reviewed for 1956, only one—the Bridgeport *Post* (Sunday circulation, 63,829) carried what could be considered a "real" editorial, i.e., one prompted by the Statement, and it was laudatory. Two newspapers—the *Washington Post-Times Herald* and the Laconia (N.H.) *Citizen*—made passing reference to the Statement to highlight their arguments that civilization is at stake. Another, the Youngstown (Ohio) *Vindicator*, published excerpts from the bishops' Statement on the editorial page with no other comment.

The proposed Statement for 1956 was "The Right of the Church to Teach,"[4] but because of the changing international situation, at the

---

[4]With slight changes, "The Right of the Church to Teach" was issued by the American bishops in 1958 as *The Teaching Mission of the Church.*

suggestion of Edward Cardinal Mooney, the subject was changed to *Peace and Unity: The Hope of Mankind,* most fortunate in its topic and timeliness. Russia had just ruthlessly crushed the freedom fighters of Hungary; Great Britain and France were clamoring for UN police action in Egypt. No adverse criticism of the Pastoral was noted in any of the ninety-one papers examined. The general press received it favorably and with fairness, often coupling it with headlines about Hungary and Egypt.

Both the Associated Press and United Press ran two accompanying stories. One dealt with the Statement itself, the other related to statistics on persecution supplied by the Bureau of Information of NCWC office as supporting what the bishops had said about Hungary. AP, in addition, carried the full twelve hundred-word text of the Statement. The five hundred fifty-word main story of the Associated Press opened: "The Catholic bishops of the United States, declaring the world 'is poised on the brink of disaster,' called today for a 'veritable crusade of prayer' for peace." International News Service liked the "brink of disaster" idea, but linked it with the bishops' praise for President Eisenhower's "vigorous leadership" in its headlines. The *New York Times* saw newsworthiness in the declaration that the United Nations offers the world the only present promise for sustained peace.

United Press picked out the plea for "basic sanity among men and nations" to outlaw Communist banditry. The news service listed four major points of the statement: the President's leadership, the UN as a hope for peace, a crusade of prayer, and help for Hungary. Most of the papers examined stressed one or more of the above four major points in their leads. Eight newspapers, seven of them large metropolitan papers, carried the full text. Twenty-one of twenty-eight metropolitan papers considered the story important enough for front page play or for prominent placement in the paper. *Time* (November 26) devoted the main part of its religion section to Statements by the Catholic and Episcopal bishops, which, in the words of the magazine, "were remarkably similar in content." *Time* quoted extensively from both Statements.

Several Polish and Hungarian language papers, gave page one or other prominent coverage. The European desk of U.S. Information Agency used the text and the two accompanying releases from the NCWC Bureau of Information. The accounts went to USIA offices in London, Paris, Rome, Bonn, and Vienna. Voice of America translated and beamed the Statement in European, Near Eastern, and Far Eastern areas. The French News Agency, which serves newspapers internationally in Europe, Africa, Latin America, and the Far East, filed a seven hundred-word story and the German Press Agency carried the story as also did Reuters, a British international news agency. Further promulgation of the Statement came through the NCWC office of UN affairs whose staff members attended UN meetings and worked for the presentation of Catholic viewpoints.

So intense did the sufferings of the members of the Church of Silence become that the bishops through their Administrative Board issued a Statement *On the Persecuted Peoples* which concluded with the call upon all Catholics of our country to make Sunday, December 30, 1956, a day of prayer "that God may humble all tyrants and grant peace and friendship to those who so patiently have borne their crushing yoke." This brief but powerfully worded Statement released toward the end of the year was written by the Most Reverend Lawrence Shehan, then Bishop of Bridgeport, Connecticut.[5]

In 1957 the bishops chose as the topic of their Statement, *Censorship*. They argued for the rights of children and proclaimed that the competence of the Church in this field comes from her divine commission as teacher of morals.[6]

More than thirty-five hundred copies of the Statement and an accompanying release were distributed by the NCWC Bureau of Information. Though the dissemination was diverse, *Censorship* elicited little or no editorial response. The response was much less than the bishops expected even in Catholic circles. Several religious leaders of other faiths praised it, a few political figures, especially Mrs. Kathryn Granahan (D. Pa.), strove for implementing legislation in the Congress of the United States against pornography and indecent literature. The Statement did offer some excellent guidelines and argumentation on the delicate subject of censorship for that time but they certainly could not all be enforced legally now. In fact, it seems the Catholic Church has only limited success in this area in the United States.

Appended to *Censorship* were two other Statements: *Persecuted Peoples*, designating Sunday, December 29, 1957, as a Day of Prayer for the persecuted, especially those in Hungary; and *On Traffic Safety*, denouncing the careless and reckless use of automobiles. The key sentence seems to be: "In far too many situations where death and injury occurs in automobile accidents the driver is at fault." Unfortunately most American Catholics to this day do not know their hierarchy ever made a Statement *On Traffic Safety*.

The fifteen hundred-word 1958 Statement *Discrimination and the Christian Conscience*, issued on November 13, was most timely. In 1943 the Catholic Interracial Council was organized by Father John La Farge, SJ, who led a campaign against segregation in Catholic insti-

---

[5]Cf., Monsignor Howard Carroll, General Secretary of NCWC to Bishop Shehan, December 10, 1956, files of the Bureau of Information of the USCC.
[6]For a fuller treatment of this point cf., chapters V and VII in Vincent A. Yzermans, ed., *Pope Pius and Catholic Education* (St. Meinrad, Ind., 1957); also pertinent is Vincent A. Yzermans, ed., *Valiant Heralds of Truth, Pius XII and Arts of Communication* (Westminster, Md., 1958).

tutions. In September 1947, Archbishop Joseph E. Ritter of St. Louis declared an end to segregation in schools of his archdiocese seven years before the Supreme Court's ruling of May 1954. In 1948 the Archbishop of Washington, Patrick A. O'Boyle, integrated the schools of the archdiocese. As Monsignor Ellis notes: "The Church often has anticipated the most enlightened public sentiment on matters of this kind."[7] Louisiana was a focal point of integration difficulties in 1955 and 1956 on school and other levels. In view of that situation Archbishop Joseph E. Rummel of New Orleans issued a strong letter for integration explaining how wrong segregation is. The letter alienated many Catholics in that archdiocese, but Archbishop Rummel never wavered in his stand.

Widely covered by the press, television, and radio, the vast majority of the stories on *Discrimination and the Christian Conscience* originated with the two wire services, Associated Press and United Press International. AP's first lead read: "The Roman Catholic bishops of the United States Thursday expressed the view that enforced racial segregation cannot be 'reconciled with the Christian view of our fellow man.'" The three hundred-word story further emphasized the legal and historical reasons cited for the judgment that segregation is wrong, quoted the bishops' call for prudence, and the need to "seize the mantle of leadership from the agitator and the racist." The coincidental statement of the Methodist bishops on the racial issue was incorporated in AP's later lead: "The struggle to end racial segregation has drawn renewed backing from the bishops of the two major religious groups in the United States." UPI's initial story noted: "The Roman Catholic bishops of the United States Thursday urged sober-minded Americans of all faiths to 'seize the mantle of leadership from the agitator and the racist . . . before it is too late.'" The story ran about five hundred words, and covered more points than did AP.

The Charleston (S.C.) *News & Courier* elicited this comment from the diocese's recently installed Bishop Paul J. Hallinan: "The statement of the American Catholic bishops made last week calls for exercise of two virtues: charity and prudence. Since I am a bishop of the Catholic Church, my principles, of course, can be found expressed in the full statement." The *New York Times*' dispatch began: "The Catholic bishops of the United States called Thursday for decisive but prudent action to eradicate racial segregation in our nation."

Of the nine Southern editorials examined, the Hearst chain's San Antonio *Light* was the only Southern newspaper that gave unqualified approval to the Statement. The same editorial was carried in at least nine Northern papers of the Hearst chain. The Hearst papers called the Statement "beautifully written" and "a historic declaration." "The Catholic Church has always preached against racial intolerance," the

---

[7]John Tracy Ellis, *American Catholicism* (Chicago, 1955), p. 146.

editorial continued, "but the tremendous impact of the statement by the Catholic bishops, including the two American cardinals, lies in the fact that this is the Church itself, in all its power saying: 'It is vital that we act now decisively . . . to seize the mantle of leadership from the agitator and racist.'" Critical comments appeared in the Natchez (Miss.) *Times*, the Chattanooga (Tenn.) *News-Free Press*, and the Montgomery (Ala.) *Journal*. The Natchez *Times* questioned whether what the bishops "consider morally correct should be translated into law." The Chattanooga *News-Free Press* argued that the Supreme Court segregation decision was a "tyrannical usurpation by unconstitutional, dictatorial court decree." The Montgomery *Journal* thought it "not inappropriate to observe that so many of our great and distinguished religious leaders have become vocative on this race mixing issue only after the Supreme Court had acted."

Most of the favorable editorials emphasized that "the heart of the race question is moral and religious." Many also stressed the need for sober-minded leadership. "With these words," stated the *Washington Post and Times Herald*, "the Catholic bishops of the United States cut through all the emotional underbrush surrounding the controversy over civil rights in general and desegregation of public schools in particular." The *New York Times* editorialized: "There is good reason why religious leadership should come to the front in dealing with this problem. These religious leaders recognize that the basic question is not merely one of law but one of morals and have taken their stand on this ground." The Springfield (Ill.) *State Journal*, noting the racial statements by the Catholic, Methodist, and Episcopal bishops, commented: "Moral leadership is needed in this field. In time, the rightness of the views of these religious leaders will win just as the moral opposition to slavery won one hundred years ago. It is inevitable under a democracy that lives up to its name." The Trenton (N.J.) *Trentonian* called the Catholic and Methodist statements "massive understanding" as opposed to "massive resistance."

Time magazine's introduction said: "Continuing the longstanding opposition of the Roman Catholic Church to segregation, two hundred ten of the U.S.'s two hundred twenty Catholic bishops met in Washington, D.C., last week, issued a tough statement on why and how segregation offends against morality and Christianity." *Newsweek* noted that "the Catholic bishops cited the moral as well as papal mandates against racial discrimination." The magazine quoted from the concluding paragraph the necessity for prudence. *U.S. News and World Report* published the full text of the Catholic Statement, as well as the text of the Methodist Statement. On the editorial page, David Lawrence called the Catholic Statement "an eloquent defense of the rights of Negroes." However, the editor thought the Statement inadequate because it avoided "the basic question . . . namely, intermarriage between white and colored." This is "the root of the whole problem" underlying opposition to integration, Lawrence argued.

In the Negro press within a week there were several editorials and stories on the bishops' Statement. George S. Schuyler, N.Y. editor, the *Pittsburgh Courier* (largest U.S. Negro weekly): "The recent statement of the Catholic bishops was . . . forthright, intelligent, understanding and statesmanlike. . . . It was especially praiseworthy because it stressed the fact that the subject treated is not simply a matter of laws but a matter of morals." Chicago *Defender* (in an editorial): "This is the most positive declaration that has yet been issued by any religious body to date. It leaves no doubt in the public's mind as to where the Roman Catholic church stands on the issue of racial equality." Ralph J. Bunche, Undersecretary, Secretariat of the United Nations: "It is a statement of the finest Christian tradition; it is also a striking expression of the spirit and promise of American democracy and the serious challenge confronting it today in race relations. I find it particularly impressive in its strong support for the equality of man and its unqualified rejection of enforced segregation." Allan Morrison, editor of the Johnson Publishing Company (three Negro magazines with a combined circulation of three million): "I was indeed profoundly stirred by the momentous anti-segregation statement. . . . I consider the statement to be a proclamation of historic importance to Catholics and non-Catholics alike for it was issued by the highest dignitaries of the Church in the U.S. and unequivocally denounces segregation as spiritually immoral, socially destructive and in the larger sense intolerable in a free society." Roy Wilkins, executive secretary, NAACP: "The National Association for the Advancement of Colored People welcomes this momentous statement and believes that it will be a substantial contribution to the solution of our country's most vexing problem. We are heartened by its call for 'quiet and persevering courage' and its recognition that prudence should not serve as 'a cloak for inaction.'"

The business office of NCWC printed 700,000 copies of the full text to fill requests. The 1953 special Statement, *Peter's Chains* on the Communist persecution of the Church, and the 1944 Statement, *On International Order* were the only previous statements that had an NCWC printing of 500,000.

A second Statement also issued by the bishops on November 13, 1958, *The Teaching Mission of the Church* is really a national application of Pius XII's Address on *The Teaching Authority of the Church* delivered on May 31, 1954.[8] The Associated Press's lead, which caught the eye of most editors, was: "The Roman Catholic bishops of the United States said today their church must have an unfettered right to teach if freedom is to survive anywhere." AP stressed the point that sub-

---

[8] Cf. Vincent A. Yzermans, ed., *The Major Addresses of Pope Pius XII* (St. Paul, Minn., 1961) I, 284-301.

version of freedom begins with restriction of the Church. The three hundred-word story continued with quotes to the effect that the Church must morally guide mankind, and that materialism and secularism "have made heavy inroads. . . ." "The bishops, who include Francis Cardinal Spellman of New York and James Cardinal McIntyre of Los Angeles," the story noted, "said the teaching function of the church is challenged most often in this country on such matters as divorce and birth control."

United Press International's account, amounting to four hundred twenty-five words, began: "The Catholic bishops of the United States forcefully defended the Catholic Church's 'right to teach.' In an eighteen hundred-word special statement issued after their annual meeting here, they said there is 'genuine urgency' for 'reaffirming this right.'" UPI's story was more comprehensive than AP's. The story elaborated upon the four contested areas: birth control, divorce, measures of guidance, and parochial schools. That teaching is a right and not a privilege, that the right stems from the Creator, that the founding fathers had foresight, and that subversion of freedom begins with the restriction of the Church were the other points touched upon in the UPI account.

The full text of the Statement was published by five newspapers. Compared to the Statement on discrimination, editorial reaction to *The Teaching Mission of the Catholic Church* was slight. In over a hundred newspapers examined there were only two editorials: one pro and one con. *Christianity and Crisis*, a nondenominational Protestant magazine, was "at first baffled by the official statement. . . . What was the purpose of the document since no one in this nation challenged the Church's right to teach?

"When the bishops speak of 'monolithic statism,' surely they cannot mean our pluralistic society, for they are conscious of our pluralism and speak several times about the confusion of voices in a pluralistic society."

The writer was finally led to understand that "the statement was meant for the faithful living in a pluralistic community, who probably asked questions about the 'right' of the Church to guide their conscience on birth control and possibly on other issues."

At the 1958 meeting the bishops passed a resolution of gratitude to the secular press, radio, and television. In part it stated: "We, archbishops and bishops of the Catholic Church in the United States, feel that it is not only proper but just that we express the deep gratitude of our Catholic people, and our own lively thanks, for the generous and understanding manner in which the press, the radio, and the television recently have dealt with a series of news events of particular importance to Catholics."[9]

The Statement, *Freedom and Peace* was the first of three Statements approved at the conclusion of the 1959 meeting of the U.S. hierarchy in Washington and issued on November 19. A continuing series of international incidents involving the United States and threatening world peace in the late 1950s such as the Suez Canal dispute, the Formosa Straits crisis, the Soviet's threat to Berlin, and the difficulty of procuring an adequate test ban on nuclear weapons definitely influenced the American hierarchy in choosing again the peace topic. Coverage in the nation's newspapers was slight in comparison with the publicity given the second statement on artificial birth prevention. The press generally looked on the *Freedom and Peace* Letter as a restatement and clarification of the Catholic or Christian viewpoint rather than a Catholic stand on a presently controversial topic. Its reasoning in many sections paralleled Pius XII's 1956 Christmas Address, *Communism and Democracy*.[10]

The Associated Press opened its story: "The nation's Roman Catholic bishops called on the United States to uphold the principles of freedom and peace under God instead of stressing material prosperity." The nine hundred-word account mentioned that the Statement of the bishops was the sixth in a period of eighteen years on the subject of peace. It quoted the bishops heavily on basic differences between the Communist and American systems. The United Press International story stressed the necessity of firmness in dealing with Communism. Its story began: "The Catholic bishops of the United States called for firmness in dealing with Communistic powers. They warned that appeasement leads only to the peace of the conquered." Later the six hundred-word story wove in the bishops' teaching on materialism and the increasing laxity in home life and discipline.

Nine stories were prepared by Washington staff correspondents of the larger dailies, e.g., *New York Times*: "The bishops proclaimed their goal as 'nothing less than the conversion of the Communistic world'"; *Chicago Sun-Times*: "Trying to meet and defeat the Communists on their ground of materialism can prove fatal, the bishops warned"; Boston (Mass.) *Traveler*: "Anyone who is inclined to take seriously the Communist pratings about peace and friendship [Premier Kruschev's visit to the United States in September 1959] should read the *Freedom and Peace* statement of American Catholic bishops"; Miami (Fla.) *News* (November 25): "Are we too complacent? What these views [bishops' statement, et al.] suggest and what most Americans forget is that there is no guarantee of our greatness. We are

---

[9]From the NCWC files for 1958. In citing religious events covered well by the secular press the bishops mentioned the coronation of Pope John XXIII and added most prophetically: "surely destined to be a great figure of our times."
[10]Cf., Vincent A. Yzermans, ed., *The Major Addresses of Pope Pius XII* (St. Paul, Minn., 1961) II, 213-228.

facing a challenge unparalleled in our whole existence"; Savannah (Ga.) *Press* (November 24): "Roman Catholic bishops have issued a statement that expresses succinctly and accurately the proper reception of recent Communist 'peace' proposals"; Washington (D.C.) *Post and Times Herald* (November 24): "The Catholic bishops of America have contributed a strong and at the same time understanding statement to the cause of attaining freedom and peace in this 'ism-riddled' world."

In their second Statement issued in 1959, *Explosion or Backfire?*, the bishops did not attempt a detailed explanation of Catholic teaching on birth prevention. Neither did they attempt to exhaust possible solutions to the population problems. Such explanations would have been outside their immediate purpose to assert that the Catholic position on artificial birth prevention had not changed and that Catholics would not support use of public funds to promote artificial birth prevention. The bishops mentioned in *Explosion or Backfire?* that a campaign in favor of birth prevention programs had been mounting for several years. The Statement offered an effective measure in countering that campaign. However, in many areas of the country it was not followed up by the day-to-day publicity effort that would have given it full effect. Birth control groups seized on the Statement as a publicity bonanza, and in the long run gathered the major share of newspaper publicity. Officials of the St. Louis unit of the Planned Parenthood Association reported to the membership at an annual meeting in January that the controversy had boomed promotion efforts, and would aid in securing contributions.

Both the Associated Press and the United Press International covered at length the Statement *Explosion or Backfire?*. The AP story, more than five hundred words, used the following lead: "The Catholic hierarchy of the United States today described as 'simply not true' assertions that artificial birth prevention is gradually becoming acceptable to the Roman Catholic Church." The UPI story, of comparable length, chose as its lead the public funds issue: "The Roman Catholic bishops of the United States served notice Wednesday they will fight any attempt to use U.S. foreign aid funds to promote 'artificial birth prevention' programs in underdeveloped countries."

Two of the fifty-one newspapers checked, in addition to the news story, printed the entire Statement: The *New York Times*, and the *Washington Post and Times Herald*. All the newspaper stories examined were accurate. Almost all papers gave the story the length it seemed to merit in view of its significance. The birth control controversy was voted the most important religious news story of 1959 by the Religious Newswriters Association. Ten of the fifty-one papers checked gave the story front page coverage. Included among the ten were the Jackson (Miss.) *Clarion-Ledger* and the Charleston (S.C.) *News & Courier*, both published in dioceses where Catholics form less than three percent of the total population. The Associated Press based a story on the Statement using the following lead: "There are signs the 1960 presidential campaign, at least until the nominating conventions next summer, promises to be a running exercise in Roman Catholic theology and moral teaching."

On December 1, Archbishop John F. Dearden of Detroit spoke before the Economic Club of Detroit and explained why the Church could not approve artificial birth prevention. His statements were published in the Detroit papers (*News; Free Press*). Albany (N.Y.) papers printed on December 3 a statement of Bishop William A. Scully praising the "courage and logic" of President Eisenhower in ruling that the United States would not provide birth control information to other nations.

The bishops said that Catholics would not support any public assistance, at home or abroad, to "promote" artificial birth prevention. The "promotion" of birth prevention with public funds could be done in various ways. At one extreme a possible position in opposition to that expressed by the bishops would have our government refuse aid to another country unless that country adopted birth control measures. No editorial supported such a stand. A milder position would have the United States "promote" artificial birth prevention by urging it abroad, and acting positively to spread it, though not making it a condition of foreign aid. This seemed to be the position of the *New York Post* in its editorial of December 3:

"The issue is this . . . whether in a crowded, underfed world, the U.S. will actively promote the use of birth control in areas where it is desperately needed and sought. No one is advocating that we 'impose' birth control on people who reject it; the question is whether we will recognize that it is a vital weapon in the war against poverty, or whether we will, as the President suggests, pretend that the weapon does not exist."

A third position in opposition to that expressed by the bishops would have the United States foreign aid program include birth control information to countries which requested it. This was the suggestion of the President's study committee on Foreign Aid, headed by William H. Draper, and almost all newspapers which took a definite stand, took it for or against this suggestion. Eleven newspapers stated or implied support for such a position. Seventeen papers opposed it, most by expressing agreement with President Eisenhower's stand that the government should take no action to further artificial birth prevention.

This is a sample comment of a newspaper which said that it was not the government's business from the *New York Herald Tribune*, December 3, 1959: "It is difficult to see why any country should turn to the United States government for assistance in a matter of this kind, and even more difficult to see why this country should create a crisis of conscience for millions of Americans by granting such assistance. . . .

"In a pluralistic society such as ours, when a moral issue arises over which the people are so broadly and deeply divided, government neutrality is the only just and wise course. Neutrality, in this case, is a positive virtue."

The St. Louis (Mo.) *Post Dispatch*, December 3, 1959, offers a sample of a newspaper which thought it was the government's business: "The President emphatically declares that birth control is not a proper subject for government action of any kind. The United States does not intend to interfere with any other government which wants to adopt a birth control program, he says, but if such a government wants help it should go to 'professional groups' and not to the government. What the President does not seem to realize is that a discriminatory attitude of that sort would in fact amount to intervention in the other government's decision."

The question of the morality of artificial birth prevention was commented on in general, only indirectly: Minneapolis (Minn.) *Star*, November 30, 1959: ". . . the dogma underlying this [the bishops'] position is not accepted by many, probably most, Americans." *New York Post*, November 30, 1959: "What matters in this controversy . . . is whether . . . he [Kennedy] views the practice [of artificial birth prevention] as morally impermissible for all men. . . . We would raise serious doubt about a man whose political theology branded aid to the indigent as a form of mortal political sin. We can hardly voice lesser doubt about any man who, for any reason, rejects the use of birth control as an elementary weapon in the battle against poverty and squalor in the year 1959." Senator John F. Kennedy's statement, issued shortly after the bishops' statement was widely approved.

The Syracuse (N.Y.) *Herald Journal*, December 1, 1959, criticized the bishops for making the statement: "It will be a happy thing for all of us if the religious leaders of all denominations in the U.S. confine their utterances to teaching us the glories of God and refrain from political efforts which only result in the bitterness and ill will which is always the opposite of their clerical aims."

More papers granted the right of the bishops to speak, so long as there was no attempt to "dictate" policy: Washington (D.C.) *Post and Times Herald*, December 1, 1959: "The Catholic bishops are as much entitled to state a moral standard for their communicants as were the Protestant and Anglican representatives on a World Council of Churches committee a few weeks ago to assert a policy for their own faiths. The primary concern of public policy is that the dictates of neither group be enforced upon followers of the other or upon the public at large." Wilmington (Del.) *News*, December 4, 1959: "We do not see how they could have kept silent on the issue despite the fact that their statement was bound to raise the bogy of Kennedy's religion. We think that it would be a healthy thing if a Catholic were nominated and elected as president next year. His performance in office should lay to rest once and for all the fear that if a Catholic were president the United States would be ruled from the Vatican."

The Louisville (Ky.) *Courier Journal* on December 2, 1959, saw the *Explosion or Backfire?* Statement as backfiring on Catholics: "The bishops' flat claim that Catholics have a special right to dictate that their tax money be spent only for purposes they consider moral is a dangerous one and likely to backfire."

On December 6, 1959, the Tallahassee (Fla.) *Democrat*, published in the predominantly Protestant deep south, criticized the Protestants and Other Americans United for Separation of Church and State for their statement following the president's news conference: "An organization which goes to ridiculous extremes in its self-assumed role of maintaining separation of church and state promptly twisted the President's statement into some improper governmental endorsement of a Catholic position.

"The illogic of it is fantastic.

"The fact that a government official and a particular church happen to agree that it is not a governmental matter doesn't put them in collusion for violation of the constitutional prohibition against a state religion."

A number of commentators deplored the effect of *Explosion or Backfire?* on Senator John Kennedy's hope for the presidency. James Reston wrote in his syndicated column (November 28): "The current argument over policy and birth control has made at least one thing clear. This is that the hierarchy of the Roman Catholic Church is not acting in a way to promote the candidacy of Senator John F. Kennedy of Massachusetts or any other Roman Catholic."

Senator John F. Kennedy met the church-state question in his widely publicized address to the Greater Houston Ministerial Association in Houston, Texas, September 12, 1960:

"These are the real issues which should decide this campaign. And they are not religious issues—for war and hunger and ignorance and despair know no religious barrier.

"But because I am a Catholic, and no Catholic has ever been elected President, the real issues in this campaign have been obscured—perhaps deliberately in some quarters less responsible than this. So it is apparently necessary for me to state once again—not what kind of church I believe in, for that should be important only to me, but what kind of America I believe in.

"I believe in an America where the separation of church and state is absolute—where no Catholic prelate would tell the President (should he be a Catholic) how to act and no Protestant minister would tell his parishioners for whom to vote—where no church or church school is granted any public funds or political preference—and where no man is denied public office merely because his religion differs from the President who might appoint him or the people who might elect him.

"I believe in an America that is officially neither Catholic, Protestant nor Jewish—where no public official either requests or accepts instructions on public policy from the Pope, the National Council of Churches or any other ecclesiastical source—where no religious body seeks to impose its will directly or indirectly upon the general populace or the public acts of its officials—and where religious liberty is so indivisible that an act against one church is treated as an act against all. . . .

"Finally, I believe in an America where religious intolerance will someday end—where all men and all churches are treated as equal—where every man has the same right to attend or not to attend the church of his choice—where there is no Catholic vote, no anti-Catholic vote, no bloc voting of any kind—and where Catholics, Protestants, and Jews, both the lay and the pastoral level, will refrain from those attitudes of disdain and division which have so often marred their works in the past, and promote instead the American ideal of brotherhood. . . .

"I do not speak for my church on public matters—and the church does not speak for me.

"Whatever issue may come before me as President, if I should be elected—on birth control, divorce, censorship, gambling, or any other subject—I will make my decision in accordance with these views, in accordance with what my conscience tells me to be in the national interest, and without regard to outside religious pressure or dictate. And no power or threat of punishment could cause me to decide otherwise.

"But if the time should ever come—and I do not concede any conflict to be remotely possible—when my office would require me to either violate my conscience, or violate the national interest, then I would resign the office, and I hope any other conscientious public servant would do likewise.

"But I do not intend to apologize for these views to my critics of either Catholic or Protestant faith, nor do I intend to disavow either my views or my church in order to win this election. If I should lose on the real issues, I shall return to my seat in the Senate, satisfied that I tried my best and was fairly judged.

"But if this election is decided on the basis that 40 million Americans lost their chance of being President on the day they were baptized, then it is the whole of the nation that will be the loser in the eyes of Catholics and non-Catholics around the world, in the eyes of history, and in the eyes of our own people."[11]

---

[11]Theodore H. White, *The Making of the President 1960* (New York, 1961) Appendix C, pp. 391-393.

John F. Kennedy was successful in his presidential campaign. His election to the presidency of the United States seems to have ended the religious question in national elections.

The third and final Statement of 1959, *World Refugee Year and Migration*, was issued by the Administrative Board after having been read and approved by the bishops at the 1959 annual meeting. It mentioned that World Refugee Year had opened the previous July. The prelates pleaded for a Christian attitude toward the problem of migration adding: "But, when migration becomes an impractical solution because of the sheer numbers involved, then heroic measures must be taken to alleviate present misery and to institute long-range reforms, designed to raise the standard of living." After noting: "Even though our [the United States] record has been good," the bishops asked several pertinent and pointed questions, e.g., "Have we made a sufficiently urgent effort to develop to the fullest extent possible a program for distributing our food surpluses to the hungry?. . . Are we doing all within our power, particularly during World Refugee Year, to help the refugee and displaced person?" Citing the prejudicial token immigration laws for Orientals and the unjust national-origins clause, this Statement did much to demonstrate the justice, charity, and concern of the American hierarchy for all peoples regardless of their belief or nationality.

On January 16, 1960, Archbishop Karl J. Alter of Cincinnati wrote to Monsignor Paul F. Tanner, then General Secretary of the NCWC: "I am inclined to think that the Administrative Board will be expected to issue some statements with regard to the upsurge of religious and racial hatreds which have been manifested in the various countries recently.

"Even if we are not asked to make such a statement I feel it might be prudent if we were to take the initiative, not only because it is called for by a spirit of social justice but also because it would be 'bread upon the waters' in the event that further religious prejudice is manifested against us during the course of the present year.

"I am enclosing a statement which I have written, and which I would prefer to issue after the Board of Bishops has given its approval."[12]

Monsignor Tanner sent copies of the Statement to the members of the Administrative Board. To hasten the publication many of them sent their approval by telegram. John Cardinal O'Hara, Archbishop of Philadelphia, telephoned his approval to Archbishop Alter. It was not possible to circularize the entire hierarchy. The approval of the Administrative Board was deemed sufficient and the sentence opening "On behalf of the Bishops, etc." was considered adequate to include the entire hierarchy, as some bishops had requested. The

---

[12]From the files of the Bureau of Information of the United States Catholic Conference.

Protest Against Religious and Racial Bigotry was released on January 25, 1960.

"We deplore any revival of the anti-Semitic prejudice which in its earlier manifestation culminated in such terrible disaster," the Statement declared. "The fact that a malevolent spirit of hatred has found expression not only in one country, but in various countries simultaneously, would seem to indicate an organized plan of action or some common origin."

The protest added that "the danger should be immediately recognized and effective measures taken to eradicate the infection before it can spread.

"We call on all citizens, whether Christians or Jews," the bishops stated, "and on all those who love truth and justice, to protest privately and publicly against further manifestations of bigotry in all its aspects and in whatever form it may be expressed."

The timeliness of the Statement was a great boon for it. Nearly every major newspaper in the country carried a story on it and many printed it *in toto* because of its brevity. It is an excellent Statement for the historical record of a nation that has been blighted often with manifestations of bigotry even into the second half of the twentieth century.

Dissemination of the Pastoral Letter, *Personal Responsibility*, was excellent. Radio and television coverage was better than in preceding years, by reason of a "first" summarizing news release to these outlets. Printed news in the secular press coverage was good as regards accuracy and length of story, prominence of position, a by-line for the newspaper's Washington bureau writer or its religion editor, or a "Special to the *Clarion*" tag. The impact of *Personal Responsibility* was especially great in Washington, D.C., where political motives were read into it, although none were intended.

Both the Associated Press and the United Press International were favorable to the Statement. The number of editorials on the 1960 Letter, four, was small, much less than the number of editorials, fifty-four, on the *Explosion or Backfire?* in 1959 or fifty-six on *Discrimination* in 1958. However, there were not any syndicated columns on the 1958 or 1959 Statements. In 1960 there was a penetrating column by David Lawrence, "Individualism Needed, Catholic Bishops Say," which was carried in two hundred one major newspapers. Holmes Alexander's, carried in sixty-four dailies, had a definite political slant, "Bishops Supply GOP Cue." Lawrence's *U.S. News & World Report* (circulation 1,136,000), carried the 2534 words of the 1960 Letter. In *Time* (circulation 2,884,570), the treatment was lengthy. Since 1955 five or six newspapers regularly carried the full text of the Bishop's Statements. The *Post* and *Evening Star* in Washington, the *St. Louis Globe-Democrat*, and frequently the Fall River *Herald Press* (large Catholic population area). Year by year the dissemination of the State- .

ments improved as more professional techniques were employed.

In November 1961, two hundred twenty-eight bishops of the United States attending their annual meeting issued the Statement, *Unchanging Duty in a Changing World*, in which they insisted that this hour when the forces of freedom and of tyranny face a showdown is the nation's time of greatest opportunity.

"Because we have so often faltered in our course," they asserted, "and because the communist nations have profited by our mistakes to inspire false ideals and to awaken glittering but barren hopes, we must not be discouraged imagining that our hour of opportunity has passed.

"It has not passed. The hour of greatest opportunity is striking now, as the forces of freedom and of tyranny gird for a decision."

The bishops noted the historic religious origins and traditions of the United States but deplored a decline in morals and cited the need of rebuilding "a sound religious and moral foundation for America." Evidence of a moral decline was seen by the bishops in the alarming increase in crime, particularly among the young; in the sensational treatment of violence and sexuality in literature, on the stage, screen, and television; in the disclosures of greed and cynicism in government, labor, and business; in the stubborn continuance of racial prejudice and injustice; in the multiplication of divorce and the rapid disintegration of the family; and in a harsh and pagan disregard of the sacredness of human life concealed under the mantle of science. The bishops blamed much of this on "a pernicious cult of the image" and laid on popular education a measure of responsibility "for the decline and rejection of moral principles."

The bishops' Statement stressed the need to recognize and affirm the essential place of religion and morality in the formation of the human personality if America is to survive as a moral people. "In a world in which individual obligation is being denied, we must show the reality of personal responsibility—transcendent responsibility to God for all acts and attitudes, personal accountability for self, for family, for community, for nation."

The Statement emphasized that the soundness of society depends on the principles of family life: the unity and sanctity of marriage, parental duty and authority, and filial reverence and obedience. Beyond the family, the bishops appealed for adherence to "those moral principles which govern man's wider social relationships" and which "must be made to permeate all of society and its institutions. The laborer must bring them to his union meetings; the industrialist, to the business world; the teacher, to his class; the parent, to his home— each to the sphere of life in which he moves."

The prelates called attention to the principles of social justice emphasized in the recent encyclical of Pope John XXIII, *Mater et Magistra*, asking for spiritual leadership as well as material help for other nations "not as mere counter-moves against communism, but for their essential rightness, as expressions of our highest principles: love of God and love of neighbor."

A look to the future that may have influenced this Statement was evident in the report of Archbishop William E. Cousins of Milwaukee, episcopal chairman of the NCWC Social Action Department. He saw dangerous possibilities in some of the groups of anti-Communists springing up around the country. These groups, he said, in substance may unwittingly be aiding the Communist cause. They divide and confuse Americans. They not only overstress the dangers of domestic Communism arising, but often consider as Communists those whose views and positions on domestic policy happen to differ from their own. The Archbishop deplored the tendency of such groups to label political opponents as pro-Communists or Communists and to harass and persecute them.

In an American Catholicism that was beginning to split widely into the so-called progressive and conservative camps, the Statement was well received by both groups.

In a December 1, 1961, editorial, "The Bishops' Meeting," *Commonweal's* editor felt that the Statement issued by the bishops was directly relevant to the problem of Catholic opposition to Communism. He considered the great point of the Statement to be that America is threatened by a serious corrosion of moral values. "To our minds, the means chosen by many Catholics to fight Communism contribute directly to this corrosion. They are means," the editor continued, "which do little more than intensify the cynicism, secularism, and materialism that characterize so much of American life. Taken together, the report of Archbishop Cousins and the bishops' Statement are distinct contributions to our troubled times."

On December 25, 1961, an editorial in *Ave Maria*, "The Bishops Look at the Year," treating of the recent bishops' meeting, noted that "Catholicism in this country is vibrant and that the Bishops are well aware of the tides and tremors that are shaping our society." After discussing the entire meeting, the editor concluded that "the [American] Church is well aware of what has to be done in the world, and is busy doing it."

Statement on the National Council of Catholic Men

*A Statement Issued by the
Administrative Board of the National Catholic
Welfare Conference*

April 3, 1951

1. The National Council of Catholic Men was established in 1920 to coordinate, promote, and assist the activities of Catholic lay organizations of the country under the direction of the bishops. It is purely a national federation of existing Catholic men's groups, and not a duplication of established organizations.

2. Today, as never before in the years since its founding, the work of NCCM is important to the Church. The problems that press upon her from all sides call for a well planned, fully coordinated, progressive program of action by Catholic laymen.

3. Through NCCM, the mind of the bishops can be made known and an adequate program fostered for implementation by its autonomous affiliated members.

4. In addition, NCCM, as *the* national federation of Catholic men's organizations, is asked to speak for Catholic men, in accordance with the mind of the Church, on the issues of the day.

5. The strength of its voice is proportionate to the support it receives throughout the country. It is our earnest wish that the NCCM be given the cooperation that will enable it to function as a vital arm of the Church.

God's Law
The Measure of Man's Conduct

A Statement Issued by the
Bishops of the United States

November 18, 1951

1. An alarming parallel exists between the situation facing us today and that which faced the Roman Empire 1500 years ago. The problems of the Empire closely resemble those which sorely test us now—barbarism on the outside, refined materialism and moral decay within. Confronted by those problems, with what were men of that time concerned? St. Augustine, who lived in that period, gives us the answer in a memorable passage:

> They do not trouble about the moral degradation of the Empire. All that they ask is that it should be prosperous and secure. "What concerns us," they say, "is that everyone should be able to increase his wealth so that he can afford a lavish expenditure and can keep the weak in subjection. Let the laws protect the rights of property and let them leave man's morals alone. . . . Let there be sumptuous banquets where anybody can play and drink and gorge himself and be dissipated by day or night as much as he pleases or is able. Let the noise of dancing be everywhere and let the theatres resound with lewd merriment. . . . Let the man who dislikes these pleasures be regarded as a public enemy" (*City of God*, Bk. II, 20).

2. Does not all this have a modern ring? Has not a great part of our society been doing and saying much the same thing? With the threat of the barbarian on the outside, does our conduct reflect the sobriety of citizens who are conscious that a bell may be tolling for them and for civilization?

3. We have sent our young men on military expeditions to far-off lands so that justice and freedom may be kept alive in the world; and yet at home we have become careless about the foundations of justice and the roots of freedom. It cannot go well with us if we continue on this course.

4. The lessons of history are evident to those with eyes that will see. The Roman Empire disintegrated from within; moral corruption was the main cause of its decline and disappearance. The same fate will befall us if we do not awaken to the danger which threatens from within our own household. Mastery over material things will avail us nothing, if we lose mastery over ourselves.

Morality: The Need Today

5.   Mastery over self is the primary concern of morality. The right ordering of our lives in relationship to all other beings so that we may attain our true destiny is the proper function of morality. The fundamental problem which faces us, then, is a moral one.

6.   Morality involves the correct and careful regulation of three relationships: man to God, man to himself, and man to his fellow men. These relationships are so closely linked together that to disturb one is to disturb the whole moral order.

7.   Morality, therefore, viewed in its entirety, has three dimensions: height, depth, and breadth. In its height, it soars up to God the Supreme Being, from Whom it takes the definitive measure of what is true and good. In its depth, it penetrates the heart of man, laying hold of his entire personality so that even his innermost thoughts and motives are subject to its rule. In its breadth, it embraces men in every station and condition of life and establishes mutual rights and duties.

God's Will: Man's Measure in the Moral Order

8.   By nature, man is a creature, subject to his Creator and responsible to Him for all his actions. By selfish inclination, at times, he chooses to be something else, assuming the prerogatives of a Creator, establishing his own standards of conduct, and making himself the measure of all things. This prideful folly on his part brings discord into his own life, and profoundly affects the whole moral order. Frustration rather than fulfillment becomes his characteristic mark because he does not possess wholly within himself the way to fulfillment. That he can discover only in God's plan.

9.   God's will, therefore, is the measure of man. It is the standard by which all human actions must meet the test of their rightness or wrongness. What conforms to God's will is right, and what goes counter to His will is wrong. This is the great and controlling rule of the moral order. Unless man recognizes and lives by this rule, he cannot come to that abundance of life destined for him by God.

10. If man is to reach this abundance of life, which depends on the fullness of moral character, it must be through the way he lives his everyday life. He has no other course. It is idle and dangerous for him to dream otherwise. The thoughts, attitudes, motives, judgments, and deeds which make up his daily round will determine his growth in character. He must use all his powers to cultivate that growth as the condition for attaining the true purpose of his life. For

this it is necessary that he should be guided by a knowledge of what is right and what is wrong in the particular situations of everyday existence.

The Moral Order and Human Reason

11. How does he come to such knowledge? How can man know what is his place in the divine plan, and what is God's will in the moral decisions he is called upon to make? God has endowed man with intelligence. When rightly used and directed, the human intellect can discover certain fundamental spiritual truths and moral principles which will give order and harmony to man's intellectual and moral life.

12. What are these truths which right reason can discover? First in importance is the existence of a personal God, all knowing and all powerful, the eternal source from Whom all things derive their being. Next comes the spiritual and immortal nature of man's soul, its freedom, its responsibility, and the duty of rendering to God reverence, obedience, and all that is embraced under the name of religion.

13. From man's position as God's rational, free, and responsible creature, destined for eternal life, spring the unique dignity of the human individual and his essential equality with his fellow men.

14. Out of the inherent demands of human nature arises the family as the fundamental unit of human society, based on a permanent and exclusive union of man and woman in marriage. From the essential character of marriage come not only the right of parents to beget children, but also their primary right and duty to rear and educate them properly.

15. Since neither the individual nor the family is completely independent and self-sustained, there arises the necessity of organized civil society, and in turn, the mutual responsibilities of the individual and family on the one side and of the civil government on the other.

16. Man's social life becomes intolerable if not impossible unless justice and benevolence govern the operations of the state and relationships between individuals and groups. Without temperance, man can neither live in accordance with his human dignity nor fulfill his obligations to his fellow men. Without fortitude, he cannot bear the trials of life or overcome the difficulties with which he is surrounded.

17. Furthermore, it is clear that the inherent dignity of the individual and the needs of the family and of society demand a code of sexual morality within the grasp of every mature mind.

18. These are some of the basic elements of natural law, a law based on human nature; a law which can be discovered by human intelligence and which governs man's relationship with God, with himself, and with other creatures of God. The principles of the natural law, absolute, stable, and unchangeable, are applicable to all the changing conditions and circumstances in which man constantly finds himself.

Natural Law and Revelation

19. These religious and moral truths of the natural order can be known by human reason; but God, in His goodness, through Divine Revelation has helped man to know better and to preserve the natural law. In the Old Testament this revelation was given to God's chosen people. Completed and perfected in the New, it has been communicated to mankind by Jesus Christ and His apostles, and it has been entrusted to the Church which Christ Himself established to teach all men.

20. While the natural law, taught and interpreted by the Church, gives us a guide in many areas of human life, the perfection of human nature is revealed to us in Christ Himself, God-become-Man, the Word-made-Flesh, "full of grace and truth," dwelling among us to be our Way, our Truth and our Life. Prayer and the sacraments are the channels through which the grace of Christ comes to elevate human nature until it becomes like unto Him, who is true God and true man. In the supernatural order of grace Christ, the God-man, is the measure of man.

21. Divine Revelation then not only includes the natural law, it complements it, and points the way to the supernatural order of grace. The natural moral law, however, remains the foundation of the supernatural order as it is the foundation of all man's relations to God, to himself, and to his fellow men. Upon that law, clarified by Divine Revelation, man, strengthened by grace, must build his life. He need never fear that it will give way under the weight of the trials and tests which life imposes; for he has the inspired words of the psalmist to assure him: "The man whose heart is set on the law of the Lord stands firm."

22. When the human heart is so governed by the law of the Lord, all human actions, no matter how commonplace or how removed from the eyes of men, are made pleasing to God and meritorious of eternal life. This means that God's will and God's plan for man are kept constantly in mind. When man has learned to direct his thoughts, his speech, and his actions in this way, it is a sign that he has mastered the great maxim of the moral order—"not my will but Thine be done." It is an indication that he realizes he must at all times be about his Father's business. The point of reference in his life is no longer his own selfish will, for such a man sees clearly that God holds the central place in his life. He also sees that he enjoys a unique status in that God has committed to him a work which no one else can do. His only reason for existence is to perform that work faithfully and diligently. This is the thought which Cardinal Newman so beautifully expressed:

> God has created me to do Him some definite service. He has committed some work to me which he has not committed to another. I have my mission. . . . I have a part in a great work; I am a link in the chain, a bond of connection between persons. He has not created me for naught. I shall do good. I shall do His work (*Meditations & Devotions*, pp. 400-401).

Moral Integrity

23. Doing God's work means doing God's will. This requires the services of the whole man at every moment of every day he exists. There is all too frequent today the spectacle of men who divide their lives to suit their own convenience. Only when it serves their selfish purpose do they conform to God's will. Their business life, their professional life, their life in the home, at school, and in the community occupy separate compartments unified by no central force. God's claims upon such men exist, but they are not honored. Expressions such as "my life is my own affair," or "I may do as I please," or "in politics, anything goes" are all too common today. They betray a gross misunderstanding of the moral order and the interlinking relationships which find their correct measure only in God's will.

24. We must be clear on this point. Man must either acknowledge that a personal God exists or he must deny His existence altogether. There is no middle course. Once he acknowledges that God exists, then the claims of God are coextensive with all the activities of His creatures. To pretend that any part of his life can be a private affair is to violate the most basic claim which God has on man. Man is a creature. As a creature, he is subject to his Creator in all that he does. There is no time in his life when he is excused from obeying the moral law. The clergyman, the educator, the doctor, the lawyer, the politician, the employer, the employee, husbands, wives, and children are alike strictly bound. All human rights and obligations have their source in God's law; otherwise they are meaningless.

Morality and Education

25. Morality, concerned with bringing human activity into conformity with God's will, has, therefore, a bearing on everything that touches human rights and duties. It has a definite place in the educational life of a nation. The forming of character is part of the educational process, and character cannot be formed unless children are given a clear indication of what is right and what is wrong. This cannot be done without reference to the ultimate standard which determines right and wrong, namely God's law.

26. No state, no group of educators may reject a truth of the moral order to suit the claim of convenience. The process of determining moral values by the consent of the majority is false in principle and sanction. Morality has its source in God and it binds all men. It cannot be adequately taught without the motivation of religious truth. Although the training of children along moral lines is primarily the business of the parents and the Church, yet it is also the business of the school if education is to give formation to the whole human personality.

Morality and Economics

27. Morality has its place in business and industry because the conditions under which men work, the wages they get, the kind of work they do, all are subject to the jurisdiction of the moral law. When economic conditions are such that the raising of a family by working people is made dishearteningly difficult and at times impossible, then those responsible for this deplorable situation are guilty of breaking God's law and they are also accomplices in the sins resulting from their injustice.

Morality and Politics

28. In politics, the principle that "anything goes" simply because people are thought not to expect any high degree of honor in politicians is grossly wrong. We have to recover that sense of personal obligation on the part of the voter and that sense of public trust on the part of the elected official which give meaning and dignity to political life. Those who are selected for office by their fellow men are entrusted with grave responsibilities. They have been selected not for self-enrichment but for conscientious public service. In their speech and in their actions they are bound by the same laws of justice and charity which bind private individuals in every other sphere of human activity. Dishonesty, slander, detraction, and defamation of character are as truly transgressions of God's commandments when resorted to by men in political life as they are for all other men.

Moral Standard Applies Universally

29. There are not two standards of morality. There is only one. It is God's standard. That single standard covers all man's relations to God, to himself, and to the world about him. It applies to every conceivable situation in life—in the home, in business, in the school, or in the field of entertainment. By its very nature, it precludes that double standard which not only tempts man to live his life on two levels, but beguiles him into thinking that this can be done without any compromise of moral principles. This two-faced way of living explains the scandalous anomaly, evident at times in our national life, of paying lip service to God while failing completely to honor His claims in daily life.

30. One and the same standard covers stealing from the cash register and dishonest gain derived from public office. It will not do to say, by way of extenuation, that the latter can be excused or condoned because it occurs in the political order. One and the same standard prohibits false statements about private individuals, and false statements about members of minority groups and races. It will not do, by way of excuse, to say that statements of the latter kind can be excused because of long-standing prejudice.

31. This single standard of morality sets a clear, positive, and complete pattern of right living. It gives an integrity of outlook and an integrity of action to daily life. By adhering to this standard, man's life becomes all of a piece, characterized by sincere singleness of purpose. Such a life will not have its "Sunday side" in which God's claims are fully respected for a single day and its "weekday side" in which those claims are completely ignored for the remaining six. Rather, all aspects of life will be so integrated that the standard to which a man subscribes in his private life will be logically extended to his life in the community. Then, if faithful to moral principles as an individual, he will be faithful to moral principles as a citizen, as a voter, and in all his actions as a member of society.

Religion and Morality

32. To live by this single standard of morality man needs the motivations and sanctions which only religion can supply. He is not self-sufficient. He must have God's help. As a creature, he is obliged to adore his Creator, to thank Him for blessings conferred, to ask His pardon for wrongs committed and to pray daily for His help and guidance. Nothing less than the faithful discharge of these essential obligations of religion will enable him to attain integrity in his moral life.

33. We exhort Americans in every walk of life to rededicate themselves to the wisdom of our founding fathers—a wisdom which proclaimed God's rightful place in human affairs—a wisdom so memorably expressed by the Father of our country in his farewell address:

> Of all the dispositions and habits which lead to political prosperity, religion and morality are indispensable supports . . . reason and experience both forbid us to expect that national morality can prevail in exclusion of religious principle.

Statement issued November 18, 1951 by the bishops of the United States and signed in their names by the members of the Administrative Board, National Catholic Welfare Conference

Edward Cardinal Mooney, Detroit

Samuel Cardinal Stritch, Chicago

Francis Cardinal Spellman, New York

Francis P. Keough, Archbishop of Baltimore

Robert E. Lucey, Archbishop of San Antonio

Karl J. Alter, Archbishop of Cincinnati

Joseph E. Ritter, Archbishop of St. Louis

Patrick A. O'Boyle, Archbishop of Washington

John J. Mitty, Archbishop of San Francisco

John F. Noll, Bishop of Fort Wayne

Emmet M. Walsh, Coadjutor Bishop of Youngstown

Michael J. Ready, Bishop of Columbus

Matthew F. Brady, Bishop of Manchester

Persecution behind the Iron Curtain

*A Statement Issued by the NCWC
Administrative Board with the Approval of
the Bishops of the United States*

April 22, 1952

1. Reports of the banishment of Bishop Hlouch from his episcopal
see in Czechoslovakia centers our attention once more to the sad
plight of the Catholic Church in that country. It is a notorious fact
that Archbishop Beran of Prague has been held under house arrest
for the past several years and has been subjected to countless indignities at the hands of the Communist government. In these prelates
we are witnessing a repetition of the atrocities already visited upon
Archbishop Stepinac and the other heroic bishop of Yugoslavia, also
upon Cardinal Mindszenty and Archbishop Josef Groesz of Hungary.
2. In view of the new wave of terror which is being visited upon
the Church in Czechoslovakia, we the members of the Administrative
Board of the National Catholic Welfare Conference, assembled in our
regular semi-annual meeting, express our deep sympathy for the
archbishop, bishops, priests, and laity of Czechoslovakia. We pray
that God may support them in their suffering and strengthen them
in their resistance to the forces of evil.
3. Even more terrible has been the fate of the Church in Romania,
where the entire hierarchy has been liquidated; in Lithuania, whose
bishops, priests, and laity were among the first to feel the full lash
of the new terror; in Albania, whose smaller number of Catholics has
tended to obscure the greatness of the sufferings endured. If in Poland,
the woes of the Church have been less dramatic, equally persistent
and far more insidious have been the means used to win the people
from their spiritual allegiance.
4. Our present sympathies, however, go out particularly to our fellow Catholics in China. There seventy-seven bishops and vicars-general have been imprisoned or are under arrest or have been expelled
or otherwise gravely impeded in the exercise of their office. Twelve
among these are Americans. There are actually seven American bishops or vicars-general in prison. The overall number of Catholic missionaries known to be in prison is twenty-one. Almost 4,000 Catholic
foreign missionaries have been expelled or forced out since the Communists have taken over China. The number of foreign Catholic missionaries in prison at the present time is almost one hundred fifty;
more than two hundred Chinese priests have suffered the same fate.
The number of Catholic priests and religious who have been killed

by the Chinese Reds or have died as the result of maltreatment is at least one hundred. Three bishops have died in Communist prisons.

5.   Every week that passes greatly adds to the number of those who are called upon to suffer for their faith in Communist countries. We may well ask whether any decade in history has been richer in martyrdom than our own.

6.   In view of the sufferings to which all men of religious belief have been subjected, we beseech our fellow citizens to renew their prayer for all, Catholics and non-Catholics alike, who bear the heavy burden of tyranny and are persecuted under a system of government which is the acknowledged enemy of all those decencies which have been the special blessing of our own country.

Religion
Our Most Vital National Asset

A Statement Issued by the
Bishops of the United States

November 16, 1952

1. As bishops of the Catholic Church, we are intensely concerned that the teachings of Jesus Christ, our Lord and God, will bless and sanctify our country. As American citizens, our concern extends to those blessings which only true religion can bring to our beloved land. Our national spiritual assets must be greater than the national material assets which are so evident everywhere. These material assets have brought a standard of living and a degree of comfort never before attained by so many people in any nation. With them has come a position of preeminence in the world hitherto unachieved by peaceful means. In the wake of such unprecedented prosperity a deep sense of security, a national optimism might have been expected. In its stead the temper of the country would seem to be one of restless foreboding and deep insecurity.

2. It cannot be denied that this gloomy and depressing atmosphere is largely a reflection of so much suffering and hopelessness in other parts of the world. Yet it must be affirmed with equal insistence that there is a lowering of vitality in our social institutions, a deplorable pessimism that signals the presence of a cause as dangerous as it is profound. The history of nations teaches us that ultimately it is spiritual losses rather than material reverses that lead to moral bankruptcy and national ruin. Across the centuries, strewn with the wreckage of once flourishing realms, the words of the Lord of nations echo a warning in our ears: "Seek first the Kingdom of God and His justice and all these things shall be given you besides." The corollary is inescapable: "If you seek not the Kingdom of God, all these things will be taken from you."

3. Religion makes man a citizen of the Kingdom of God; for it is through religion that man gives his allegiance to his Maker. Viewed in its entirety, religion is the system of beliefs and practices by which man comes to the knowledge of the one true God, by which he gives to God the worship which is His due, by which he renders thanks for all he is and has, acknowledges and expiates his own guilt, and begs the grace that makes it possible for him to attain his true destiny. As an act, religion is the communion of man with God, the source of all life. It is this that explains the essential importance of religion to man both as an individual and as a member of society, a citizen of a nation. Religion, then, is not only the individual's most precious possession, it is also a nation's most vital asset.

Man's Need of Religion

4.   Man, as an individual, needs religion. He needs it for many reasons. He needs it because he is a creature of God, entirely dependent on his Creator, and hence must acknowledge his obligation of adoration and love. He needs it to give meaning to his present existence; for without religion this life, with its disappointments, its uncertainty, its cruelty, and its suffering, becomes

> but a walking shadow, a poor player that struts and frets his hour upon the stage and then is heard no more, . . . a tale told by an idiot full of sound and fury, signifying nothing (*Macbeth*, V,v,17).

Again, a man needs religion to give him that sense of responsibility which prevents human existence from becoming a wilderness of warring passions and aimless strivings. He needs religion because, apart from God, man is lonely and he can never find in himself or in the institutions which bear his image the means to fill up that void of loneliness which is in the human heart. Man needs religion because he is weak, and in his weakness he must have access to the source of all strength. Man needs religion because without the hope that religion alone can give, he cannot rise above that pessimism, that sense of despair, which threatens to engulf the whole of our civilization. Man needs religion because he has an impelling need to worship, and if he does not worship God he will direct his worship to base objects that will pervert his mind and heart.

Religion, a Fundamental Need of Society

5.   Religion, necessary to individual man, is necessary also to human society. From the very beginning the family, the primary unit of society, has been intimately dependent on religion, and from it has drawn its unity, its stability, and its holiness. Apart from its divine origin and sanction, parental authority, upon which the family is founded, becomes but an arbitrary application of force to be superseded by any stronger power. Where religion has grown weak the family has shown a corresponding tendency to disintegrate. When religion remains strong, it stands as a protective armor, safeguarding both individual and family. Unique as a compelling ideal is the Holy Family of Nazareth with the striking lessons of love and obedience it teaches. More than the knowledge of all the abstract principles of ethics and sociology, the example of this perfect fulfillment of God's plan has through the Christian tradition strengthened and protected the primary unit of society.

6.   Nor is the civic community less dependent on religion. Men are indeed forced by the conditions of human nature to unite and cooperate in the fulfillment of their common needs. But union and cooperation can continue to exist among free men only when justice and charity, universal in their binding force because imposed by God Himself, are embodied in law. While civic authority may have its immediate source in the consent of the governed, that authority must be recognized as coming ultimately from Him upon Whom all men depend. Unless religion with its binding force in justice and charity supplies the foundation of law and authority, there remains only human convention or brute force as the unifying element in society. In the last analysis there is no society of free men without the creative and sustaining force of religion. Civic society received its most effective support from Him Who taught us to render to Caesar the things that are Caesar's and to God the things that are God's.

7.   Nor is religion less important to the complex modern state than to the more primitive social structure. In the measure the state has excluded religion, it has shown a tendency to become an instrument of tyranny. The irreligious state sets itself up in the place of God, substituting its own arbitrary dictates for the decrees of eternal Wisdom. It demands an absolute loyalty such as can be claimed only by Truth itself, and it has no effective deterrent from violating its solemn treaties and from waging unjust and aggressive wars. Since religion is what contemporary tyrannies are attempting first to shackle and then to destroy, one can rightly conclude that it is the one thing most necessary for the preservation of free nations.

8.   Religion then is of the utmost importance to society in all its aspects and in all its stages of development. It is like the rays of the sun, bringing the light of God's wisdom and grace into man's whole social life. It lights up and purifies the city of man and turns it into the city of God. Without these sustaining influences, the city of man is gradually overrun by a Mayan-like jungle of human passions, in whose rank undergrowth of greed and cruelty and every other vice man lives his life in terror—and in the end perishes.

Religious Influences in American Traditions

9.   All society, particularly our own, is intimately dependent on religion. In the beginning of our own nation, at the very time when the

revolutionary movement on the continent of Europe was planning to destroy all influence of religion on public life, it is a remarkable fact that our founding fathers based their own revolutionary action on the rights inherent in man as a creature of God, and placed their trust in His divine providence. The concept of man, which they set forth in the Declaration of Independence and on which they based the Constitution and our Bill of Rights, is essentially a religious concept— a concept inherited from Christian tradition. Human equality stems from the fact that all men have been created by God and equally endowed by Him with rights rooted in human nature itself. Against any other background, human equality has no meaning. Freedom, too, is essentially bound up with the religious concept of man. In any context that separates man from the creative and sustaining hand of God, there can be no freedom. The same is true of all man's inalienable rights. The enjoyment of such rights is safe only in a society which acknowledges the supreme and omnipotent God. The whole idea of government, dedicated to the welfare of the human person in the common good and subject to God's eternal law, is derived from the religious concepts of man and society which our founders inherited from their Christian tradition.

10. The founders of this country were deeply conscious of this debt to religion. The long deliberations to which they submitted the First Amendment to the Constitution and the many revisions it underwent before adoption bear witness to the important place religion occupied in the minds of the first Congress. Certainly it was not their purpose to eliminate the influence of religion on public life. On the contrary it was their intention to guarantee to religion its essential freedom. In a country of divided religious allegiance, the federal government was indeed prohibited from setting up any established religion; but it was also prohibited from interfering in any way with any religious institution or with the freedom of the individual in the practice of the religion of his conscientious choice. That nothing other than this was intended, that the federal government was not prevented from encouraging and even aiding religion, so long as no particular form of religion should be established by the state, is clear not only from the wording of the First Amendment but also from the fact that from the beginning, under the Constitution and its amendments, many practices have flourished which have continued to give great help to religion.

11. Apart from the record of deliberation and the wording of the First Amendment itself, there is abundant evidence that this carefully thought out solution was not indicative of indifference and still less of hostility to religion. Both the Northwest and Southwest Ordinances, passed by the very men who were responsible for the amendment, speak of religion and morality as "necessary for good government and the happiness of mankind." And even more pointed are the words used by our first president in his farewell address:

> Of all the dispositions and habits which lead to political prosperity, religion and morality are indispensable supports. . . . Reason and experience both forbid us to expect that national morality can prevail in exclusion of religious principle.

12. Such were the prevailing convictions of the founders of this country. Such, too, were the traditions which have in large measure determined the course of its development. No one has better expressed American traditions or has contributed more to their development than Abraham Lincoln. Eight times during the term of his presidency he issued proclamations of thanksgiving and of days of prayer and fasting which strongly emphasize this nation's need of religion. The proclamation of March 30, 1863 seems even more pertinent today than it was at the time it was issued.

> We have been the recipients of the choicest bounties of Heaven; we have been preserved, these many years, in peace and prosperity . . . but we have forgotten God. We have forgotten the gracious hand which preserved us in peace, and multiplied and enriched and strengthened us; and we have vainly imagined, in the deceitfulness of our hearts, that all these blessings were produced by some superior wisdom and virtue of our own. Intoxicated with unbroken success, we have become too self-sufficient to feel the necessity of redeeming and preserving grace, too proud to pray to the God that made us.

The Threat of Secularism

13. These words of Lincoln not only recall to us our national traditions relative to the importance of religion; they also remind us of the constant temptation for this country to turn away from God and to become immersed in material pursuits. In our own day widespread yielding to this temptation has given rise to an even greater danger— the way of life we call secularism. Those who follow this way of life distort and blot out our religious traditions, and seek to remove all influence of religion from public life. Their main efforts are centered on the divorce of religion from education. Their strategy seems to be: first to secularize completely the public school and then to claim for it a total monopoly of education.

14. To teach moral and spiritual values divorced from religion and based solely on social convention, as these men claim to do, is not enough. Unless man's conscience is enlightened by the knowledge of principles that express God's law, there can be no firm and lasting morality. Without religion, morality becomes simply a matter of individual taste, of public opinion or majority vote. The moral law must derive its validity and its binding force from the truths of religion.

Without religious education, moral education is impossible.

15. In criticizing this secularist trend in education, let it not be said that we are enemies of public education. We recognize that the state has a legitimate and even necessary concern with education. But if religion is important to good citizenship—and that is the burden of our national tradition—then the state must give recognition to its importance in public education. The state, therefore, has the duty to help parents fulfill their task of religious instruction and training. When the state fails in this help, when it makes the task more difficult and even penalizes parents who try to fulfill this duty according to conscience, by depriving their children of their right under our Federal Constitution to auxiliary services, this can only be regarded as an utterly unfair and short-sighted policy.

16. Even more alarming are the efforts to create a monopoly of education for a secularized public school. To one who cherishes the American tradition, it is alarming to hear all nonpublic education denounced as divisive. Not all differences are divisive, and not all divisions are harmful. There are political and social differences and divisions which are simply the manifestations of our fundamental freedom. The differences which are harmful to our country are those which divide our people in their duty of loyalty, patriotism, and good citizenship. Education of children in schools under religious auspices has no such effect. On the contrary, the religious instruction children receive in such schools inculcates the duties of loyalty, patriotism, and civic service based on love of God, of neighbor, and of country. Education that is truly religious is then a unifying rather than a dividing force.

17. Particularly difficult to understand is the attitude of some few who, while occupying positions of leadership in various religious groups, yet, in almost every question involving the influence of religion in public life and education, throw the weight of their influence behind secularism. In the days when Communism was posing as a new and advanced kind of democracy, some of these persons were loud in their praise of practically everything that came out of the realms of atheism and tyranny. Now that it is no longer fashionable to regard Communism as other than the avowed enemy of our own country, they indeed maintain a discreet silence on the subject of Communistic virtues, but they still throw the weight of their influence behind such totalitarian movements as an all-embracing state-controlled school system and education completely devoid of religion. Although they often lay claim to the title of Christian, they are rather devotees of the pseudo-religion of progress; and they always think of progress in terms of materialistic or secularistic evolution. Consciously or unconsciously, in eliminating the influence of religion and in working for the absolutism of majority vote, they are promoting the disintegration of those social institutions whose foundations are in religion—freedom, equality, human dignity, the stable family, and that constitutional democracy which has been characteristic of this country.

Irreligion, Our Real Danger

18. The real danger to our country comes not from any division likely to result from religious education or profession. It comes rather from the threatening disintegration of our social life, due to the weakening of religion as a constructive force. With the decline of religious belief, the increase of divorce and family disintegration has become a national scandal. With the break-up of the family, juvenile delinquency has shown an alarming increase. Consequent upon the weakening of religion there has been a lowering of moral standards which has resulted in public corruption—and this in turn threatens all respect for law and public authority. The imminent threat to our country comes not from religious divisiveness but from irreligious social decay. The truly religious man is certain to be one who treasures all those ideals which religion helped to build into this nation. To the man who is lacking in religious belief, nothing in the end is likely to be sacred, nothing worth preserving. In that direction lies the real danger to our country.

Fundamental Obligations of a Religious People

19. Although there have been many evidences of the weakening of religion among our people, in recent times there have been unmistakable signs of a renewed religious interest. The number of religious books which have attained wide circulation, the frequent serious discussion of religious topics in the daily papers and influential periodicals, the reported increase everywhere in Church attendance, the frequent and effective use of radio and television for religious programs—all these are encouraging signs. Moreover the vitality of the religious tradition of our country has recently been attested by the Supreme Court, when in its majority opinion it stated that "We are a religious people whose institutions presuppose a Supreme Being," and when it declared that "when the state encourages religious instruction or cooperates with religious authorities . . . it follows the best of our traditions."

20. But our best religious traditions are not fulfilled by mere theoretical acknowledgement of religion as a possible aid in solving our problems, or by a perfunctory attendance at Sunday devotions, or even by a stiff bow on the part of government in the general direction of God. If our country is truly religious, the influence of religion will permeate every part of our national life. The state will not merely tolerate religion; it will honor and welcome it as an indispensable aid in building the complete good life of its citizens—much as the influence of religion has been welcomed in our Armed Forces.

21. In its internal and external affairs the state will uphold, and it will expect its citizens and its officials to uphold, that standard of morality which flows necessarily from belief in God and God's law. From its own officials and employees it will demand an even stricter observance of the moral standard than it can enforce upon individual citizens or business institutions. In dealing with the latter, the state is often using its police power, rightly restricted by constitutional and other legal guarantees. In the case of public servants the state is dealing with individuals whose public employment is conditioned on their honesty, their honor, their truthfulness, their efficiency, and their devotion to the national welfare and the public good.

22. Religion requires that justice, tempered by charity, must prevail in the state's legislation and policy relative to economic groups. It will also inspire and guide the employer in the fulfillment of his duties towards his employees in the spirit of justice and charity. In the workingman's struggle for his rights, the religious conscience of the nation was not among the least of the forces that sustained him. Now that those rights have been largely vindicated, religion still insists on his responsibility to his employer and to society in the achievement of a right economic solidarity.

23. Religion will lead a nation not only to hold forth its bounty to the needy of other nations but also, in a spirit of charity and justice, to do its part to alleviate the plight of the homeless and dispossessed of other lands.

24. A religious people is a people which prays. If the spirit of religion has declined in our times, it is because many, immersed in worldly pursuits, have ceased to pray. Most earnestly, therefore, we urge a return to a life sanctified by prayer. But prayer itself can be effective only when it is the fruit of calm and ordered reflection of the great spiritual realities which underlie our whole existence. Once the opportunity of such reflection was afforded largely by the reverent observance of Sunday, the day of the Lord. We call upon our people to return to the proper religious observance of the Lord's day and the practice of family prayer.

25. It is a cherished tradition for our government to call its citizens to prayer and public worship. Too often the proclamation of days of prayer, traditional in our country, has come to be regarded by many as a pious formality. The realization of the immeasurable benefits we have received from Almighty God, the further realization that only under God's guidance can we hope to solve our problems and overcome our perils will restore to these days their sacred character. The truly religious observance of such days as our religious feasts and national holidays will deepen and enrich the spiritual life of the whole nation.

The Role of Christian Faith

26. One of the constant dangers to the religious spirit in a country such as ours is the tendency to regard religion itself simply as the fruit of pious sentiment; or to hold, as the doctrinal basis of religion, what we may call the common factor in the religious opinions held by various groups; or to be content with the great religious truths of the natural order which can be known by unaided human reason. It is true that the founders of this country, in their public utterances, gave as the religious foundation of their work only the truths of the natural order—belief in God as the omnipotent Creator; belief in man as God's free creature endowed with inalienable rights; belief in the eternal truth and universality of the moral law. But it is also true that these convictions were part of their Christian tradition. Historically these truths had been received and elaborated by intellects illumined by faith and guided by revelation. It would be wrong to imagine that these truths are sufficient for the religious life of the individual, or that they can of themselves guarantee the firm foundation of society. After all, the truths which can be known by reason are but a part of religious truth. It is through supernatural faith alone that man comes to the knowledge of religious truth in its fullness. Man is not free to pick and choose among the truths God has made known either through reason or revelation. His obligation is to accept the whole of God's truth.

27. Man himself is not merely a creature of the natural order. At the moment of creation he was elevated by God to the supernatural state and destined to an everlasting and supernatural life. To the fall of man from this high estate are traceable all the woes which have marked human history. To save man from the eternal consequences of his fall, to pay the penalty of his sins and to restore him to his supernatural state and destiny, the Son of God became man, suffered and died on the cross for the salvation of all mankind. In the accomplishment of the work of redemption, Christ has given us the fullness of God's revelation. To attain to his destiny, therefore, man needs not merely the truths which reason can discover; he needs also the truths which Christ has revealed; he needs the Church which Christ has established.

28. All the religious truths, natural and supernatural, are parts of one integral whole. Ultimately in man's mind they must stand or fall together. Subtract one part and you distort the rest; deny one part and in the end you deny the whole. Nor, in the light of divine revelation, can the principles of natural ethics be separated from the principles of Christian morality. Only the life of Christian faith can guarantee to man in his present state the moral life; and the Christian life is lived in its entirety only through the one true Church of Christ. **29.** In our present day world it has become clear that denial of supernatural truth tends finally to the denial of all religious truth. "I will show you the truth and the truth will make you free." In Christ's design truth and freedom stand together. If today Christianity stands for freedom, it is because Christianity is truth.

Statement issued November 16, 1952 by the bishops of the United States and signed in their names by members of the Administrative Board, National Catholic Welfare Conference

Edward Cardinal Mooney, Detroit

Samuel Cardinal Stritch, Chicago

Francis Cardinal Spellman, New York

Francis J. Keough, Archbishop of Baltimore

John J. Mitty, Archbishop of San Francisco

Richard J. Cushing, Archbishop of Boston

Joseph E. Ritter, Archbishop of St. Louis

Patrick A. O'Boyle, Archbishop of Washington

Karl J. Alter, Archbishop of Cincinnati

John F. Noll, Bishop of Fort Wayne

Emmet M. Walsh, Coadjutor Bishop of Youngstown

Thomas K. Gorman, Coadjutor Bishop of Dallas

Matthew F. Brady, Bishop of Manchester

Communist Persecution Particularly in China

*A Statement Issued by the NCWC
Administrative Board in the Name of the
Catholic Hierarchy of the United States*

November 27, 1952

1. The bishops of the United States of America bow their heads in reverent homage to the multitude of contemporary martyrs and confessors who in these latter days have suffered for their faith in Jesus Christ.

2. Their name is legion. They are citizens of many lands. Never before in history have so many men and women fallen victim to religious persecution. The modern Bede-roll of Christian heroes enshrines the names of two cardinals, one hundred thirty bishops, tens of thousands of priests and religious, and millions of faithful Catholics. The list lengthens with each passing day. Indignity, prison, torture, death—this is the lot of those who profess the faith of Jesus Christ in countries conquered by the hosts of atheistic materialism.

3. To the Holy Father, whose heart grieves sorely for his afflicted children, we send the assurance of our filial sympathy and affectionate solidarity.

4. To the prelates and priests and to our fellow Catholics of the Church of Silence we pledge the continuing aid of our prayers and the encouragement of every help which lies within our power.

5. And to our Catholic priests and people in this free land of America, we issue a call to intercession and prayer that God in His loving providence may shorten these days of trial and restore peace and tranquility to the Church and to the world.

6. It is our prayer that the lesson of our contemporary martyrs and confessors be not lost on a distraught world. If Catholic bishops, priests, and laymen are the first on the enemies' list of proscription, is it not because our Holy Church, today as always, stands as a bulwark against those who would destroy the practice of justice and charity among men? Is it not because the Church is the most powerful defender, against the new barbarism, of all the gains of 2,000 years of Christian civilization? Is it not because the Church, faithful to its divine commission, is the uncompromising custodian of the truth which saves and sets men free?

7. These are sad but glorious days for the Church of Jesus Christ. Of old, the Prince of Apostles was crucified on Vatican Hill, and the

Prince of Missionaries was beheaded outside the walls of Rome. It is significant that the chroniclers of that day failed to record events which have since been treasured by centuries.

8.   The blood of those early martyrs was the seed of the Church, and the eloquent witness throughout the world to that faith which was to shape our era and to give it its Christian name.

9.   The confessors and martyrs of today are part of our Christian heritage. Let us write their deeds upon our hearts as a sequel to the epic story of St. Peter and St. Paul, of the early Christians, and of the myriads in every age who were deemed worthy to suffer for the faith of Christ. Let us tell this story to our people and to our children for their inspiration and for their emulation.

10. God grant that the glorious death of our martyrs may be the source of new life to millions of their fellow men in every land, and may their example hasten the return of the modern world to Christ. From the lips of these contemporary witnesses to Christ, let us catch and reecho those words of life which for twenty centuries have been the rallying cry of Christian civilization: "Long live Christ the King."

Persecution in Poland

*A Statement Issued by the Chairman of the
NCWC Administrative Board*[1]

September 29, 1953

1.　With the arrest of His Eminence Stefan Cardinal Wyszynski, the Polish Communist regime has struck one more infamous blow against a heroic and helpless people whose only defense against wanton and brutal tyranny is the strong armor of their faith.

2.　Cardinal Wyszynski has stood firm in the face of ruthless efforts by men devoid of decency or conscience to deprive his beloved people of rights, which because they derive from God, are more precious to them than life itself.

3.　His people will now tearfully but proudly add his name to the litany of heroes and martyrs who have given such luster to the long and glorious history of the Polish nation.

4.　Men everywhere who grasp the significance of the present struggle between good and evil, between freedom and slavery, will acclaim him as a symbol of magnificent Christian leadership.

5.　The Church in the United States, bishops, clergy, and laity alike, embrace their fellow Catholics of Poland in the bonds of love and affection in this, one of the darkest hours of their history.

6.　We reassure them of our sympathy and of our admiration for their courage, fidelity, and Christian fortitude.

7.　We join with them in the most earnest prayer that their beloved shepherd may be strengthened in his bitter plight, and that both he and they, in the inscrutable designs of Providence, may come speedily to the end of their tragic *Via Crucis*.

---

[1]A statement issued outside of a meeting in the name of the American bishops by Archbishop Patrick A. O'Boyle of Washington, acting chairman of the Administrative Board of the National Catholic Welfare Conference.

Peter's Chains

*A Statement Issued by the Catholic Bishops of
the United States*[1]

November 21, 1953

1.   The heroic constancy of the martyrs and the unwavering witness of the confessors have always been preeminent among the signs that distinguish and identify the true Church of Jesus Christ. Look where you will in Europe and in Asia, in every land now shrouded in the gloom of Communism, and you will see the solid phalanx of bishops, priests, religious, and faithful, our modern martyrs and confessors, gathered around the cross of Christ, the standard of salvation—the one steady light which still shines in the general darkness. We in the free countries still speak of a cold war; these men and women are enduring the bitterest, the bloodiest persecution in all history.

2.   Shepherds of the flock of Christ are hunted down, imprisoned, debased, tortured, slain. Sick and helpless sisters are dragged from their convents, condemned to the slow death of forced labor on roads, in forests, and in mines, or to the quicker death of starvation. Peasants are slaughtered and flung upon the pyres of their burning churches. Innocent children are torn from the arms of their Christian mothers and handed over to atheist debauchers.

Extent of Religious Persecution

3.   It is a war against all who believe in God and His Christ, against all who dare to claim for man the liberty of the sons of God. It rages from Korea to China and to Indochina; from Russia to the Baltic lands; from Poland and Lithuania to Yugoslavia; from the Ukraine to Albania; from Czechoslovakia to Hungary, to Romania and Bulgaria; it rages in the eastern parts of Austria and Germany. And everywhere the Church of God, her sacred ministers, and her faithful children are the first targets of the persecution. Millions of them have already died for the faith. Who shall count the numbers of those who are now suffering and marked for death?

4.   This is a war against the true religion of Jesus Christ. When will men in the free world come to realize that the crisis of today is first of all a crisis of religion, that the Communist debaser of man is essentially a hater of God, that his long-range and his short-range purpose

---

[1]This statement was published unsigned.

is the destruction of Christianity. From Marx to Malenkov, the Communist sees Christ as the enemy to be exterminated.

5.   Is it not, then, the strange anomaly of our times that a calculated confusion has been able to hide from so many of our people the primary, the changeless purpose of the enemy? How few there are who understand that the struggle for liberty is a warfare against the fanatical foes of Christ! How few there are who know that millions of Catholics have already died that the rest of us might live!

6.   Here is a story of epic nobility, of unsurpassed human grandeur, of deathless spiritual devotion. Our martyrs and confessors are the glory of the age in which we live. One would have thought that the Western world would rise as one man to do them reverence, would write their deeds of valor in letters of enduring gold. Instead, indifference, scant notice, or silence. Only in the Catholic press will you find the martyrology which the historians of tomorrow will account the greatest glory of today.

7.   Who can now recall the chroniclers of Nero's day? But the names of Peter and of Paul have endured throughout the centuries; above their tombs rise the noblest temples of Christendom, and pilgrims come in multitudes unnumbered to remember and to pray.

8.   Nor can history be kind to those men of state who retreated to the refuge of a polite neutralism while the crucial battle of our times was being fought.

9.   History can record only in reprobation that while Nero raged in the East against the true Church of Christ, the Voltaires of the West raised their olden cry *"Ecrasez l'Infame"* and sought to crush these valiant fighters for God and human freedom. Genuine philosophy must list Nero and Voltaire as allies. History will register the fact of that alliance in the Warsaw maneuver which would cut off from help the champions of the authentic liberties.

10.   And what shall we say of those ungenerous men, who in the crisis of our times have been found so sadly wanting—those narrow sectarians who allowed their petty or their imagined grievances to obscure the true greatness of our blessed martyrs and confessors. We shall leave them to God and to the worm of conscience, as we pray "Father, forgive them, for they know not what they do."

Prayers for the Church of Silence

11.   The Catholic bishops of the United States of America, gathered together in their annual assembly at Washington, proclaim to all their faithful priests and people the solemn duty of instant and constant prayer for our suffering brethren of the Church of Silence. When Peter was in prison, the Church prayed without ceasing for him, and

the Angel of the Lord touched him and the chains fell off from his hands. Peter is again in chains.

12. Let there then be supplication to God and penance that His grace be poured out in superabundant measure to strengthen those who hold the place of honor and of danger in the new warfare launched against the Church. Let us all cherish in our hearts the epic story of our own martyrs and confessors. Let us tell this story to our children that they may learn the names of Stepinac and Mindszenty and Wyszynski, of Beran, of Cule, of Ford, and of Byrne, along with the heroes of the faith in ages past; that they may understand how great it is to be a Catholic.

13. And let us raise our voices, in a unison of protest, a protest that will penetrate into the consciences of all decent men, into all the chancelleries of the world, against this new scourge of God and man.

14. To our brother bishops, to the priests, religious, and people of the Church of Silence, we send affectionate greeting and the tribute of our devotion, of our admiration, of our entire solidarity. We salute you; we embrace you; we minister in spirit to your necessities; we bind in prayer the wounds you suffer for justice sake. For you are blessed when the enemies of Christ persecute and revile you. You are the light of the world, giving to our generation that saving example of fidelity spoken of by St. Paul: "Who shall separate us from the love of Christ? Shall privation or distress, or famine or nakedness, or danger, or persecution or the sword?" As it is written: "For Thy sake, we are put to death all the day long. We are accounted as sheep for the slaughter."

15. "But in all these things we overcome because of Him that hath loved us."

16. Indeed your faith is the victory which overcometh the world. By your stripes will the modern world be healed.

17. Peter's successor who is Pius spoke the deepest sentiments of our own hearts when he said to you: "We embrace you with a special love and we kneel to kiss your chains."

A Statement on Man's Dignity

*A Statement Issued by the NCWC
Administrative Board in the Name of the
Bishops of the United States*

November 21, 1953

1. Every man knows instinctively that he is, somehow, a superior being. He knows he is superior to the land he tills, the machine he operates, or the animals which are at his service. Even when unable to define this superiority in terms of "honor" and "dignity," if a man enjoys the fruits of his nobility, he is content and accepts that status as his due; lacking honor and dignity for any cause, a man is restless, depressed, even rebellious because something proper to him, as a man, is withheld or denied.

2. The Catholic Church has always taught and defended the natural dignity of every human being. She has preached the burden of individual responsibility and has insisted upon the importance of personal conscience. She has reminded mankind that there is a great division between "things" and "men." She has never forgotten that "things were made for men" and that "men were made for God."

3. In thus holding up a mirror to men that they may see their own greatness and realize their personal dignity, the Catholic Church has taught that man's true honor is from God, has been enhanced spiritually by divine grace, and is preserved without degradation only when the honor and dignity of God Himself are first maintained.

4. Often in times past men have failed to live up to the honor of their state. They have degraded their dignity in many ways. But, always till now, violence and vice, injustice and oppression or any other assaults on human dignity were recognized as abominations and were so abhorred. It has remained for our day to attempt to disregard human personality and to fortify such disregard with the force of legislation or the approbation of custom, as if a man were only a "thing." The present has been described as a rationally established inhumanity working with all the expedients of administrative and mechanical techniques. Our Holy Father, Pope Pius XII, in his 1952 Christmas allocution, gave warning of the attempted mechanization of mankind and protested the stripping of personality from men by legal or social devices. The bishops of the United States, conscious of the growing depersonalization of man, reaffirm man's essential dignity and reassert the rights which flow from it.

Roots of Human Dignity

5.   Man's essential worth derives from a threefold source: from the fact of his creation, from the mode of his existence, and from the nobility of his destiny.

6.   The mere fact that any creature exists at all requires the creative and sustaining power of God. When God exercises this power to summon any possible reality into actual existence, that reality is thereby sealed with value from within. Such a dignity man shares with the animal and material world around him.

7.   But his special type of existence confers on man a special claim to honor. Though immersed in a universe of fleeting and random sensations, he is endowed with an intellect able to pierce the flux of passing images and discover beneath them enduring patterns of truth. Though subjected to the pressures of his environment, and a prey to unthinking appetites, he is endowed with a self-determining will capable of choosing wisely within the framework of law.

8.   Intellect and will, then, are man's distinctive adornments. It is their distinctive role to allow a finite creature to grasp truth consciously and to choose goodness freely, and thus to mirror the Infinite Creator Who is conscious Truth and absolute Goodness.

9.   Man's natural honor, however, has been enhanced by grace, conferred at creation, lost through sin, but restored through the incarnation and redemption of our Lord and Savior, Jesus Christ. When the Son of God took human flesh as an instrument of salvation, all human flesh was honored by His association with it. Through His death and resurrection Christ demonstrated the role and destiny, the honor and dignity of every man for whom He lived and suffered. Since those days of Christ on earth, no man lives by his body alone, nor by the natural powers of his soul alone; every man is sanctified, made holy, made more worthy and more honorable by the enjoyment of the special spiritual life which flows from the cross, or by the possibility that this life will one day be his, to raise him above the limitations of nature, to honor him in unending union with the God Who became man.

10. Such is the triple fountain of man's dignity. To the extent these truths cease to energize the sense of reverence in every man, assaults upon the majesty of the human person must increase and intensify. Heedless that his nature has God for its origin and destiny, and reason and revelation for its divinely commissioned guide, man will do what no other creature can—he will deny his true nature and will destroy all that is good within himself.

Man's Dignity and the Body

11. Such a process of degradation is viciously at work in our own country, where the deification of the flesh continues to enlist new devotees. Through its liturgy of advertisement, entertainment, and literature, this cult bids fair to corrode our national sense of decency. When reason abdicates its sovereignty over bodily energies, their purpose is destroyed; and, by a sort of instinctive vengeance, they themselves become destroyers. Like wild animals, these energies are hard to tame, and remain dangerous even when tamed. But whatever lawful use an animal may serve, it is not wisdom for man to accept as his master the lion who seeks to devour him.

12. The Catholic Church, however, has never failed to accord the human body an immense measure of honor. She affirms that it was originally created by God; in one instance actually assumed by Him; in every instance meant to be on earth His special temple, and destined eventually to rejoin the soul in His beatific presence. Whatever is uncompromising in her teaching about the body stems from her realism on two points: the body, though good, is not the highest good; and the undisciplined body is notoriously bad.

13. Other sacrileges against personality flow from errors less crude perhaps, but hardly less injurious. Such are some prevailing misconceptions about society, liberty, economics, labor, and education.

Man's Dignity and Society

14. The practical social theory of the last century enthroned the individual but not the person. An individual can be a thing: as for instance an individual tree; but in virtue of his rational soul, a person is more than a thing. Yet the depersonalized view of man gained ascendancy, and generated a society which was a crisscross of individual egotisms, and in which each man sought his own.

15. Against this error our century has seen a reaction which has sought to overcome the isolation of man from man by imposing upon rebellious individuals a pattern of compulsory and all-embracing state organization, with unlimited power in the hands of the civil government. Hence socialism in its various guises has appeared as forcible organization imposed upon the confusion which resulted from false concepts of human freedom.

16. The Christian concept of man, however, is that he is both personal and social. As a person he has rights independent of the state; as a member of society he has social obligations. Parents and society contribute to the making of a man, hence man is indebted to the social order. At the same time, since his soul comes not from society but from God, a man has rights which no society may violate. The state is a creature of man, but man is a creature of God; hence the state exists for man, not man for the state.

Man's Dignity and Liberty

17. The Christian view, then, avoids the opposing extremes of individualism and collectivism, both of which are grounded on false concepts of liberty—either the unfettered liberty of individualism, which gives the "individual" the right to ignore society; or the unfettered liberty of dictatorship, which gives the government the right to ignore the person by absorbing him into a race or class, thus destroying his freedom of choice. The false liberty of individualism wrecks society by defining freedom as individual license; the false liberty of dictatorship wrecks humanity by defining freedom as the right of a dictator to nullify the person—a right which he claims to derive from social necessity.

18. Concerning the results of such false notions of liberty, Leo XIII issued these warnings:

> The true liberty of human society does not consist in every man doing what he pleases, for this would simply end in turmoil and confusion, and bring on the overthrow of the state . . . likewise, liberty does not consist in the power of those in authority to lay unreasonable and capricious demands upon their subjects, a course which would be equally criminal, and would lead to the ruin of the commonwealth.

19. Liberty in political life may be described as the condition in which the individual finds himself unhampered in the discharge of his duties and in the exercise of his rights. Liberty, however, is something more than a political phenomenon as tyrannical dictatorship contends; it is more than an economic phenomenon as some disciples of free enterprise maintain. It is something more mature than that dream of rights without responsibilities which historic liberalism envisioned; it is certainly different from that terrorism of responsibilities without rights which Communism imposes. It is something wiser than free thought, and something freer than dictated thought. For freedom has its roots in man's spiritual nature. It does not arise out of any social organization, or any constitution, or any party, but out of the soul of man. Hence to the whole tradition of the Western world, liberty does not come essentially from improved conditions of living, either political or economic, but is rather the spring out of which better conditions must flow. A free spirit creates free institutions; a slave spirit permits the creation of tyrannical ones.

Man's Dignity and Economics

20. Closely connected with freedom and human dignity is the right of private property. On the question of private property the afore-mentioned misconceptions of liberty beget two other extremes: first the belief that a man's right to property is absolute, and that he may do with it what he pleases, without regard for the moral law or social justice, and, second, the reactionary error of Communism, which denies all personal rights and lodges all property in the hands of the state.

21. The Christian position maintains that the right to property is personal, while the use of property is also social. Unrestrained capitalism makes its mistake by divorcing property rights from social use; Communism hits wide of the mark by considering social use apart from personal rights.

22. Much of our economic restlessness, however, is the festering of man's wounded dignity. Karl Marx himself was perceptive enough to see that "Democracy is based on the principle of the sovereign worth of the individual, which, in turn, is based on the dream of Christianity that man has an immortal soul" (*Marx-Engels Historical-Critical Edition*, Karl Marx Institute, Moscow, Vol. I, No. 1, p. 590).

23. Ignoring the testimony of both reason and revelation and believing the "dream" to be only a dream, modern men have tended to concentrate almost exclusively on economic security and to pursue it at times with the fervor of religious devotion.

24. Often the hope is voiced that man will turn to the cultivation of the spirit after all his economic needs are supplied. We are reminded of the delusion of Jean Jacques Rousseau that man, good in himself, has been corrupted only by society. Marxism, changing the formula, gives the same false primacy to external circumstances—man's good-ness will depend upon the economic system under which he lives. But the exclusive dependence on economic security and social reform to right the wrongs of mankind is by no means confined to Marxism. It affects the thought of great masses of men who reject the funda-mental tenets of Marxism.

25. While we have deep sympathy with all people in their craving for economic security and while we acknowledge the evils, individual and spiritual as well as social, which often flourish in a society when many are forced to live in conditions of degrading poverty, yet we cannot refrain from pointing out the fact that man's goodness is from within. It depends upon man's personal convictions and upon his efforts aided by God's grace. Economic and social reform, to be effec-tive, must be preceded by personal reform. The perfection of a society may not be measured by the moral goodness of the individuals who compose it; but the goodness of a society cannot rise above the goodness of its members.

26. The position of the Church relative to the economic order is based on the principle that the rights man possesses as an individual and the function he fulfills in society are inseparable. Many of the rights of the individual depend upon the function he fulfills in society. Capital and labor from this point of view are related and made inseparable by the common good of society. This is a prime principle of social justice. The right of the capitalist to his business and to his profits and interest, and the right of the laborer to his wages and his union, are both conditioned by their service to the common good.

Man's Dignity and Labor

27. It is only in the light of the spiritual worth of man that the dignity and importance of labor become evident. Labor is not something detached from the rest of life. Economically, it is bound up with capital as a copartner in production. Socially, it is bound up with leisure as an avenue to cultural enrichment. Spiritually, it is bound up with the soul's development and with salvation. The worker is not a hand, as individualistic capitalism contends; not a stomach to be fed by commissars, as Communism thinks; but a person who through his labor establishes three relations: with God, with his neighbor, and with the whole natural world.

28. First of all, work unites us to God not only by its ascetic character and through the discipline it imposes on man by subjugating his lower passions to order and reason, but principally because, through the intention of the worker, the material universe is brought back again to God.

29. Second, labor is also the bond uniting man to man, a kind of school of social service, a base of human solidarity, a testimonial to man's insufficiency without his neighbor. In working with others, man ratifies his social dependence and performs an act of natural charity, because he helps create utility for others and thus promotes the happiness of his fellow men. The Catholic view, it will be noted here, adds that labor must always be used, not to dissociate ourselves from our neighbor, but to unite us with him. The greater the material advancement of any country, therefore, the more energetic should be its spirit of neighborliness.

30. Finally, work unites us with nature. It does this by enabling us to share in the creative work of God and by making each of us, in the language of St. Paul, "a helper of God." God, the supreme artist, has communicated artistic causality to men, so that they can now make things and shape events to the image and likeness of their own ideas. The marriage of man's intelligence and will with the material world and the natural forces with which he is surrounded becomes a fruitful union, and from them is generated a culture.

Man's Dignity and Education

31. In transmitting culture from generation to generation, it is the purpose of education to safeguard and develop the dignity of man. At the end of the eighteenth century our first president spoke of religion and morality as indispensable supports of political prosperity. At the end of the nineteenth century our highest court declared that "The reasons presented affirm and reaffirm that this is a religious nation." What is true of our political prosperity and our nation is true as well of our Western culture in general. Yet everywhere modern education is being drained of moral content through the movement which is known as secularism. It has been well said that the education of the soul is the soul of education. Therefore when education tries to thrive in a religious and moral vacuum, and does not aspire to impart a set of principles and a hierarchy of values, it degenerates into a dead and deadening juxtaposition of facts.

32. And even worse. For though it tries to thrive in such a vacuum, education can never really be neutral in practice. It has been truly said that "men must be governed by God or they will be ruled by tyrants." Similarly, education must inculcate a religious and moral outlook, or it will inculcate a materialistic one. And there is no word for dignity in the vocabulary of materialism.

Conclusion

33. Every day in Holy Mass, Almighty God is addressed as He Who wondrously established the dignity of man, and restored it more wondrously still. Only by regaining our reverence for God can we of America in the twentieth century rediscover both our own value and the solid basis on which it rests. We must at the same time expend every effort to see that this dignity is reflected in our sense of decency, made aware of itself by education, nurtured by society, guarded by the state, stabilized by private ownership, and exercised through creative activity.

34. The alternative is increasing chaos. The words of a contemporary historian of culture may serve to summarize the issues at stake:

> Unless we find a way to restore the contact between the life of society and the life of the spirit, our civilization will be destroyed by forces which it has had the knowledge to create but not the wisdom to control.

Signed by the members of the Administrative Board, National Catholic Welfare Conference, in the names of the bishops of the United States

Edward Cardinal Mooney, Archbishop of Detroit

Samuel Cardinal Stritch, Archbishop of Chicago

Francis Cardinal Spellman, Archbishop of New York

James Francis Cardinal McIntyre, Archbishop of Los Angeles

John J. Mitty, Archbishop of San Francisco

Richard J. Cushing, Archbishop of Boston

Patrick A. O'Boyle, Archbishop of Washington

John F. O'Hara, Archbishop of Philadelphia

Karl J. Alter, Archbishop of Cincinnati

John F. Noll, Bishop of Fort Wayne

Michael J. Ready, Bishop of Columbus

Emmet M. Walsh, Coadjutor Bishop of Youngstown

Thomas K. Gorman, Coadjutor Bishop of Dallas

Matthew F. Brady, Bishop of Manchester

Victory . . . Our Faith

*A Statement Issued by the Catholic Bishops of
the United States*

November 19, 1954

1. The bishops of the United States of America, gathered in annual assembly at Washington, send greeting and paternal blessing to all their priests, religious, and people.

2. This greeting and blessing we send to you with mixed hope and concern. For while our hope is in the blessing of Christ and His Church, our concern is aroused by a tyranny already imposed upon a billion souls. It threatens the destruction of our own land as it has already attacked the culture of others. That tyranny is atheistic materialism, whether revealed in Communism or in godless humanism.

3. The battle is joined. If our nation is to escape the fate of Poland and of China, of Yugoslavia and of Hungary, and of so many others, if we are to survive as a free Christian nation, then we must be clear-eyed and we must be strong. It is the blind and the weak who fall into the pit.

First, Identify the Enemy

4. We need, first of all, to identify our enemy; to recognize it for what it really is. Some see the enemy only as a political state or group of states, or merely as an economic system. Spiritual vision gives better intelligence of the fact. The enemy is atheistic materialism. Whether it be entrenched in the organs of a foreign state, or in one of our own domestic institutions, it is atheistic materialism that seeks to destroy us. This is the enemy.

5. In the second place, we must be strong. Material strength is necessary, of course, and its proper organization and disposition are of immediate urgency. But material strength, like physical vision, is not enough. This nation must look to its spiritual strength. Our vast physical resources and our masterly technical skills will avail us nothing unless we are a people strong in the faith which gives purpose to action, and in the morality which fosters discipline and courage. The true strength of a Christian nation is in the power of God which outweighs all force of arms.

6. Unfortunately, in recent times the drift from God and from the spiritual and supernatural view of life has seriously weakened this country. It is true that a rise in church membership has been reported

172

during the past few years, but in the light of other evidence, one is forced to question how significant such mere statistics may be. One looks in vain for any corresponding increase of religion's beneficent influence upon the nation's life. Indeed, the trend in public and private morality has been downward; there is an alarming disregard in practice for God's teaching and for God's law. Is there any need to instance the growing evils in family life, the lustful self-indulgence which leads from birth prevention to divorce, from broken homes to the broken lives of youthful delinquents? Need we adduce in evidence the appalling circulation of indecent literature, and the low moral level of so much of the public entertainment in these days.

Absorption with the Material World

7.   It is not that the existence of God is expressly or generally denied; it is rather that so many ignore Him and His law in their absorption with the material world which He created. There is not yet a deliberate turning away from God, but there is an excessive preoccupation with creatures. This form of materialism reveals itself as secularism in politics and government, as avarice in business and in the professions, and as paganism in the personal lives and relations of all too many men and women. "This people honors me with their lips, but their heart is far from me" (Mk 7:6).

8.   Materialism has brought about a decline in the influence of religion upon American life. Confusion in our thinking and a sort of paralysis of the national will have been the inevitable results of this decline. Here, then, we have the source of that weakness which is causing so much concern to men of good will. Unless we arrest this religious decline, unless we push back the domestic invasion of materialism, we shall not be able, as history clearly attests, to withstand the enemy from without.

9.   Materialism is the real enemy, at home as well as abroad. In its varieties, there is little difference of kind; the difference is largely one of degree. Both are deadly for America. The way of matter and of the flesh is the way of death; the way of God and of the spirit is the way of life. If we would have life, we must renew and reaffirm our faith in God and in His Christ; we must cling again to that Christian moral code which is the American way of life at its purest and its best.

Faith Is the First Essential

10. We need faith, first of all; belief in God and in the Son whom He sent us, Jesus Christ. Faith is the first essential of human living. But let us be clear about what we mean by this wondrous word. Faith is not sentiment of reverence in the presence of goodness and beauty, or of awe in the presence of mystery. Faith has to do with knowing, not with feeling. It is knowledge in its highest and surest form. Faith is the intellectual act by which, under the influence of grace, we accept on the authority of God the truths by Him revealed.

11. By faith, we know. It is a key to knowledge, to knowledge of the highest and noblest character. By faith, we rise above the things of earth and of time and glimpse the things of Heaven and of eternity. From this high point of vantage, we sweep the horizon of human life from origin to destiny, and make the discovery that God is our beginning and our end. With faith we break through the barriers of nature to the supernatural vision of grace. How they misunderstand who consider faith a mere pious emotion! It is, instead, the surest of all forms of cognition; the word of Him who knows unerringly and speaks with truth because He can neither deceive nor be deceived. God Himself is both revealer and guarantor of the truths of faith. Let us be clear, too, as to what we mean when we utter the sacred name of God. Those who have confused the notion of faith, have also falsified the wonder which is God. To the timid who retreat before any positive assertion, there can be no understanding of the majesty of pure being, infinite affirmation, which is God.

12. Shallow men prattle of a shadowy world spirit or essence of things; of a dim projection of the ego, of a hypothetical construction of the mind for the purpose of explaining the hidden laws of nature. The reality is so inexpressibly greater, warmer, more uplifting, more comforting, more profoundly influential in our lives. *God is.* He is self-subsisting, perfect being. He is personal God, all-wise, all-powerful, all-good, all-just, all-holy. He is changeless, eternal, infinite. He is one God in three Divine Persons. He created us innocent and holy. He redeemed us after our fall into sin. He sanctifies us. He is our beginning and our final purpose or end. He loves us as our Father with a tender love, and He wants our filial love in return. He gave us His Son as our brother, and with the love that surpasses all other loves, our brother laid down His life for us to give us life eternal.

The Answer to All Our
Questioning

13. Here is the answer to all our questioning; the satisfaction for all our needs. The purpose of human life can be summed up in the three luminous propositions which define our relationship to God: we were created to know Him, to love Him, to serve Him. We were created by Him and for Him. We shall find no rest until we rest in Him. He is the fulfillment of all our aspirations—truth and goodness and beauty. He is the beginning and the end, our origin and our destiny. He is our only hope for happiness.

14. The most perfect revelation of God to man is made in His Son, Jesus Christ. He is Emmanuel, *God with us.* Just as the Creator brought light and order to the ancient chaos at the dawn of creation, so His divine Son, Jesus Christ, restored light and order to a world sunk in error and evil. The mission and message of Christ complete the earlier, partial revelations of God, and launch the world on the Christian era.

15. The era of Christ! In the sign of the cross, Christ conquers the paganism which has enslaved mankind, and He sets man's feet on the highroad of faith, hope, and love; the highroad of happiness through harmony with God, with fellow man, and with himself. Jesus Christ restored meaning and purpose and love to human life; He warmed and illumined our life where before it had been cold and dark. He rescued man from the wild wandering and the black despair of the atheistic materialism of that day. In this day of the new paganism, we Christians can again triumph in the sign of the same cross of Christ.

16. Christ is the prophet and the teacher, in whose doctrines are the truths which inspire and satisfy the souls of men. He speaks to us with power and authority. He has the words of life eternal.

17. Christ is the priest, the mediator. His is the great atonement. By His sacrifice, we are redeemed from our sins. The cross of Calvary stands for that great love which throughout the centuries has drawn men powerfully to Christ—that love by which He laid down His life for His friends.

To Serve Is to Reign

18. And Christ is King, the Lord of Heaven and earth, whose Kingdom endures forever and ever. He is the lawgiver, laying down the code of conduct that binds the consciences of men. He is the judge, merciful and just, Who rewards the good and punishes the evil. He is the ruler Who reaches from end to end mightily and disposes all things well. From Him alone do earthly magistrates receive their power of governance. He is the King of Kings. Worship and obedience, order and discipline, filial love—these He exacts from His subjects, but in return He gives His Father's love and His Father's home, rich largesse of grace and abiding peace of soul. Truly, to serve Him is to reign.

19. This, then, is what we mean by the faith; this is the truth about God and Jesus Christ. This is why we repeat without ceasing that God and His Christ afford the answer to all our problems, and provide that solution to all our difficulties. Those who have never known the Christian religion, or who have not known it in its fullness as taught by the Catholic Church, should turn to it now, and examine its credentials. It is the answer to their quest.

20. The Western World, with its law of fraternal charity and its humane culture, was created by this faith in God and in His Son, Jesus Christ. At its best, our civilization was the fine flowering of the Christian faith. Now that the West has fallen from its former greatness, let us recognize that it is because so many have fallen away from the faith, or have denatured it by dilution and compromise. We have fallen down before idols of flesh and of gold. It is not the true faith that has failed us; it is we who have failed the faith. A weak and vacillating Christianity, a partial, truncated Christianity, paying lip service to God and to the spirit, but devoted in practice to man and to matter, can never triumph in the battle with total, determined materialism.

21. Our nation, if it is to survive, must recover and renew its Christian faith. Here alone can we find purpose to end the present confusion; strength instead of weakness; a dynamic zeal to overcome the difficulties of life; an uplifting, soul-stirring motive for the fight to the death against a total materialist enemy. In the sign of Christ's cross our ancestors in the faith conquered the ancient paganism and gave mankind the golden ages of the Christian era. We in our day shall conquer the new paganism, atheistic materialism, in the same triumphant sign.

Statement issued November 19, 1954, by the bishops of the United States and signed in their names by the Administrative Board of the National Catholic Welfare Conference, whose members are:

Edward Cardinal Mooney, Detroit

Samuel Cardinal Stritch, Chicago

Francis Cardinal Spellman, New York

James F. Cardinal McIntyre, Los Angeles

Karl J. Alter, Archbishop of Cincinnati

Francis P. Keough, Archbishop of Baltimore

John J. Mitty, Archbishop of
San Francisco

Richard J. Cushing, Archbishop
of Boston

Joseph E. Ritter, Archbishop of
St. Louis

Patrick A. O'Boyle, Archbishop
of Washington

John F. O'Hara, Archbishop of
Philadelphia

Thomas K. Gorman, Bishop of
Dallas-Fort Worth

Matthew F. Brady, Bishop of
Manchester

Michael J. Ready, Bishop of
Columbus

A Plea for Justice

*A Statement Issued by the Catholic Bishops of
the United States*[1]

November 20, 1954

1. We, the bishops of the United States, cannot adjourn our meeting here without a statement of protest against persecution and a word of consolation to all who suffer. A year ago our thoughts were with the persecuted of Eastern Europe, long afflicted and much tried. Today we add to these the people of Vietnam and its neighbor nations who most recently have come upon days of disaster and now face the persecution so often known in the Church of Christ.

2. We cannot end this meeting which has been held in the freedom of our beloved country without a plea to all who love justice and hate iniquity that they will stand with us in prayer and in protest; in prayer for the afflicted; in protest against misuse of power. For we cannot be so blind as to imagine that Asia or Europe stands alone. Rather, there seems to be a master plan of oppression, worldwide. In it, we of America are included by intent as others elsewhere are included in grim reality.

3. The grim reality is that men are in prison, men are broken, families live in fear or are disrupted, nations are threatened or under attack. The grim reality is that such oppression is an attempt to break man's faith in God or to divide men from their Savior or their Church.

4. We pray then that God will restrain the tyrant and relieve the anguish of the afflicted. We beg our Catholic people to cherish well the blessings of freedom they enjoy and to pray fervently for those whose freedom has been lost or is in danger.

5. We beg our neighbors—all of them in the United States, all to whom the blessings of our liberties here are a cherished heritage—that by our united prayers, our sympathetic understanding, and by action (as far as action lies within our power) we may give comfort to those who are tortured in body or in spirit, and that the power of God will quickly restore to them in justice the freedom which their souls crave and their nature demands.

---

[1]This statement was not signed.

Private and Church-Related Schools in American Education

*A Statement Issued by the NCWC
Administrative Board in the Name of the
Bishops of the United States*

November 20, 1955

1. Freedom under God is America's dearest treasure. Its roots lie deep in her Christian heritage, and its germ is the concept of man's personal responsibility to his Creator for his temporal and eternal salvation. Here in America freedom has flowered in an ordered democracy, which guarantees to her citizens the widest latitude of individual expression within the framework of commonly held principles of justice, decency, and law.

Schools Must Teach Freedom

2. To preserve freedom America must teach freedom. It is in the schools of the nation, preeminently, that this educative process is carried on. It is in the classroom that the principles underlying our Christian concept of human liberty must be defined and inculcated, if future generations are to appreciate, defend, and preserve it. But that this be done, it is an absolutely necessary condition that the schools of America should themselves be guaranteed their rightful freedom to teach the truth.

3. Historically and actually our nation has been blessed with educational freedom. Her school system is not a closed, unitary creation of the state, a servile instrument of governmental monopoly, but one which embraces, together with the state-supported schools, a whole enormous cluster of private and church-related schools, including many of the most honored names in the entire educational world, and devoted to the education of many millions of the nation's youth.

4. That these private and church-related schools serve a minority in America, by sheer numerical computation, is a purely incidental factor, and it is plainly unrealistic thinking to discount their importance on that score. Indeed, it is unrealistic to belittle in any way the schools in which more than five million young Americans are currently receiving their education. These schools, emphatically, are an integral part of the American educational system. And so long as our nation is faithful to her principles of justice and due process of law, these schools will remain a permanent part of that system.

Private Schools Produced First
Leaders

5.   It is not without significance that the private and church-related schools were the first in the field of American education. For well-nigh two centuries, during our colonial and early national periods, they occupied that field alone. It was from such schools, as from fruitful seedbeds, that there came the guiding intellectual and moral impulses which led to the definition and establishment of American freedom, no less than the leadership which launched the young republic on her career in history. The familiar pride of a Daniel Webster in his alma mater, which was both private and church-related, is echoed by countless other Americans in all walks of life and at all stages of our growth. And it is demonstrably a faulty interpretation of the mind of such a liberal theorist as Thomas Jefferson which would present him as champion of a monopolistic state system of education.

6.   As Catholics, our memory is stirred by the recollection of the valiant efforts of our religious founders in this country to provide, out of their slender resources, for the educational needs of their people. We think of young John Carroll, destined to be our first bishop, conning his lessons at Bohemia Manor, in colonial Maryland. The torch he grasped there was to be carried by myriad hands to enkindle brighter fires from end to end of our expanding nation. It is with honest pride that we survey the development of Catholic education in America, so intimately a part of her cultural growth, so deeply intertwined with the traditions and aspirations of her people. The Catholic school has matured with the Church, a joint product of the foresight of the bishops and the enlightened generosity of her faithful. It is no foreign importation, no alien growth, but a sturdy native plant, a conspicuous example of a common religious impulse working under the favorable conditions of our republic.

Accomplishment of Public
Schools

7.   The rise and vigorous expansion of the American educational system is cited, correctly, as one of the major achievements of Western civilization. During the past hundred years, in particular, general education, sponsored by states and communities, religious groups and private bodies, has come very near to the goal of providing adequate educational opportunities for every American. It would be blind prejudice which would refuse to acknowledge, in this connection,

the tremendous accomplishment of the public educational agencies. Whatever uneasiness may or must be felt on the score of educational theory and philosophy as illustrated in large areas of American teaching, the plain physical fact of the school system is a matter for unanimous congratulation. This, at least in part, is what freedom has achieved.

8.   But if the unparalleled growth of the schools supported by public funds is a mighty tribute to America's zeal for learning and her ambition to build an intelligent democratic society, no less astonishing has been the growth and accomplishment of the private and church-related schools during the same relative period. In candor, it deserves to be said that their record affords an even more impressive example of the American spirit at work, for it has been brought about not by the advantage of public funds nor by the spur of legislative mandate, but by the free cooperation of those convinced of their importance and necessity. It is, incidentally, wholly erroneous to conceive that these schools represent a diminishing force in the American educational system. Their growth today, proportionately, equals where it does not actually exceed that of schools maintained by public authority.

9.   Let this be fully understood: Private and church-related schools in America exist not by sufferance but by right. The right is implicit in the whole concept of American freedom and immunity from totalitarian oppression and in the constitutional framework of our federal government and of the several states. Under attack it has been rendered explicit by the decision of the Supreme Court of the United States in the celebrated Oregon School Case. Thus far, happily, the right of the parent to educate the child has not been successfully challenged in any American court. The country agrees that this right is basic to the definition of freedom. Be that education provided by the state-supported school, the private school, or the church-affiliated school, the choice of the parent is decisive. If the state has a concurrent right to decree a minimal education for its citizens, as a vital necessity in a modern democratic society, that right does not extend to an arbitrary designation of the school or the educational agency. It is, rather, a general right, limited by the primary right of the parent to exercise his choice according to his best wisdom and his conscience. Indeed, it is worth remarking that while the state may usefully engage in the business of education, as demonstrated in our national experience, it has no authority either to monopolize the field or to arrogate to itself exclusive privileges and powers. The state, by definition, is not itself primarily an educative agency.

10.   The right of the parent to attend to the child's education is, moreover, antecedent to any human law or institution. It is vested in his very nature and is demanded as a fulfillment of his actual parenthood. In this it reflects the inviolability of the human person and his freedom under God. It is indeed a right which must be exercised in accordance with sound reason and consistently with the just demands of society, but it remains fundamentally intact in the parents' keeping. It is a manifestation of the law of nature in concrete action. So it is that private and religious education in America rests upon the law of nature as well as upon the law of the land.

The Positive Training of Children

11. For Catholic parents there is an additional imperative. As they willingly accept the obligations of their faith, they realize that the mind of the Church on so important a subject as education cannot in conscience be ignored. As this mind is interpreted for them by their spiritual leaders, the bishops, they know that the circumstances of modern life demand the positive training of their children in the fundamentals of religion, a training which cannot be soundly imparted elsewhere than in schools dedicated to the purpose. As conscientious Catholics, they "think with the Church"; with supreme confidence in a divine wisdom, and with magnificent generosity, they have provided the indicated means, a Catholic school.

12. It is dangerous thinking to suppose that the existence of the private school is an infringement upon the domain of the school supported by public funds. The private school is a concrete demonstration of the fact that education is not a monopoly of public authority. It should be added, moreover, that the private school provides a saving and challenging variety in the total system, beneficial to the whole and manifestly fruitful in its effects. Those who would seek to abolish the private school would not only sin against justice, they would destroy something very precious in American life.

13. Neither is the church-related school a limitation on the right of the state to insure an educated citizenry. It exists not only to fulfill the function of education in our democratic society, but specifically to educate the Christian for his dual citizenship in time and eternity. It exists to teach not only the content of the accepted curriculum, but that which the tax-supported school under present conditions may not teach, namely, positive religion. Other nations, with varying success, have attempted general educational systems in which provision is made for religious instruction in separate church-related schools. Practical considerations, in view of wide religious differences, almost from the outset prevented the American tax-supported schools from following this pattern. There are those now, even among public school educators, who regret the development, involving, as it has, the risk of religious indifferentism and secularism. The solution of the problem is indeed difficult. The alternative, so far as the religious bodies who believe education essential to their mission are concerned, is the school under religious auspices.

14. The Catholic Church in America, to cite only a major example, recognized this alternative as far back as 1852, when the First Plenary Council of her bishops earnestly recommended the parochial school as the necessary safeguard of the faith of her children. Thirty-two years later, at the Third Plenary Council, the recommendation was strengthened and enacted as law: the school was to be a part of every well-organized parish. Today, with a total enrollment, from kindergarten to graduate school, of more than four million American youth, the vision of the fathers has taken on monumental impressiveness. Fully in keeping with the American tradition, it is perhaps the greatest achievement in general education under religious auspices and without government support the world has ever known.

15. The fact, we submit, bears repetition: The private and church-related schools are part of the American system. Manifestly, they exist; they exist by right; and they are unquestionably carrying a large share of the educational burden. Their teachers, religious and lay, have dedicated themselves to a high purpose, have labored hard to acquit themselves worthily, and the entire nation is their debtor. These schools have every claim in fact and in justice to be recognized as powerful contributing factors in the building of a better and freer country.

16. They have their critics, and among them none more vocal than those who assert that these schools introduce an element of divisiveness into American society. It is idle to attempt to argue the point with those who deliberately employ it to foment disagreement, but for the sake of those who are honestly confused, it is worth examining the charge. Upon what does it rest? Is it justified in the observation that private schooling and religious education have actually tended toward a sundering of the bonds of civic unity and common loyalty?

17. It is true that in the case of the religious schools there is a difference, inasmuch as they exist to teach positive religion as the integrating element of the curriculum. But surely, religion itself is not a discordant factor in American life. Surely, Christianity, with its primary inculcation of love of God and love of neighbor is not divisive. Only those who teach hatred teach division; those who teach love teach unity. How can it be, then, that religion in the school should be accused of sowing the seeds of national discord? Rather, is it not obvious that positive Christian training, with its emphasis on the sanction of divine law, of the natural law, and of civil law, on the social nature of the virtues of justice and charity, on the moral obligations of patriotism and public service, provides the strongest cement that can possibly bind a nation together? Criticism of these schools at times seems to forget that we are a pluralistic society that postulates not uniformity but rather unity in variety.

18. Church-related schools reflect nothing so clearly as that American spirit which demands unity in the essentials of citizenship while defending to the death those things in which the citizen is guaranteed his freedom.

19. What, then, is the place of the private and church-related schools in America? Their place is one dictated by nothing more than justice and equity, and accorded the recognition of their worth. They have, we repeat, full right to be considered and dealt with as components of the American educational system. They protest against the kind of thinking that would reduce them to a secondary level, and against unfair and discriminatory treatment which would, in effect, write them off as less wholly dedicated to the public welfare than the state-supported schools. The students of these schools have the right to benefit from those measures, grants, or aids, which are manifestly designed for the health, safety, and welfare of American youth, irrespective of the school attended.

20. This statement is submitted in quiet confidence that the national sense of justice will stand firm, and that a cordial appreciation of private and church-related schools, both for what they are and for what they have done for America, will see to it that they are preserved and upheld so long as this is a nation of free men.

Signed by members of the Administrative Board, National Catholic Welfare Conference, in the name of the bishops of the United States

Edward Cardinal Mooney, Detroit

Samuel Cardinal Stritch, Chicago

Francis Cardinal Spellman, New York

James Francis Cardinal McIntyre, Los Angeles

Karl J. Alter, Archbishop of Cincinnati

Francis P. Keough, Archbishop of Baltimore

John J. Mitty, Archbishop of San Francisco

Richard J. Cushing, Archbishop of Boston

Joseph E. Ritter, Archbishop of St. Louis

John F. O'Hara, Archbishop of Philadelphia

Emmet M. Walsh, Bishop of Youngstown

Thomas K. Gorman, Bishop of Dallas-Fort Worth

Matthew F. Brady, Bishop of Manchester

Michael J. Ready, Bishop of Columbus

Religious Persecution and Prayer Plan

*A Statement Issued by the Chairman of the
Administrative Board of the National Catholic
Welfare Conference[1]*

December 25, 1955

1. Still deeply involved in the contemporary struggle for the souls and bodies of men are the millions who suffer bitter persecution for the cause of Christ. Countless numbers of them in both the East and the West continue to be subjected to inhuman treatment at the hands of tyrants and despots because of their loyalty to conscience, their faith in God, and their attachment to Christ and His Church. Unjust imprisonment, frightful physical and mental torture, economic ruin are the price that innocent men, women, and children in many lands must pay for the crime of loving their Creator.

2. We, their brethren in the faith, cannot ever permit their plight to be forgotten or ignored. Indeed, all men of good will, impressed by their cause, and moved by their courage, at times heroic, in the face of such brutal and overwhelming pressure will surely continue to protest against such stark injustice and to plead before God and before men that it be speedily ended.

3. Rooted solidly in Christian teaching and tradition is the cherished truth that all members of the Church suffer with any who suffer. We are mindful that St. Peter himself, saddened by the afflictions of the flock in his own day, gave expression to that consoling thought when he wrote them:

> Beloved, do not be startled at the trial by fire that is taking place among you to prove you, as if something strange were happening to you; but insofar as you are partakers of the sufferings of Christ, rejoice that you may also rejoice with exultation in the revelation of His glory. If you are upbraided for the name of Christ, blessed will you be, because the honor, the glory, and the power of God and His Spirit rest upon you.

4. As we, bishops, priests, and people throughout the nation join again on New Year's Day, in prayer and intercession for our own afflicted brethren, we salute them in affection and in admiration. By their wounds may the modern world be healed. By their merits may it deserve to achieve in our time that measure of peace with justice and charity which is the fervent hope of men of good will everywhere.

---

[1] This statement was released in the name of the American hierarchy by the Most Reverend Francis P. Keough, Archbishop of Baltimore, and chairman of the Administrative Board of the National Catholic Welfare Conference.

Peace and Unity
The Hope of Mankind

*A Statement Issued by the NCWC
Administrative Board in the Name of the
Bishops of the United States*

November 15, 1956

1. Once again in our time the alarm bell is ringing in the night.[1] The world, inured as it is to tragedy, is apprised of tragedy still more profound. In the events of this hour at which the bishops of the American hierarchy meet in annual session, they and all men concerned with human welfare under God read the threat of catastrophe so dire as to destroy the last bulwarks of civilization.

Stern Warning of Madness

2. One voice, urgent and clear, has made itself heard above the tumult of the nations. The common father of Christendom, Pope Pius XII, has spoken out with unhesitating forthrightness. To those peoples who have been made the victims of a brutality so gross as to defy historic comparison, he has addressed words of compassion which could only come from a father's heart. To those nations bent upon aggression and which have ignored the sacred rights of humanity and the instruments of justice upon which they rest, he has issued stern warning of their madness. To all, whether inspired by selfish interest or led astray by rash counsel, who would jeopardize the delicate balance of world peace, he has recalled the primacy of law and order in the settlement of human disagreements.
3. In this crisis we can only add our voice to his. We echo his burning reproof of those who have dared to unleash the hounds of war in a world which has already suffered so long and so bitterly. With him we denounce with all our strength this fresh outbreak of aggression which sets at utter defiance the hard-won concert of the nations for the outlawing of international banditry. With him we plead for a renewal of that basic sanity among men and nations which will establish peace upon its only enduring foundations of justice and charity. With him we urge upon the world not the counsels of despair which

---

[1] The originally planned statement, *The Right of the Church to Teach*, was drafted but deferred until 1958 when it appeared as *The Teaching Church*. The above statement was issued because of the new threat of a third World War.

would describe the situation as beyond salvation, but the promise of a better hope implicit in the dawning recognition of human solidarity under the universal fatherhood of God.

Heroic People of Hungary

4. We share his anguish for those whose unmerited sufferings have again filled the cup of human misery to overflowing. Our eyes follow his as he surveys the ravaged cities, the desolated countrysides, the charred ruins of a thousand homes and shrines. We count with him the ghastly casualties of modern warfare, the broken bodies, the dead in their silent windrows. Foremost, inevitably, in our thinking are the heroic people of Hungary. For centuries they have been a bastion of Christendom against the outer perils, and for centuries their blood has been spilled for the ideal of a united Christian society. Now again they have received the full brunt of a calculated fury and have written a matchless chapter in the annals of freedom. To them, in their darkest hour, we offer the sympathy of our common faith and we pledge our unremitting efforts to help them achieve that ultimate liberty for which their sons and daughters have died, surely not in vain.

World on Brink of Disaster

5. It is not mere rhetoric to say that at this juncture the world is poised on the brink of disaster: It is grim realism. Yet war in modern terms would be a nightmare of unimaginable horrors. It can only annihilate; it has no power to solve our problems. If, in the ultimate resort, it is the duty of man to resist naked aggression, still it is obvious that every possible means consistent with divine law and human dignity must be employed and exhausted to avoid the final arbitrament of nuclear warfare. It has been the hope of humankind that a means adequate to the necessity might be found in the concert of the United Nations. This is neither the time nor the place to review its history or to pass judgment on its achievement. If there have been mistakes in its decisions and faltering in its procedures, that is no more than a commentary on our human condition. The fact remains that it offers the only present promise we have for sustained peace in our time; peace with any approximation of justice. The implication of our Holy Father's recent impassioned messages, clearly revealed in their context, is that the nations must employ their unity with such revived strength and purpose as to banish the spectre of war. It is division which tempts the aggressor; it is unity which gives him pause. Nothing could be conceived more disheartening for the cause of peace, nothing more discreditable to the honor of nations which have pledged themselves to peace, than the disunity which threatens to disrupt our immediate counsels and dissipates our strength. With the Sovereign Pontiff we recognize the urgency of prompt and effective intervention to silence the guns of war and to enforce the pacific arbitration of conflicting claims. With him, also, we emphasize the paramount need for a heightened concept of the universal validity of law among nations as among men. For unless God and His justice are acknowledged as basic to the very substance of law, there is no foundation upon which men may hope to build a lasting citadel of peace. There, for those who will read it, is the poignant warning of our present tragedy.

Our Own Government Praised

6.   It is with genuine satisfaction, amid all this distress, that we as Americans have followed the course set by our own government for the avoidance of international calamity. Worthy of highest praise are its efforts, rising above considerations of party and politics, to bring the problems before the tribunal of the nations, to restore mutual confidence in all those who seek justice, and to counter the threat of anarchy by marshalling the full strength of those forces of law and order which the world commands. Our president, indeed, has set a pattern of vigorous leadership, and has emphasized many of the points which have been dwelt upon by Pope Pius XII. He too is alert to the overriding need of a developed reverence for international law, clearly mindful, as he stressed in his recent address to the American people, that without law there can be no peace.

Ask Crusade of Prayer

7.   "If you wish peace," said the pagan axiom, "prepare for war." Christianity has revised that saying: "If you wish peace, prepare for peace." Though the hour is late indeed, it is not yet too late. There is the Divinity which governs the destinies of this world, and the supreme folly is to leave God out of our reckoning. As the bishops of the United States, we solemnly call upon the faithful throughout the land to pledge themselves to a veritable crusade of prayer. Let it be for the specific ends that international sanity will triumph over war; that justice may be vindicated by the nations united under law; and that our own beloved country, under God, may lead the way to that better hope for all mankind. Nor let us forget those who have suffered and who suffer now; that out of the crucible of their sacrifice may come the minted gold of freedom. We stand with the Vicar of Christ, and our prayer is for peace for our country and all the world— a peace with justice and charity.

Signed November 15, 1956, by the Administrative Board, National Catholic Welfare Conference, in the name of the bishops of the United States

Edward Cardinal Mooney, Archbishop of Detroit

Samuel Cardinal Stritch, Archbishop of Chicago

Francis Cardinal Spellman, Archbishop of New York

James Francis Cardinal McIntyre, Archbishop of Los Angeles

Francis P. Keough, Archbishop of Baltimore

Patrick A. O'Boyle, Archbishop of Washington

Joseph E. Ritter, Archbishop of St. Louis

John F. O'Hara, C.S.C., Archbishop of Philadelphia

Richard J. Cushing, Archbishop of Boston

Leo Binz, Archbishop of Dubuque

Matthew F. Brady, Bishop of Manchester

Emmet M. Walsh, Bishop of Youngstown

Thomas K. Gorman, Bishop of Dallas-Fort Worth

Michael J. Ready, Bishop of Columbus

A Statement on Persecuted Peoples

*A Statement Issued by the
Administrative Board of the National Catholic
Welfare Conference*[1]

December 20, 1956

1. With the sound of the Hungarian tragedy still ringing in our ears, there is little likelihood that we of the free world will forget the sufferings of our fellow Christians of that nation as they end this year in the darkness of renewed slavery. In one heroic gesture, they have laid bare to the whole world the unchanging evil character of the Soviet regime; they have clearly shown that the human spirit cannot be warped and moulded by brute force and that love of freedom cannot be killed by even the most cruel and complete oppression. Their noble uprising and the frightfulness of their repression serve as a vivid reminder of all those who for so long have borne the yoke of atheistic Communism.

2. For forty years now in domains that have come under that evil and inhuman rule, members of the Church of Silence have suffered, bled, and died for their Christian faith. Never in history has any body of Christians borne such widespread and unrelenting persecution. Even in the pagan days of the Caesars there were intervals of quiet and places where the poor and obscure were left unmolested. In our own day, however, throughout the whole vast territory under Red domination in Eastern Europe and in Asia, a constant, grinding terror has everywhere and at all times made itself felt. Perhaps from their ancient exemplars modern tyrants have learned the lesson that, as long as even a few of the faithful are left, they are certain to raise up from the seed of their martyred brothers a Christian Church which in the end will prevail.

3. Truth crushed to earth will rise again. In spite of long years of persecution, all evidence bespeaks a still large body of Christians whose faith has been but deepened by their trials. We are confident that, with the grace of God, they will endure steadfast and will bear to the Church of Christ fruit a hundredfold.

4. Because the sufferings of these our brothers require special graces of fortitude and perseverance, at this season when we stand near the beginning of another year of plenty and hope, and they on the brink

---

[1]This statement by the Administrative Board with the approval of the bishops of the United States was issued outside of the annual meeting and unsigned.

190

of another desolate year of persecution and terror, we call upon all Catholics of our country to unite on Sunday, December 30, in a day of prayer[2]—and in this we beseech all men of good will to join us—that God may speedily humble all tyrants and grant peace and freedom to those who so patiently have borne their crushing yoke.

---

[2]This was not the first day of prayer for the persecuted. In their 1955 meeting the bishops passed a resolution "urging that in all dioceses of the country Sunday, January 1, 1956 be designated as a Day of Prayer for the Persecuted."

A Statement on Censorship

A Statement Issued by the Catholic Bishops of
the United States

November 17, 1957

1. Censorship is today a provocative and sometimes misleading word.
It generates controversy by provoking those who would deny in fact
any restrictions, legal or moral, upon freedom of expression. It misleads,
since few approach the problems of censorship without emotion.

2. Obviously the state does have some power of censorship. In times
of war or great national danger, few will deny it a preventive power.
In normal circumstances, however, the state exercises only a punitive
function, placing restraint on those who misuse liberty to deny equal
or greater rights to others. The state's power of censorship is not
unlimited.

Teacher of Morals

3. Morally, the Church can and does exercise what is called censorship. This right is hers from her office as teacher of morals and
guardian of divine truth. Her decisions bind her people but her sanctions upon them are only spiritual and moral. She does, nevertheless,
express her judgments to all men of good will, soliciting their rea-
soned understanding and their freely given acceptance and support.

4. Most commonly in civil affairs the particular freedom that is
involved in discussions of the subject is freedom of the press, not
only in newspapers and other publications, but also such dramatic
expression as is represented in the theater, motion pictures, radio,
and television.

5. Because in modern times the press has been a major instrument
in the development of knowledge and the chief means of its diffusion,
freedom of the press is closely bound up with man's right to knowledge. Man's patient plodding ascent to the heights of truth evidences
the spiritual powers given him by God and at the same time their
wounding by sin. His search for truth is an enriching and ennobling
experience, uniquely proper to man.

6. The right to know the truth is evidently broad and sweeping. Is
the right to express this knowledge, whether through speech or press,
equally broad? That man has a right to communicate his ideas through
the spoken or written word is beyond challenge. And yet it can be
recognized at the outset that expression adds a new element to knowl-

192

edge. Directed as it is to others, it is an act that has social implications. Society itself must take cognizance of it. Although man must claim and hold to freedom of expression, he must also recognize his duty to exercise it with a sense of responsibility.

7.   This is a freedom that is intimately bound up with other freedoms that man prizes. Freedom of the press is patently a key safeguard of civil liberty. Democracy does not exist without it. The day free expression of opinion is extinguished and all are constrained to fall into a single pattern of political thought and action, democracy has died.

8.   As indispensable as is freedom of expression to us as citizens, it is no less indispensable to the Church in carrying out her mission to preach the Gospel. The content of man's knowledge of God derived through the use of his native powers has been immeasurably enriched and perfected and has been given certainty by the revelation made by God to man through Jesus Christ. This knowledge has been attained not through man's effort, but through the goodness and mercy of God. It is accepted by an act of faith made with the help of divine grace. Of this deposit of revealed truth the Church is the divinely appointed custodian.

9.   Without an unfettered means of communication, the teaching office of the Church is sorely hampered. She counts among her special blessings in our own country the important and fruitful Catholic press.

10.   Because freedom of the press is a basic right to be respected and safeguarded, it must be understood and defended not as license, but as true rational freedom. The kind of uncritical claims for and defense of liberty which so often have been made in our day actually places that liberty in jeopardy. For this reason we feel that light must be thrown not only on its meaning but also on its limits.

Serve the Common Good

11.   To speak of limits is to indicate that freedom of expression is not an absolute freedom. Not infrequently it is so presented. It is alleged that this freedom can suffer no curtailment or limitation without being destroyed. The traditional and sounder understanding of freedom, and specifically freedom of the press, is more temperate. It recognizes that liberty has a moral dimension. Man is true to himself as a free being when he acts in accord with the laws of right reason. As a member of society his liberty is exercised within bounds fixed by the multiple demands of social living. In the concrete this means that the common good is to be served. It will entail, among other things, a respect for the rights of others, a regard for public order, and a positive deference to those human, moral, and social values which are our common Christian heritage. It is within this context that freedom of expression is rightly understood.

12. This recognition of limitations has been given statement in recent decisions of the Supreme Court of the United States: "We hold that obscenity is not within the area of constitutionally protected speech or press." (Roth v. United States, 77 S. Ct. 1304, Alberts v. California, 77 S. Ct. 1304—June 24, 1957.) The decisions touching on this subject are encouraging to those who have been deeply concerned over trends that threatened to destroy the traditional authority exercised by the state over expressions and displays of obscenity.

Obscenity Demands Restraint

13. Contrary to this trend, the court has held that there is such a thing as obscenity susceptible of legal determination and demanding legal restraint; that laws forbidding the circulation of obscene literature are not as such in violation of the Constitution; that the federal government may ban such publications from the mail; that a state may act against obscene literature and punish those who sell or advertise it. The decisions reasserted the traditional conviction that freedom of expression is exercised within the defined limits of law. Obscenity cannot be permitted as a proper exercise of a basic human freedom. Civil enactments as well as the moral law both indicate that the exercise of this freedom cannot be unrestrained.

14. Ideally, we could wish that no man-made legal restraints were ever necessary. Thus, restraint on any human freedom would be imposed rather by one's own reason than by external authority. In any case, restraint's best justification is that it is imposed for the sake of a greater freedom. Since, however, individuals do act in an irresponsible way and do threaten social and moral harm, society must face its responsibility and exercise its authority. The exigencies of social living demand it.

15. In his recent encyclical of September 8, 1957, Our Holy Father has spoken not only of the competence of public administrators, but also of their strict duty to exercise supervision over the more modern media of communication and entertainment—radio and television. He warns public officials that they must look on this matter not from a merely political standpoint—but also from that of public morals, the sure foundation of which rests on the natural law. What he has said applies with even greater force to the older media—the press and motion pictures—since they have been and continue to be subject to even greater abuse and supply so much of the material used in the programs presented through the more modern media. Pope Pius XII writes:

> Nor can it be asserted that this watchful care of the state's officials is an unfair limitation on the liberty of individual citizens, for it is concerned not with the private citizens as such but rather with the whole of human society with whom these arts are being shared.

16. Although civil authority has the right and duty to exercise such control over the various media of communications as is necessary to safeguard public morals, yet civil law, especially in those areas which are constitutionally protected, will define as narrowly as possible the limitations placed on freedom. The one purpose which will guide legislators in establishing necessary restraints to freedom is the securing of the general welfare through the prevention of grave and harmful abuse. Our juridical system has been dedicated from the beginning to the principle of minimal restraint. Those who may become impatient with the reluctance of the state through its laws to curb and curtail human freedom should bear in mind that this is a principle which serves to safeguard all our vital freedoms—to curb less rather than more; to hold for liberty rather than for restraint.

Discretion and Prudence

17. In practice the exercise of any such curbs by the state calls for the highest discretion and prudence. This is particularly true in the area of the press. For here an unbridled power to curb and repress can make a tyrant of government, and can wrest from the people one by one their most cherished liberties.

18. Prudence will always demand, as is true under our governmental system, that the courts be in a position to protect the people against arbitrary repressive action. While they uphold the authority of government to suppress that which not only has no social value, but is actually harmful, as is the case with the obscene, the courts will be the traditional bulwark of the people's liberties.

Legislation Not Enough

19. Within the bounds essential to the preservation of a free press, human action and human expression may fall short of what is legally punishable and may still defy the moral standards of a notable number in the community. Between the legally punishable and the morally good there exists a wide gap. If we are content to accept as morally inoffensive all that is legally unpunishable, we have lowered greatly our moral standards. It must be recognized that civil legislation by itself does not constitute an adequate standard of morality.

20. An understanding of this truth together with the knowledge that offensive materials on the stage and screen and in publications have a harmful effect moved the bishops of the United States to set up agencies to work in the field—for motion pictures, the National Legion of Decency; for printed publications, the National Office for Decent Literature.

21. The function of these agencies is related in character. Each evaluates and offers the evaluation to those interested. Each seeks to enlist in a proper and lawful manner the cooperation of those who can curb the evil. Each invites the help of all people in the support of its objectives. Each endeavors through positive action to form habits of artistic taste which will move people to seek out and patronize the good. In their work they reflect the moral teaching of the Church. Neither agency exercises censorship in any true sense of the word.

22. The competence of the Church in this field comes from her divine commission as teacher of morals. Moral values are here clearly involved. Her standards of evaluation are drawn from revelation, reason, and Christian tradition and from the basic norms of the moral law. These are the standards on which our nation was founded and their preservation will be a safeguard to national integrity. A judgment of moral values in these areas is of prime importance to the whole nation.

23. Although the Church is primarily concerned with morals and not aesthetics, the two are clearly related. Art that is false to morality is not true art. While good taste cannot supply the norm for moral judgment on literature or art, yet it must be admitted that good taste will inevitably narrow the field of what is morally objectionable.

24. Who can deny that in modern American life there are many grave moral problems? This is not the judgment solely of the Catholic Church. When the Select Committee of the U.S. House of Representatives calls pornography big business, a national disgrace, and a menace to our civic welfare; when the National Council of Juvenile Court Judges attacks vicious and evil publications as a major cause of the change of juvenile delinquency from the thoughtless and mischievous acts of children into crimes of violence, armed robbery, rape, torture, and even homicide; when the New York State Joint Legislative Committee at the end of its five-year survey assures us that by actual count trash and smut on the newsstands have the advantage of numbers and that those same stands reflect an acceptance of and growing concentration on lewdness—in the face of all this we can only say that we are confronted with conditions which are fraught with peril.

Legion of Decency and NODL

25. Through the National Legion of Decency and the National Office for Decent Literature, we Catholics give public expression to our opinion on this subject. Through these agencies we voice our concern over conditions which, tolerated, merit expression of public indignation. But we assert that our activities as carried out by these organizations cannot justly be termed an attempt to exercise censorship.

26. The right to speak out in favor of good morals can hardly be challenged in a democracy such as ours. It is a long-standing tradition of this country that groups large and small have given expression of their concern over injustice: political, social, and economic. Their efforts, put forth within the framework of the law, have been directed toward dislodging evils against which the law itself is powerless. In many instances such efforts have made a valuable contribution to the community.

The Right of Children

27. It is in full accord with this tradition that the work of the Legion of Decency and the National Office for Decent Literature is carried on. The rights these agencies seek to protect are among the most important and sacred—the right of parents to bring up their children in an atmosphere reasonably free from defilement, the right of children to be protected from grave and insidious moral danger, the right of all not to be assailed at every turn by a display of indecency. Through the work of these agencies, the Church is able to give concrete expression of her concern.

28. The evaluations of these agencies have been a guide to our Catholic people. At the same time, they have enlisted the support of many others who share our concern. No one can fail to be stirred by the evident desire of so many people to remedy an unwholesome situation. And surely all those who are conscious of the gravity of the problem will applaud the efforts of the Church to safeguard the moral standards of the society in which we live.

Agencies Must Continue

29. It would be most gratifying to find it unnecessary to carry on this work. One could wish that the sense of responsibility of those who write and those who produce motion pictures would make superfluous action of this nature. Past experience, however, does not permit us to look forward to a day when this sort of evaluation will no longer be called for. Far from curtailing the work of these agencies, we must have them continue. Nor can we fail to be watchful over the fields of radio and television. Meanwhile, our existing agencies must be prepared to meet a continuing evil with an unremitting effort.

30. As a nation, we are intensely jealous of our freedoms. We are filled with pride that they have been so fully assured to us in our democracy. The reverence in which we hold our Constitution is due in great part to the care with which it has set down for all to know basic human freedoms that are inviolable. From childhood, these truths are taught us; they become the support of our adult life.

31. A freedom perceived in its true essence, in its exact limits, in its context of responsibility, is a freedom doubly secure; a freedom misunderstood risks becoming a freedom lost.

Signed in the name of the bishops of the United States by members of the Administrative Board, National Catholic Welfare Conference

Edward Cardinal Mooney, Archbishop of Detroit

Samuel Cardinal Stritch, Archbishop of Chicago

Francis Cardinal Spellman, Archbishop of New York

James Francis Cardinal McIntyre, Archbishop of Los Angeles

Francis P. Keough, Archbishop of Baltimore

Joseph E. Ritter, Archbishop of St. Louis

Patrick A. O'Boyle, Archbishop of Washington

Leo Binz, Archbishop of Dubuque

Karl J. Alter, Archbishop of Cincinnati

John F. O'Hara, C.S.C., Archbishop of Philadelphia

Albert G. Meyer, Archbishop of Milwaukee

Emmet M. Walsh, Bishop of Youngstown

Thomas K. Gorman, Bishop of Dallas-Fort Worth

Joseph M. Gilmore, Bishop of Helena

A Statement on Persecuted Peoples

A Statement Issued by the Catholic Bishops of the United States[1]

November 17, 1957

1. Little more than a year has elapsed since the agonized cry of the Hungarian people broke through the silence that enveloped them and millions of others who are suffering the most frightful persecution in history. Brute force speedily and ruthlessly stifled their heroic effort. Yet in a larger sense they have triumphed. For in God's loving providence they sounded a tocsin to which no man of good will could be deaf. In the midst of our grief over the atrocities perpetrated upon them and our other brothers beneath the heel of the Communist slavery, we thrill to the striking evidence they have given that faith and hope still shine in lands of darkness and that not all the might of wicked men can overcome the strength which is of God.

2. While millions of human beings live under the rule of terror and bitter oppression, it is imperative for us to recall that in the arsenal of Christianity, in reach of all men of good will, there is the invincible weapon of prayer. It has prevailed against apparently hopeless odds in ages past. It is unthinkable that we should in our day neglect to petition the infinite Creator and Ruler of the universe in behalf of these modern martyrs.

3. We, the Catholic bishops of the United States, with profound reliance on the unfailing power of prayer, call upon our people and upon all who "love justice and hate iniquity" to unite on Sunday, December twenty-ninth, in a day of prayer. Let us all beg God, our common Father, to stretch forth His mighty arm, to restrain those who have so long crushed His children, to strengthen and console the heroic souls who have endured so much and to lead them speedily to the enjoyment of the freedom of the Sons of God.

---

[1] This statement and the following *On Traffic Safety* were appended to that on *Censorship.*

A Statement on Traffic Safety

*A Statement Issued by the Catholic Bishops of
the United States*

November 17, 1957

1. God has commanded: Thou shalt not kill. The conscience of mankind rightly extends this law to all actions which without due reason,
endanger the health and physical integrity of any person. Suicide and
reckless actions which endanger one's life or safety are as reprehen-
sible as murder and mayhem.

2. And yet, in our time, a singular blind spot has developed in the
consciences of many people who are in all other matters law-abiding
and conscientious. We refer to the careless and even reckless use of
the automobile. Many who would never dream of handling a gun or
knife carelessly seem to lose all moral sense behind the wheel of an
automobile.

3. In far too many situations where death or injury occurs in automobile accidents, the driver is at fault. His carelessness, neglect, or
reckless conduct causes the death or injury. From a legal viewpoint,
such conduct is a crime. From a moral and religious viewpoint, these
actions are sinful.

4. Each of us has an obligation to seek an enlightened and educated
conscience. It is for this reason we urge, with the utmost seriousness,
that every driver reflect upon the moral obligations he assumes.

5. The distinctive mark of the follower of Christ is his love for his
fellow man. The mark of the upright and conscientious man is his
strict regard for the rights of others. On the basis of both justice and
Christian love we appeal to our fellow American citizens to join in a
crusade to keep our highways safe.

Discrimination and Christian Conscience

*A Statement Issued by the Catholic Bishops of
the United States*

November 14, 1958

1. Fifteen years ago, when this nation was devoting its energies to a World War designed to maintain human freedom, the Catholic bishops of the United States issued a prayerful warning to their fellow citizens. We called for the extension of full freedom within the confines of our beloved country. Specifically, we noted the problems faced by Negroes in obtaining the rights that are theirs as Americans. The statement of 1943 said in part:

2. "In the providence of God there are among us millions of fellow citizens of the Negro race. We owe to these fellow citizens, who have contributed so largely to the development of our country, and for whose welfare history imposes on us a special obligation of justice, to see that they have in fact the rights which are given them in our Constitution. This means not only political equality, but also fair economic and educational opportunities, a just share in public welfare projects, good housing without exploitation, and a full chance for the social advancement of their race."

Progress Made

3. In the intervening years, considerable progress was made in achieving these goals. The Negro race, brought to this country in slavery, continued its quiet but determined march toward the goal of equal rights and equal opportunity. During and after the Second World War, great and even spectacular advances were made in the obtaining of voting rights, good education, better-paying jobs, and adequate housing. Through the efforts of men of good will, of every race and creed and from all parts of the nation, the barriers of prejudice and discrimination were slowly but inevitably eroded.

4. Because this method of quiet conciliation produced such excellent results, we have preferred the path of action to that of exhortation. Unfortunately, however, it appears that in recent years the issues have become confused and the march toward justice and equality has been slowed if not halted in some areas. The transcendent moral issues involved have become obscured, and possibly forgotten.

5.   Our nation now stands divided by the problem of compulsory segregation of the races and the opposing demand for racial justice. No region of our land is immune from strife and division resulting from this problem. In one area, the key issue may concern the schools. In another it may be conflicts over housing. Job discrimination may be the focal point in still other sectors. But all these issues have one main point in common. They reflect the determination of our Negro people, and we hope the overwhelming majority of our white citizens, to see that our colored citizens obtain their full rights as given to them by God, the Creator of all, and guaranteed by the democratic traditions of our nation. There are many facets to the problems raised by the quest for racial justice. There are issues of law, of history, of economics, and of sociology. There are questions of procedure and technique. There are conflicts in cultures. Volumes have been written on each of these phases. Their importance we do not deny. But the time has come, in our considered and prayerful judgment, to cut through the maze of secondary or less essential issues and to come to the heart of the problem.

Question Is Moral and Religious

6.   The heart of the race question is moral and religious. It concerns the rights of man and our attitude toward our fellow man. If our attitude is governed by the great Christian law of love of neighbor and respect for his rights, then we can work out harmoniously the techniques for making legal, educational, economic, and social adjustments. But if our hearts are poisoned by hatred, or even by indifference toward the welfare and rights of our fellow men, then our nation faces a grave internal crisis.

7.   No one who bears the name of Christian can deny the universal love of God for all mankind. When our Lord and Savior, Jesus Christ, "took on the form of man" (Phil 2:7) and walked among men, He taught as the first two laws of life the love of God and the love of fellow man. "By this shall all men know that you are my disciples, that you have love, one for the other" (Jn 13:35). He offered His life in sacrifice for all mankind. His parting mandate to His followers was to "teach all nations" (Mt 28:19).

8.   Our Christian faith is of its nature universal. It knows not the distinctions of race, color, or nationhood. The missionaries of the Church have spread throughout the world, visiting with equal impartiality nations such as China and India, whose ancient cultures antedate the coming of the Savior, and the primitive tribes of the Americas. The love of Christ, and the love of the Christian, knows no bounds. In the words of Pope Pius XII, addressed to American Negro publishers twelve years ago, "All men are brothered in Jesus Christ;

for He, though God, became also man, became a member of the human family, a brother of all" (May 27, 1946).

9. Even those who do not accept our Christian tradition should at least acknowledge that God has implanted in the souls of all men some knowledge of the natural moral law and a respect for its teachings. Reason alone taught philosophers through the ages respect for the sacred dignity of each human being and the fundamental rights of man. Every man has an equal right to life, to justice before the law, to marry and rear a family under humane conditions, and to an equitable opportunity to use the goods of this earth for his needs and those of his family.

10. From these solemn truths, there follow certain conclusions vital for a proper approach to the problems that trouble us today. First, we must repeat the principle—embodied in our Declaration of Independence—that all men are equal in the sight of God. By equal we mean that they are created by God and redeemed by His Divine Son, that they are bound by His Law, and that God desires them as His friends in the eternity of Heaven. This fact confers upon all men human dignity and human rights.

Personal Differences among Men

11. Men are unequal in talent and achievement. They differ in culture and personal characteristics. Some are saintly, some seem to be evil, most are men of good will, though beset with human frailty. On the basis of personal differences we may distinguish among our fellow men, remembering always the admonition: "Let him who is without sin . . . cast the first stone . . ." (Jn 8:7). But discrimination based on the accidental fact of race or color, and as such injurious to human rights regardless of personal qualities or achievements, cannot be reconciled with the truth that God has created all men with equal rights and equal dignity.

12. Second, we are bound to love our fellow man. The Christian love we bespeak is not a matter of emotional likes or dislikes. It is a firm purpose to do good to all men, to the extent that ability and opportunity permit.

13. Among all races and national groups, class distinctions are inevitably made on the basis of like-mindedness or a community of interests. Such distinctions are normal and constitute a universal social phenomenon. They are accidental, however, and are subject to change as conditions change. It is unreasonable and injurious to the rights of others that a factor such as race, by and of itself, should be made a cause of discrimination and a basis for unequal treatment in our mutual relations.

Enforced Segregation

14. The question then arises: can enforced segregation be reconciled with the Christian view of our fellow man? In our judgment it cannot, and this for two fundamental reasons.

15. (1) Legal segregation, or any form of compulsory segregation, in itself and by its very nature imposes a stigma of inferiority upon the segregated people. Even if the now obsolete court doctrine of "separate but equal" had been carried out to the fullest extent, so that all public and semipublic facilities were in fact equal, there is nonetheless the judgment that an entire race, by the sole fact of race and regardless of individual qualities, is not fit to associate on equal terms with members of another race. We cannot reconcile such a judgment with the Christian view of man's nature and rights. Here again it is appropriate to cite the language of Pope Pius XII:

> God did not create a human family made up of segregated, dissociated, mutually independent members. No; He would have them all united by the bond of total love of Him and consequent self-dedication to assisting each other to maintain that bond intact (September 7, 1956).

16. (2) It is a matter of historical fact that segregation in our country has led to oppressive conditions and the denial of basic human rights for the Negro. This is evident in the fundamental fields of education, job opportunity, and housing. Flowing from these areas of neglect and discrimination are problems of health and the sordid train of evils so often associated with the consequent slum conditions. Surely Pope Pius XII must have had these conditions in mind when he said just two months ago:

> It is only too well known, alas, to what excesses pride of race and racial hate can lead. The Church has always been energetically opposed to attempts of genocide or practices arising from what is called the "color bar" (September 5, 1958).

Economic and Educational Opportunity

17. One of the tragedies of racial oppression is that the evils we have cited are being used as excuses to continue the very conditions that so strongly fostered such evils. Today we are told that Negroes, Indians, and also some Spanish-speaking Americans differ too much in culture and achievements to be assimilated in our schools, factories, and neighborhoods. Some decades back the same charge was made against the immigrant Irish, Jewish, Italian, Polish, Hungarian, German, Russian. In both instances differences were used by some as a basis for discrimination and even for bigoted ill-treatment. The immigrant, fortunately, has achieved his rightful status in the American community. Economic opportunity was wide open and educational equality was not denied to him.

18. Negro citizens seek these same opportunities. They wish an education that does not carry with it any stigma of inferiority. They wish economic advancement based on merit and skill. They wish their civil rights as American citizens. They wish acceptance based upon proved ability and achievement. No one who truly loves God's children will deny them this opportunity.

19. To work for this principle amid passions and misunderstandings will not be easy. It will take courage. But quiet and persevering courage has always been the mark of a true follower of Christ.

Plans Should Be Based on Prudence

20. We urge that concrete plans in this field be based on prudence. Prudence may be called a virtue that inclines us to view problems in their proper perspective. It aids us to use the proper means to secure our aim.

21. The problems we inherit today are rooted in decades, even centuries, of custom and cultural patterns. Changes in deep-rooted attitudes are not made overnight. When we are confronted with complex and far-reaching evils, it is not a sign of weakness or timidity to distinguish among remedies and reforms. Some changes are more necessary than others. Some are relatively easy to achieve. Others seem impossible at this time. What may succeed in one area may fail in another.

22. It is a sign of wisdom, rather than weakness, to study carefully the problems we face, to prepare for advances, and to by-pass the nonessential if it interferes with essential progress. We may well deplore a gradualism that is merely a cloak for inaction. But we equally deplore rash impetuosity that would sacrifice the achievements of decades in ill-timed and ill-considered ventures. In concrete matters we distinguish between prudence and inaction by asking the question: Are we sincerely and earnestly acting to solve these problems? We distinguish between prudence and rashness by seeking the prayerful and considered judgment of experienced counselors who have achieved success in meeting similar problems.

Vital That We Act Now

23. For this reason we hope and earnestly pray that responsible and soberminded Americans of all religious faiths, in all areas of our land, will seize the mantle of leadership from the agitator and the racist. It is vital that we act now and act decisively. All must act quietly, courageously, and prayerfully before it is too late.

24. For the welfare of our nation we call upon all to root out from their hearts bitterness and hatred. The tasks we face are indeed difficult. But hearts inspired by Christian love will surmount these difficulties.

25. Clearly, then, these problems are vital and urgent. May God give this nation the grace to meet the challenge it faces. For the sake of generations of future Americans, and indeed of all humanity, we cannot fail.

Signed by members of the Administrative Board, National Catholic Welfare Conference, in the name of the bishops of the United States

Francis Cardinal Spellman, Archbishop of New York

James Francis Cardinal McIntyre, Archbishop of Los Angeles

Francis P. Keough, Archbishop of Baltimore

Karl J. Alter, Archbishop of Cincinnati

Joseph E. Ritter, Archbishop of St. Louis

William O. Brady, Archbishop of St. Paul

Albert G. Meyer, Archbishop of Chicago

Patrick A. O'Boyle, Archbishop of Washington

Leo Binz, Archbishop of Dubuque

Emmet M. Walsh, Bishop of Youngstown

Joseph M. Gilmore, Bishop of Helena

Albert R. Zuroweste, Bishop of Belleville

A Statement on the Teaching Mission of the Catholic Church

*A Statement Issued by the Catholic Bishops of
the United States*

November 16, 1958[1]

1. For nearly two thousand years the Catholic Church has taught the children of men. The divine impetus of the first Pentecost has carried with undiminished force through the centuries to our own day, so that the name of Christ is known throughout the whole world as the name above all names.

2. In the midst of society the Church proclaims her right to teach. She asserts this not as a privilege which may or may not be conceded to her by any temporal authority, but as a power vested in her directly by her Divine Founder Himself. From His lips came the command, "Going into the whole world, preach the Gospel to every creature" (Mk 16:15). With instant obedience and literal fidelity, the apostles at once set forth upon their teaching mission. It was not by virtue of any imperial permission that they began the evangelization of the Roman world, nor has the Church in all the succeeding centuries ever sought the sanction of any dynasty or government as conferring upon her the right to engage in her universal mission. Her claim is that she holds her authority from the Author of Truth Himself; any lesser source would be meaningless for her.

3. The purpose of this Statement is to reaffirm this right in the confusion of modern pluralism. It is to clarify for her own children and for men of good will the objects which are embraced by this right and the nature of the obedience which she demands of those who know that hearing her, they hear Christ Himself.

Subject of Genuine Urgency

4. There is a genuine urgency for dwelling upon the subject at this time. We live in a sundered and divided world, a world harassed by conflicting voices and warring philosophies. Materialism and secularism, in particular, have made heavy inroads on the official and popular thinking of men and nations. The basic tenet of those ideologies is that man's sole concern is with the here and now, with the

---

[1]The bishops issued two separate statements at the 1958 meeting.

actual politics and economics of this world, to the exclusion, theoretical or practical, of the things of the spirit and their relegation to
the realm of pure fantasy. They, moreover, have seized upon the
democratic principle of popular suffrage and have distorted its meaning into a denial of all rights save those which derive from majority
opinion, of the social and political realities of our temporal condition.
But man's spiritual nature, his supernatural origin and immortal destiny, are not annihilated by being ignored; nor is the fact of man's
redemption by the blood of Christ obliterated by being denied.

5.   The Church holds that she is the teacher of men and nations
because she is divinely commissioned by Jesus Christ. She cannot
admit, therefore, that any earthly power can deprive her of her right
to teach. That right inheres in her very nature as autonomous society,
one whose constitution is altogether independent of the state. If the
Church were not allowed to teach she would be bereft of one of her
basic functions; she would be condemned, as under Communist totalitarianism today, to a twilight existence, and, by every human augury,
to gradual extinction. The right of the Church to exist implies and
demands her full competence to teach.

The Herald of God's Revelation

6.   Now it is certainly true that faith alone, a supernatural gift, enables the individual soul to acknowledge and accept the Church as
the authentic herald of God's revelation to mankind. This is eminently
a judgment and a decision based upon the credentials of the divinity
of her founder and the indefectibility of His word. Faith is the mys-
terious union of human freedom and the grace of God which results
in the highest act of the mind: *Credo*, I believe.

7.   But it is also true that in the natural order the Church's right to
exist and to teach has its roots in man's freedom, an essential attribute
of his nature, the sanctity and inviolability of which has long been
recognized as a fundamental of Western civilization. If man is truly
free, he is free to accept the revelation of our Lord and to embrace
the society He established. It is this freedom, essentially, which is
attacked and denied by modern secularism.

8.   Can it be said that our country is historically committed to the
secularist view of man's nature and human society? To the contrary,
our American founders, throwing off the bonds of tyranny, postulated as a right for themselves and their posterity, life, liberty, and
the pursuit of happiness. By the very terms of our Constitution, particularly as expressed in the first and ninth Amendments, those rights
are guaranteed not only to citizens as individuals, but also to the
associations and the religious societies to which they belong.

Freedom to Teach Essential

9. But life for the Church is dependent upon her freedom to teach; liberty for her must be broad enough to encompass her unfettered competence to proclaim the truth of her mission; and happiness, which for her is the fulfillment of God's will to redeem mankind, is no more than a mockery unless she is free to work for that end. It is an enduring tribute to the wisdom of the men who framed American freedom that they placed no hindrance in the way of the Church as teacher. Fidelity to their restraint is a proof of our national greatness.

10. The sanctity of the right of the Church to teach involves all other rights asserted for individuals and institutions. For this there is the uniform testimony of history. Under whatever form of tyranny, from Caesarism to Sovietism, the subversion of human freedom has almost invariably begun with the restriction or denial of the right of the Church to teach. The record extends from the imperialism of Rome to our contemporary examples of state socialism with wearisome repetition. Once the Church has been muzzled then other freedoms fall ready prey to those powers which would darken the mind and control the will of man. The irony, indeed, of many of the modern regimes which have passed as liberal is that they have vitiated their claim, only too often by a radical intolerance in regard to the Church as a teacher.

11. It is more than a question of history, however. The right of the Church to teach is deeply rooted in man's primary right to know the truths necessary for his salvation. There is no right anterior to this in value or importance, and there is no consideration which could justify the slightest infringement of it. The fact that in our modern pluralistic society all men are not agreed upon these truths, or, more specifically, are not united in recognizing the Church as the voice of God revealing, does not affect the essential nature of the problem.

12. What in practice does the Church regard as essential for the exercise of her right to teach men? The answer is very simple: the right to a hearing.

13. What does the Church claim it is her right to teach? Obviously, the total content of the deposit of faith revealed by Jesus Christ through His apostles, developed and unfolded through the ages under the guidance of the Holy Spirit whose abiding presence was promised her by the Divine Master. She can acknowledge no temporal authority as empowered to change or modify in any respect the least part of this deposit, and many of her most anguished conflicts have been fought out on that issue with those who would dictate her creed. It is her right, moreover, to teach those moral principles which flow from the natural law and the positive law of God, and which are binding upon all men, either as written, in St. Paul's phrase, on the tablets of their hearts, or as faith illumines their rightness and necessity.

Debate Is on Moral Teaching

14. It is significant of the temper of our times that only rarely now are undisguised attempts made to contest the right of the Church to proclaim her dogmatic truth. The debate more closely centers around her freedom to assert her moral teaching in a world which has increasingly tended to acknowledge no objective standard. It is questioned, thus, whether she has the right to preach her own concept of the holiness and inviolability of the marriage bond in a society which has legalized divorce and has advanced very far toward accepting it as a normal solution for marital problems of any kind. Again, there is vehement opposition raised when she states her principles on contraception. In another field it is contended that the Church is not justified in adopting measures to protect the faith of her children in a mixed society where established principles are at a discount. Her position on the moral necessity of Christian education is denounced as divisive, or, more properly, as running counter to the interests of a monopolistic statism. The list could well be extended, for there are many areas in which the stand of the Church is contested and her right to legislate for the consciences of her children is denied.

15. As freedom is fundamental to faith, so is freedom fundamental to conscience. The Church has never wavered in her adherence to these principles. But freedom does not mean intellectual or moral anarchy. It is not, as some would interpret it, merely freedom *from* something. It is spiritual power of man's very soul, inherent in his personality, by which he can rise to the fulfillment of God's will in his regard. Its deepest realization is in the voluntary acceptance of truth in obedience to God's law. When the Church legislates for conscience she does no more than make application of the imperatives of the divine law for the moral governance of mankind.

The Right to Define Virtue

16. The Church must exercise her right to teach men their duty. As in matters of faith she has the right and power to teach truth and to distinguish it from heresy, so in the field of morals she has the right to define virtue and to distinguish it from sin. What is sometimes misunderstood is that the Church is not a debating society but a divinely founded organization committed to a definite body of teachings and proclaiming a positive way of salvation.

17. In these modern times, the Church has ample reason to be grateful for those astonishing developments in the field of communication which render it possible for her voice to be heard and her truth to be pondered by far greater numbers than ever before in her long history. She is confident that her truth, fully known, will bring forth its fruits in the hearts of men.

Signed by members of the Administrative Board, National Catholic Welfare Conference, in the name of the bishops of the United States

Francis Cardinal Spellman, Archbishop of New York

James Francis Cardinal McIntyre, Archbishop of Los Angeles

Francis P. Keough, Archbishop of Baltimore

Karl J. Alter, Archbishop of Cincinnati

Joseph E. Ritter, Archbishop of St. Louis

William O. Brady, Archbishop of St. Paul

Albert G. Meyer, Archbishop of Chicago

Patrick A. O'Boyle, Archbishop of Washington

Leo Binz, Archbishop of Dubuque

Emmet M. Walsh, Bishop of Youngstown

Joseph M. Gilmore, Bishop of Helena

Albert R. Zuroweste, Bishop of Belleville

A Resolution on the Catholic Press and Bureau of Information

*A Resolution Passed by the
Administrative Board of the National Catholic
Welfare Conference*

November 1958

1. The Catholic Press of the United States, growing steadily and on firm foundations, has recorded some of its finest accomplishments in the last year.

2. Month after month, events of transcending importance and interest to Catholics have followed close upon one another. These have come to pass in many places, but notably in Rome in the last nine months. Particularly, the news coverage from the Eternal City by our press has been impressive with its completeness and variety. Our Catholic people have looked to their press for reports on these developments and they have not been disappointed. They have had their news in impressive volume, but with authenticity and detail.

3. This vigorous but careful reporting has brought a steadily expanding Catholic reading public. Today, our publications in this country reach a total of more than 23,000,000 subscribers. They have also created a greater interest in things Catholic on the part of the secular press.

4. We are proud of our press and we pledge it our continuing interest and support. We have a justifiable pride, we feel, in the contribution the archbishops and bishops have made to its growth through the establishment of the NCWC Press Department, some forty years ago, and in more recent years the organization of the Bureau of Information, whose primary purpose is to supply correct news stories and information to secular newspapers, radio, and television, of all events affecting Catholic life. The NCWC News Service, issued by the Press Department, has won many commendations from religious and secular sources as the finest agency of its kind in the world today.

5. We salute our Catholic Press, and we invoke God's blessings on it.

A Resolution on the Secular Press, Radio, and TV

A Resolution Passed by the
Administrative Board of the National Catholic
Welfare Conference

November 1958

1. We, archbishops and bishops of the Catholic Church in the United States, feel that it is not only proper but just that we express the deep gratitude of our Catholic people, and our own lively thanks, for the generous and understanding manner in which the press, the radio and the television recently have dealt with a series of news events of particular importance to Catholics.

2. These include the appointment of His Eminence, Samuel Cardinal Stritch, to be Pro-Prefect of the Sacred Congregation for the Propagation of the Faith; the illness and death of the Cardinal shortly after his arrival in Rome to take up this high office; the illness and death of His Holiness, Pope Pius XII; the death in Rome of His Eminence, Edward Cardinal Mooney; and the election and coronation of His Holiness, Pope John XXIII.

3. Pope Pius was reverenced by many millions of Americans. The two cardinals who have died commanded deep esteem also by millions. Pope John XXIII is surely destined to be a great figure of our times. Our communications media, in recounting the news of these events, has given an example of completeness, perception, and appreciation that is admirable and to their lasting credit.

4. We believe we are speaking for all our Catholic people when we commend these media and their staff.

A Statement on Freedom and Peace

A Statement Issued by the Catholic Bishops of the United States

November 19, 1959[1]

1. All the world craves peace. Without freedom under God for every man and for every nation there can be no peace.

2. On his recent visit to our country the Communist spokesman took every opportunity to compare unfavorably, capitalism with communism in their economic aspects. This is not the basic issue. The choice that men and nations must make today is between freedom and coercion.

3. Such words as *democracy, republic, peace,* and *friendship* are words to which the Western World is long accustomed. These words have been taken into their current vocabulary by the proponents of Communism. But while we may use the same words, we are not speaking the same language. By *peace* the Communist means submission to his program. By *friendship* he means the acceptance on the part of others of his formula for coexistence.

4. Freedom is not the product of any political or social system; it is man's natural birthright, and, in the words of Pope Leo XIII, "the highest of man's natural endowments."

5. This freedom under God permits man to use his faculties for his own just benefit and for the service of his fellow man in accordance with the law of God. Furthermore, to protect the freedom and rights of its citizens, each nation has the right to be free.

Freedom: The American Ideal

6. Our country was "conceived in liberty and dedicated to the proposition that all men are created equal." This recognition of the dignity of every citizen, endowed with inalienable rights that are God-given, is indelibly woven into the origin and history of the American republic.

7. Ours is a tradition of freedom under God with justice and charity for all. It seems opportune to emphasize the importance of this heritage of freedom. In it lies the moral strength that makes the contribution of America to the world's rebuilding unique and distinctive.

8. Above and beyond the material aid that we distribute so generously around the globe to those in need, we should be equally con-

---

[1]There are actually three statements for 1959: this and the two following.

cerned in sharing our ideals of liberty and justice. Proper standards of living and material prosperity are not enough. These are but means to an end and not in themselves the goal we would attain, if world peace is, as it should be, the aim of all our efforts.

The Foundations of Peace

9.   Peace, as demonstrated by our nation's experience, rests on disciplined freedom with its attendant virtues. True peace for nations as well as for individuals comes from justice, from charity, from the faithful observance of the moral law. The might of arms can do no more for peace than to discourage aggressors that are belligerent. Pacts and treaties can bring at best an uneasy truce, restraining an open hostility without achieving friendship or understanding. Not even international organizations and international law, essential as they are for order in the world, can bring about world peace. Fundamentally, that peace depends on the acceptance by men and nations of a fixed, unchangeable, universal moral law.

10. There is no need to retell the noble efforts that have been made in behalf of peace since the dawn of the present century. Nor is there need to retell disappointments that have laid low the hopes of men. The two most destructive wars in history have left their indelible mark on the first half of our century. Now, well into the second half, men live under the threat of a third world war that would be immeasurably more destructive.

Present Obstacles to Peace and Freedom

11. We would recognize that the chief obstacles to peace are the obstacles to real freedom. First among the main obstacles to peace and freedom in our present world is obviously world Communism. Communists do indeed preach peace and freedom and preach it incessantly; their actions, however, belie their word. They stir up hatred and mistrust. They reopen the old wounds of people who had real grievances in the days when they were subject to alien rule. While they themselves enslave whole nations over whom they have no shadow of claim, they seize wherever possible, upon economic and racial injustice to incite class warfare and violent revolution.

12. Thus, the Communist world poses a twofold threat to peace: first, that of military aggression of which the more recent instances continue to exemplify both ruthlessness and perfidy; second, the widespread sowing of the seed of hatred within nations and among nations.

To meet this constant threat to peace is the free world's greatest problem.

13. A second obstacle to peace and freedom, personal and national, is the spirit of excessive nationalism. The worldwide movement toward independence is in itself good and laudable, and we rejoice that many nations formerly subjected to external control now guide their own destinies. But all too often a morbid preoccupation with past grievances arouses a spirit of revenge that defrauds certain minorities of freedom and obstructs the clear vision of the constructive and peaceful paths that lead to national greatness.

14. A third obstacle to freedom and peace is found in the inhuman conditions that prevail among so many millions of the world's population. Poverty, hunger, disease, and the bitterness engendered by social injustice are their common lot. Embittered by the contrast between their own wretchedness and the wealth of the rich and powerful in their own lands, and between the nations, they are ripe for exploitation by both the communists and extreme nationalists.

15. Nor can we be unmindful of the plight of the millions of refugees whose present status is a challenge to all who believe in freedom and peace. Victims of totalitarian tyranny, deprived of family, of homeland, of liberty itself, they pose no threat to the peace and security of any land that may be their haven. But continued apathy to the problem of their resettlement is a reproach to the conscience of the free world.

Obstacles to Peace at Home

16. We must also recognize that conditions at home which threaten our moral integrity seriously threaten the cause of freedom and peace.

17. Our attention is directed to the subversive and evil forces that may undermine the moral strength of the nation. Chief among these currently are racial injustice, laxity in home life and discipline, preoccupation with the sensual, selfishness and self-seeking in economic life, and the excessive desire for wealth and ease.

18. The forces of religion in this country face no problem more pressing than the restoration within our people of respect for the moral law as God's law, and the inculcation of those virtues on which the soundness of family and civic life depends. Reverence for God's law, the keeping of His commandments, the practice of self-restraint, of justice, and charity will contribute beyond measure to the strength and unity of our country, which are so essential for effective leadership in the cause of freedom and of peace.

Roads to Peace and Freedom

19. Although Communism is the overriding danger to peace and freedom, our preoccupation with Communism should not deter us from seeking to solve other problems that may endanger peace and freedom. The social and economic problems of the world, and particularly those of Asia, Africa, and some areas in Latin America, pose a twofold challenge that can be met. In the first place, our Christian sense of justice and mercy impels us to do all that we can to help those who suffer from avoidable poverty, ignorance, and disease. Second, we know that tensions engendered by these conditions tend to foment both militant nationalism and Communist infiltration. Hungry and desperate people may grasp at short-range solutions in the effort to compress within a few decades a progress that elsewhere took centuries.

20. Our people have been generous in responding to the appeals of the afflicted victims of war and famine. But the needs of the world will not be met by charitable aid alone. The greater charity is to help people to help themselves. Programs of education, technical assistance, and developmental aid, now being carried out both by individual governments and by international bodies, can do much to build the foundations for prosperity and peace in nations suffering from poverty and hunger.

21. In the long run, at least, the cause of peace and freedom so intimately connected with the independence of nations would be better served if we could rely less upon programs of governmental aid and more on private investment and international trade adequately regulated for the good of all nations. In view of such serious problems as the pressure of population in some areas upon resources, the world needs every element of cooperation and good will to step up production and distribution of food and fibers. The potential abundance made possible by modern technology should be made a reality, as a result of programs inspired by our love of our fellow man and the quest for peace and freedom.

22. In regard to Communism, our goal is nothing less than the conversion of the Communist world. Our moral judgment is absolute: Communism is godless, it is aggressive and belligerent, it is unbelievably cruel. Witness the commune system in China! Hungary and Tibet are but the more recent manifestations of its total disregard for human rights and human dignity. Nevertheless, conscious of Christ's example and the infinite power of grace, we pray for the Red persecutors and for the persecuted. We wish no conquest except that of the spirit. We wish those who constructed the Iron Curtain to tear down the barbed wire and the machine gun posts and to join us in the enjoyment of God's freedom and peace.

23. Even today there are signs that the tyranny of Communism is not the same in every nation under its sway. There are indications that the spirit of man will not stay crushed. We should storm Heaven with prayer and penance, knowing that what to man seems impossible, God will grant to those who pray to Him with humble hearts, free of hatred and a spirit of revenge. As the early Christians converted their persecutors, we can seek to move those whose hearts seem hardened by blasphemous contempt for God and inhuman disregard for their fellow men.

24. In this spirit, statesmen of the world must continue their often disheartening quest for peace, reductions in armament, and the introduction of the rule of law into the society of nations. They must be firm in upholding principle and justice, knowing that appeasement in such matters leads only to the peace of the conquered. It is a delusion to place hope in seeking real understanding when the true problem is a conflict of essential principles, not lack of understanding.

25. While negotiating unceasingly for better relations with the Communist regimes, we must never forget that their system and ours are as basically different as slavery and freedom. To palliate the difference is to subvert the cause of freedom and peace. Recently the Communists have been cleverly veiling the sharp differences between the systems, as witnessed by the statement of a member of the Russian press group, "Our systems are different but there is not a single obstacle which would deny us peace of friendship or cooperation." In other words, Red slavery is only different, not opposed to our system of peace and freedom under God.

26. Ultimately, the problem of Communism as a threat to peace and freedom will be met only when we exemplify the principles that we proclaim as Christian members of a nation dedicated to God's law. There must be a searching reappraisal of our devotion to the principles we proclaim. We cannot live as materialists and expect to convert others to our system of freedom and peace under God.

27. Instead of upholding boldly the principles of peace and freedom under God we have emphasized the material fruits of our freedom, material wealth from industrialization and education. Instead of proclaiming freedom under God as we did in a more robust time in our history, we have so praised a program of supplying machines and calories and pleasure that these fruits of freedom and peace are made its substitutes. Today throughout the world, too often it is thought that when we speak of our American way of life we are speaking only of a high standard of living.

28. We have often acted in our international relations as if the products of industry and methods of production were our only contribution to the welfare of our neighbors. We have given the impression that material progress is our sovereign if not our exclusive concern.

In particular, we have fostered industrialization and education as the ends and not the means of elevating nations. Insofar as we have done this, we have tacitly accepted the materialistic philosophy of Communism as our way of life. We have aimed our efforts at satisfying the body, and, paradoxically, have allowed the Communists to capture the minds of men.

29. We must convince the world that our industry, our education, our technology are made not only to serve the body but the free spirit of man, that the grandeur of our heritage and extent of our contribution to the world is not measured in dollars and machines, but in the spirit of God's freedom and the dignity of the human person. Our motive in gladly pouring out our resources is not simply a natural pity for the misery of our fellow man or a damper to conflict, but recognition of his dignity as an equal son of God endowed with freedom.

30. To accomplish this we must be totally dedicated to our beliefs in God, the source of freedom and peace. We must be ready to give our country's principles the same unlimited measure of devotion that led to the birth of our nation. Mankind will follow only those who give it a higher cause and the leadership of their dedication. It is up to us to give that leadership to mankind in the cause of God's freedom and peace.

Signed by members of the Administrative Board, National Catholic Welfare Conference, in the name of the bishops of the United States

Francis Cardinal Spellman, Archbishop of New York

James Francis Cardinal McIntyre, Archbishop of Los Angeles

John Cardinal O'Hara, C.S.C., Archbishop of Philadelphia

Richard Cardinal Cushing, Archbishop of Boston

Aloisius Muench, Cardinal Designate, Bishop of Fargo, North Dakota

Albert Meyer, Cardinal Designate, Archbishop of Chicago

Karl J. Alter, Archbishop of Cincinnati

William O. Brady, Archbishop of St. Paul

Patrick A. O'Boyle, Archbishop of Washington

Leo Binz, Archbishop of Dubuque

Emmet M. Walsh, Bishop of Youngstown

Joseph M. Gilmore, Bishop of Helena

Albert R. Zuroweste, Bishop of Belleville

Joseph T. McGucken, Bishop of Sacramento

Allen J. Babcock, Bishop of Grand Rapids

Lawrence J. Shehan, Bishop of Bridgeport

Explosion or Backfire?

*A Statement Issued by the Catholic Bishops of
the United States*

November 19, 1959

1. For the past several years a campaign of propaganda has been gaining momentum to influence international, national, and personal opinion in favor of birth prevention programs. The vehicle for this propaganda is the recently coined terror technique phrase, "population explosion." The phrase, indeed, alerts all to the attention that must be given to population pressures, but it also provides a smoke screen behind which a moral evil may be foisted on the public and for obscuring the many factors that must be considered in this vital question.

2. More alarming is the present attempt of some representatives of Christian bodies who endeavor to elaborate the plan into a theological doctrine which envisages artificial birth prevention within the married state as the "will of God." Strangely too, simply because of these efforts and with callous disregard of the thinking of hundreds of millions of Christians and others who reject the position, some international and national figures have made the statement that artificial birth prevention within the married state is gradually becoming acceptable even in the Catholic Church. This is simply not true.

3. The perennial teaching of the Catholic Church has distinguished artificial birth prevention, which is a frustration of the marital act, from other forms of control of birth which are morally permissible. Method alone, however, is not the only question involved. Equally important is the sincere and objective examination of the motives and intentions of the couples involved, in view of the nature of the marriage contract itself. As long as due recognition is not given to these fundamental questions, there can be no genuine understanding of the problem.

4. At the present time, too, there is abundant evidence of a systematic, concerted effort to convince United States public opinion, legislators, and policy makers that United States national agencies, as well as international bodies, should provide with public funds and support, assistance in promoting artificial birth prevention for economically underdeveloped countries. The alleged purpose, as already remarked, is to prevent a hypothetical "population explosion." Experts, however, have not yet reached agreement on the exact meaning of this phrase. It is still a hypothesis that must stand the test of science. Yet, pessimistic population predictors seizing on the popular acceptance of the phrase, take little account of economic, social, and cultural factors and changes. Moreover, it would seem that if the predictors of population explosion wish to avail themselves of the right to foretell *population increases*, they must concede the right to predict *production increases* of food as well as of employment and educational opportunities.

5.   The position of United States Catholics to the growing and needy population of the world is a realistic one which is grounded in the natural law (which, it should be made clear, is not the law of the jungle, as sometimes erroneously supposed) and in respect for the human person, his origin, freedom, responsibility, and destiny. They believe that the goods of the earth were created by God for the use of all men and that men should not be arbitrarily tailored to fit a niggling and static image of what they are entitled to, as conceived by those who are more fortunate, greedy, or lazy. The thus far hidden reservoirs of science and of the earth unquestionably will be uncovered in this era of marvels and offered to humanity by dedicated persons with faith in mankind, and not by those seeking short cuts to comfort at the expense of the heritage of their own or other peoples.

6.   United States Catholics believe that the promotion of artificial birth prevention is a morally, humanly, psychologically, and politically disastrous approach to the population problem. Not only is such an approach ineffective in its own aims, but it spurns the basis of the real solution, sustained effort in a sense of human solidarity. Catholics are prepared to dedicate themselves to this effort, already so promisingly initiated in national and international circles. They will not, however, support any public assistance, either at home or abroad, to promote artificial birth prevention, abortion, or sterilization whether through direct aid or by means of international organizations.

7.   The fundamental reason for this position is the well-considered objection to promoting a moral evil—an objection not founded solely on any typically or exclusively Catholic doctrine, but on the natural law and on basic ethical considerations. However, quite apart from the moral issue, there are other cogent reasons why Catholics would not wish to see any official support or even favor given such specious methods of "assistance."

Social Development

8.   Man himself is the most valuable productive agent. Therefore, economic development and progress are best promoted by *creating conditions* favorable to his *highest development*. Such progress implies discipline, self-control, and the disposition to postpone present satisfactions for future gains. The widespread use of contraceptives would hinder rather than promote the acquisition of these qualities needed

for the social and economic changes in underdeveloped countries.

Immigration

9. Immigration and emigration—even within the same country—have their role to play in solving the population problem. It has been said that migration to other countries is no ultimate solution because of difficulties of absorbing populations into other economies. But it is a matter of record that migration has helped as a solution. Sixty million people migrated successfully from Europe to the Americas in the last one hundred fifty years. When the nomadic Indians roamed the uncultivated plains of North America before the coming of these immigrants, the entire country with its estimated Indian population of only 500,000 and its shortage of food, would have been regarded as "overpopulated" according to the norms of the exponents of Planned Parenthood. Yet, the same plains today are being retired into a "land bank" because they are overproductive in a land of 175 million. It is, therefore, apparent that to speak of a population explosion in the United States in these circumstances is the sheerest kind of nonsense.

Political and Psychological

10. The Soviets in their wooing of economically underdeveloped countries do not press artificial birth prevention propaganda on them as a remedy for their ills. Rather they allure them into the Communist orbit by offering education, loans, technical assistance, and trade, and they boast that their economic system is able to use human beings in constructive work and to meet all their needs. The Russian delegate to the relatively recent meeting of the United Nations Economic Commission on Asia and the Far East proclaimed, "The key to progress does not lie in a limitation of population through artificial reduction of the birthrate, but in the speedy defeat of the economic backwardness of these countries." The Communist record of contempt for the value of human life gives the lie to this hypocritical propaganda, but to peoples aspiring to economic development and political status, the deceit is not immediately evident. Confronted on the one hand by the prospect of achieving their goals without sacrificing natural fertility and on the other by the insistence that reducing natural fertility is essential to the achievement of such goals, how could these peoples be reasonably expected to reject Communism? Yet, the prophets of "population explosion" in alleging that contraception will thwart Communism naively emphasize its specious attractiveness in these areas.

Food and Agriculture

11. United States Catholics do not wish to ignore or minimize the problem of population pressure, but they do deplore the studious omission of adequate reference to the role of modern agriculture in food production. The "population explosion" alarmists do not place in proper focus the idea of increasing the acreage or the acreage yield to meet the food demands of an increasing population. By hysterical terrorism and bland misrepresentation of data they dismiss these ideas as requiring too much time for the development of extensive education and new distribution methods and for the elimination of apathy, greed, and superstition. Such arguments merely beg the question, for the implementation of their own program demands the fulfillment of the same conditions. It seems never to dawn on them that in a chronic condition where we have more people than food, the logical answer would be, not to decrease the number of people but to increase the food supply which is almost unlimited in potential.

12. We make these observations to direct attention to the very real problem of population pressures. Such remarks are not intended to exhaust this complex subject, nor to discourage demographers, economists, agricultural experts, and political scientists in their endeavors to solve the problem. Rather, our intention is to reaffirm the position of the Catholic Church that the only true solutions are those that are morally acceptable under the natural law of God. Never should we allow the unilateral "guesstimates" of special pleaders to stampede or terrorize the United States into a national or international policy inimical to human dignity. For, the adoption of the morally objectionable means advocated to forestall the so-called "population explosion" may backfire on the human race.[1]

Signed by members of the Administrative Board, National Catholic Welfare Conference, in the name of the bishops of the United States

Francis Cardinal Spellman, Archbishop of New York

James Francis Cardinal McIntyre, Archbishop of Los Angeles

John Cardinal O'Hara, C.S.C., Archbishop of Philadelphia

Richard Cardinal Cushing, Archbishop of Boston

Aloisius Muench, Cardinal Designate, Bishop of Fargo, North Dakota

---

[1] After the signatures of the Administrative Board there is appended a lengthy quotation from "An Address to the Association for Large Families of Rome and Italy" by Pius XII, January 20, 1958.

Albert Meyer, Cardinal
Designate, Archbishop of
Chicago

Karl J. Alter, Archbishop of
Cincinnati

William O. Brady, Archbishop
of St. Paul

Patrick A. O'Boyle, Archbishop
of Washington

Leo Binz, Archbishop of
Dubuque

Emmet M. Walsh, Bishop of
Youngstown

Joseph M. Gilmore, Bishop of
Helena

Albert R. Zuroweste, Bishop of
Belleville

Joseph T. McGucken, Bishop of
Sacramento

Allen J. Babcock, Bishop of
Grand Rapids

Lawrence J. Shehan, Bishop of
Bridgeport

World Refugee Year and Migration

*A Statement Issued by the NCWC
Administrative Board in the Name of the
Bishops of the United States*

November 19, 1959

1. World Refugee Year began last July on a note of high hope for the homeless refugees of the world. His Holiness Pope John XXIII added his voice to the chorus of those earnestly seeking to remind nations of their obligations:

> We raise our voice on behalf of refugees, and we paternally exhort all our children in every part of the world to collaborate generously and efficaciously in making a success of this World Refugee Year, an undertaking inspired by aims so noble and disinterested, to which it pleases us to pay tribute.

2. The earliest records of history indicate that migration and resettlement are common occurrences in the life of men. People move from their native land for various reasons. Some seek opportunity and adventure. Others flee from the disasters of nature, or of war and the aftermath of war. In many instances the tyranny of rulers, or economic and political pressures, or religious and social tensions force countless families to seek new homes in distant lands.

3. Migration is as much a part of current history as of past history. In the present-day world there are two groups of potential migrants, those forced to flee as refugees and displaced persons, and those who emigrate voluntarily.

4. Those who are refugees and displaced persons have lost their homes because of war, persecution, or political pressures. Some are refugees from Communist persecution. Others are expelled, or subjected to intolerable pressure, as minority groups in a highly nationalistic society.

5. The second group of potential migrants comprises those seeking better living conditions or aspiring to a more abundant life.

6. Even in relatively prosperous nations of Western Europe there are millions who either lack work or who barely subsist on the products of their labor, however diligent. In Asia, Africa, and Latin America there are literally millions living in sheer destitution. They do not have even the utter minimum of food, shelter, clothing, and medical care needed for a truly human life.

7. Any assertion that migration is the ultimate solution for all refugees or for the economically destitute can certainly be challenged.

In many instances, vigorous and realistic plans for economic development might more effectively serve the purpose of aid.

8.   The fact remains, however, that great numbers of these people understandably clamor for the chance to seek a new home where they can more adequately meet their needs and those of their families.

9.   Their plea and their plight should be heard and examined in the light of Christian principles.

A Christian Attitude toward the Problem

10.   The attitude of the Christian toward his fellow man is based on the second of the two great laws of God, "Thou shalt love thy neighbor as thyself." Christ Himself insisted on love of neighbor as essential to the life of His followers. He even singled it out as a test for salvation:

11.   "If anyone says, 'I love God,' and hates his brother, he is a liar. For how can he who does not love his brother, whom he sees, love God, whom he does not see? And this commandment we have from Him, that he who loves God should love his brother also."

12.   Love of neighbor is fundamental and it must transcend nation, race, creed, and status.

13.   From this principle springs the basic moral considerations for formulating national policy on behalf of potential migrants in other countries. True love of neighbor will motivate us to assist these people in attaining the measure of justice that is rightfully theirs and to share with them in charity the temporal abundance God has given us.

14.   Migration is a right due in justice to the individual.

15.   Pope Pius XII spoke of the "natural right of the individual to be unhampered in immigration or emigration." It is the right of human beings to have access to the resources of the earth created by God for the good of man. In the present order of things, it is necessary for nations to make laws to insure the use of these resources in a reasonable and orderly fashion, but the tenor of the law should be such as to facilitate, not impede, access to them.

16.   It must be recognized, however, that migration is not the only solution, nor always the best solution for the problem of poverty in overcrowded lands.

17.   True, for many of those who are refugees and displaced persons there is no other hope but migration. Those, however, who are victims of disrupted economic and social conditions may prefer to remain in their homeland if these conditions are improved. A few years ago, for example, the world was deeply concerned about refugees and expellees from East Germany and from German lands now occupied by other powers. Today many of these persons have been absorbed by a prospering West German economy.

18. On the other hand, in some countries such as Italy, Greece, the Netherlands, and Japan, there is no apparent prospect in the immediate future for an expansion of the economy sufficient to provide a decent livelihood for all of their people.

19. Accordingly, the nations of the world, especially those that are prosperous, should unite in effective long-range programs designed to raise productivity and thus make such nations as self-supporting as possible.

20. Sometimes migration is impossible because of the sheer numbers involved. Also migration is slow, and in the meantime many millions are destitute, homeless, and hungry. Here the obligation of charity, love for neighbor, strikes directly at the Christian conscience.

21. The plight of these people cannot be ignored. Each nation, in a manner commensurate with true ability and wealth, must provide needed food, shelter, clothing, and medical care. To neglect these people is to neglect the human family.

22. To summarize, migration is an absolute need for many refugees and displaced peoples. It is a solution for economic and social pressures in some areas where there seems to be little hope for internal economic and social improvement.

23. But, when migration becomes an impractical solution because of the sheer numbers involved, then heroic measures must be taken to alleviate present misery and to institute long-range reforms, designed to raise the standard of living.

The United States Is Involved

24. The moral principles just stated, and the applications outlined above, have special relevance for a nation such as ours which is so lavishly blessed with God's bounty.

25. Our obligation is fourfold: to share our own abundance; to welcome the immigrant; to promote and cooperate with world policies of resettlement; and to aid underdeveloped nations.

26. There is no need to restate here completely our record in this regard. Traditionally we have been generous in helping others in need. Until recent decades, we have been relatively liberal in accepting immigrants. In present restrictive immigration laws, we have made exceptions for refugees and displaced persons. Since World War II, our aid to nations and peoples in distress has been extensive indeed.

27. Even though our record has been good, it is, nevertheless, not inappropriate to conduct a careful examination of the needs of the world to see whether we have done all within our power to aid the homeless and the hungry. The following questions might legitimately be raised:

28. Have we made a sufficiently urgent effort to develop to the fullest possible a program for distributing our food surpluses to the hungry? The difficulties involved are formidable, ranging from the political to the purely logistic. But could not these difficulties be overcome, were we determined to do so?

29. Are we meeting, according to our abilities the needs of other nations, the demands for technical assistance, development loans, and stimulation of private investment in newly developing nations? Should we increase our efforts to influence other comparatively wealthy nations to associate with us in international programs of this type?

30. Are we doing all within our power, particularly during this World Refugee Year, to help the refugee and displaced person? Could we do more in accepting the homeless within our own borders, or in helping them to find homes elsewhere in a suitable or desirable environment?

31. Do our own laws tend to discriminate against the "difficult to resettle" and "hardship" cases? Many students of our immigration laws feel they are designed to favor the best educated, the strongest, and the healthiest immigrants. This in effect bleeds a nation troubled with population problems of its best citizens, leaving behind those who can contribute least to national prosperity. Such ungenerous laws seem to bespeak a spirit of selfishness rather than a genuine desire by a privileged people to help those in need.

32. Are our basic laws sufficiently sensitive to problems of compassion, such as reuniting of families or the provision of homes for orphan children?

33. Are we observing the precepts of justice and charity by keeping in our laws prejudicial elements such as token quotas for Orientals or a national-origins clause? Do not these laws in effect favor nations whose people show the least desire for emigration?

34. Have we considered the possibility that some regulations designed to keep out criminals and subversives may affront the human dignity of immigrants not belonging to this category? Could we not find less offensive methods for securing the same purpose?

35. Is the total number of quota immigrants too low, considering the immense economic strength of our nation? It is certainly no kindness to admit immigrants if there are no jobs available, but the ability of our economy to offer jobs has steadily and vigorously risen. Even doubling the present effective quota immigrant level would be an insignificant factor in adding to our work force.

36. Is our effort to help the immigrant adjust adequate to the problem? Could we not display warmer understanding toward him in his struggle with the new and complex difficulties involved in the process of social assimilation?

37. These questions are raised to stimulate Christian thinking on the concrete problems connected with migration and immigration. They are raised at a time when most Americans are acutely aware of the sacrifices they are making, especially in the form of taxes to meet the costs of national defense and an expanding population.

38. The burdens we have been carrying are admittedly heavy, especially since they have been prolonged over many years, but sacrifice is essentially comparative. How many of us, even with heavy taxes and extensive programs of aid, are deprived of luxuries and possibly some comforts? There are few employed Americans whose lot is not incomparably better than that of the overwhelming majority of workers in the rest of the world.

39. When we realize that a great portion of the world's population goes to bed hungry each night and that preventable disease is endemic in whole countries, we know that our sacrifices are relatively minor.

40. In the light of these problems the thoughtful Christian will read again the words of our Savior:

> I was hungry and you gave me to eat; I was thirsty and you gave me to drink; I was a stranger and you took me in; Naked and you covered me; Sick and you visited me; I was in prison and you came to me. . . . Amen, I say to you, as long as you did it for one of these, the least of my brethren, you did it for me (Mt 25:35-40).

Statement issued by members of the Administrative Board, National Catholic Welfare Conference, in the name of the bishops of the United States

Francis Cardinal Spellman, Archbishop of New York

James Francis Cardinal McIntyre, Archbishop of Los Angeles

John Cardinal O'Hara, C.S.C., Archbishop of Philadelphia

Richard Cardinal Cushing, Archbishop of Boston

Aloisius Muench, Cardinal Designate, Archbishop of Fargo, North Dakota

Albert Meyer, Cardinal Designate, Archbishop of Chicago

Karl J. Alter, Archbishop of Cincinnati

William O. Brady, Archbishop of St. Paul

Patrick A. O'Boyle, Archbishop of Washington

Leo Binz, Archbishop of Dubuque

Emmet M. Walsh, Bishop of
Youngstown

Joseph M. Gilmore, Bishop of
Helena

Albert R. Zuroweste, Bishop of
Belleville

Joseph T. McGucken, Bishop of
Sacramento

Allen J. Babcock, Bishop of
Grand Rapids

Lawrence J. Shehan, Bishop of
Bridgeport

Protest against Bigotry

A Statement Issued in the Name of the
NCWC Administrative Board with the
Approval of the Catholic Bishops of the
United States[1]

January 25, 1960

Anti-Semitism

1. The widespread eruption of religious and racial bigotry recorded
in recent press dispatches has not only shocked the whole civilized
world but calls insistently for a vigorous and public repudiation of
the evil by all right-minded citizens. We deplore any revival of the
anti-Semitic prejudice which in its earlier manifestations culminated
in such terrible disaster. The fact that a malevolent spirit of hatred
has found expression not only in one country, but in various countries
simultaneously, would seem to indicate an organized plan of action
or some common origin. Whatever may be the source of the evil or
the sinister purpose to be served, the danger should be immediately
recognized and effective measures taken to eradicate the infection
before it can spread.

Widespread Religious and Racial Hatred

2. The defilement of various synagogues, churches, schools, and
other buildings with derogatory symbols has revealed the existence
of racial hatred. It has not been confined to any one group. Various
Catholic and other Christian churches have been desecrated as well
as Jewish temples, indicating that religious and racial hatred is widespread and constitutes a common motivation of the outrages.
3. Speaking for the Administrative Board of Bishops of the National
Catholic Welfare Conference, I wish to declare our sympathy with
those who have suffered injury. On behalf of the bishops I express
our detestation of any and every kind of hatred and bigotry, no matter
what its source or against whom it may have been registered. We call
on all citizens, whether Christians or Jews, and on all those who love
truth and justice, to protest privately and publicly against further
manifestation of bigotry in all its aspects and in whatever form it may

[1]This statement was written by and issued upon the initiative of Archbishop Karl Alter
of Cincinnati, cf., Alter to Paul Tanner, January 16, 1960, files of the then NCWC.

be expressed. We urge that all right-minded people refrain from any word or deed which might seem to condone the circulation of rumors, false reports, or misrepresentation which embitters our mutual relations and retards the advancement of our common welfare.

Karl J. Alter
Archbishop of Cincinnati
Chairman of the Board
NCWC

A Statement on Personal Responsibility

A Statement Issued by the Catholic Bishops of the United States

November 20, 1960

1. The history and achievements of America stand as a monument to the personal responsibility of free men. Our institutions and our industry, the fruit of the American sense of responsibility, have in the past inspired, guided, and helped many other nations of the world. If our future is to be worthy of our past, if the fruit of America's promise is not to wither before it has reached full maturity, our present preeminent need is to reaffirm the sense of individual obligation, to place clearly before ourselves the foundation on which personal responsibility rests, to determine the causes of its decay and to seek the means by which it can be revived.

2. The foremost signs of the decline of personal responsibility are to be found in the family. Marriage, a sacred and binding contract, all too often is considered merely as an arbitrary arrangement to satisfy the instinct of pleasure. The failure of parents to fulfill their responsibilities, as revealed in the frequency of divorce, desertion, and broken homes, is a national disgrace. Any delinquency of parents may well be reflected in the delinquency of youth, which is now commonly considered our greatest national domestic problem.

Personal Responsibility and Industry

3. Equally conspicuous is the evidence of decline in the sense of responsibility within our industrial organization and in our general economic life. At a time when so much depends upon the soundness of our economy and upon our ability to produce to meet the needs of a rapidly developing world, we have been faced by a frequent lack of truly responsible leadership, both on the part of management and of labor. Among the evident instances of the breakdown of personal responsibility most deplorable has been the widespread cynical reaction to the recent revelation of dishonesty, waste, and malfeasance in industrial relations.

4. Although personal responsibility and initiative have been our national characteristics, explaining in large measure our country's progress in human welfare, yet pressures are growing for a constantly greater reliance on the collectivity rather than on the individual. An inordinate demand for benefits, most easily secured by the pressures of organization, has led an ever-growing number of our people to relinquish their rights and to abdicate their responsibilities. This concession creates a widening spiral of increasing demands and pressures with a further infringement on personal freedom and responsibility. The result is the condition recently noted by our Holy Father: "Modern man sees that the sphere in which he can think for himself, act on his own initiative, exercise his responsibilities, and affirm and enrich his personality is in many cases restricted to an excessive degree" (Letter of July 12, 1960, to the "Semaine Sociale" in Grenoble). Intensive socialization can achieve mass benefits, but man and morality can be seriously hurt in the process.

5.   This tendency to delegate excessive responsibility to an organization is discernible also in the realm of international affairs. Some manifest no sense of personal responsibility in the affairs of the international community. On the other hand, many citizens seem to feel that our mere adherence to the United Nations absolves us from further responsibility in the international order and that decisions made by the United Nations, regardless of their objective value, are always to be regarded as morally right. Admitting the undoubted value of a policy of supporting the United Nations and recognizing the genuine contribution it has made in many areas, we must understand clearly that the citizens of this country, and of all countries, have a responsibility to judge and to evaluate the United Nations' deliberations and decisions according to objective norms of morality universally binding. This involves also the duty of citizens to make proper representation of such judgment to their respective governments.

Rejection of Personal Responsibility

6.   However varied the above-mentioned evils, ranging from the single act of wrongdoing to the moral laxity of the mass mind, the root cause is the same—the rejection of personal responsibility. This is a moral evil, as are all the major ills that beset the present world. As such their cure is largely within the power of individual persons. A godly society is the work of godly men. Even the most universal evil and the threatened mechanization of man can be made to yield before the just and determined will of individual persons.

7.   Our Holy Father has pointed out the capacity of the individual in the face of such problems.

Does it follow that the process of socialization is impossible to control and that, increasing constantly in its breadth and depth, it will one day surely reduce men to the role of automatons? Certainly not. For socialization is not the result of forces of nature acting according to determinism that cannot be changed. It is the work of man, of a free being conscious of and responsible for his acts (Letter of July 12, 1960, to "Semaine Sociale" in Grenoble).

8.   In our national life we have experienced the truth of this statement. Our progress has been achieved chiefly according to the measure of individual commitment to responsibility. The heroes of our history have not been blind forces but stouthearted persons; our worthy national goals have been achieved not as a result of environment but by men who made their environment. A strong and responsible nation is fashioned by responsible persons, not group pressures. As Pope Pius XII stated: "The people live from the fullness of the life of the men who make it up; each of them in his place and in the manner proper to him is a person conscious of his own convictions" (Christmas Message, 1944).

9.   What is personal responsibility in the context of man's relation to the world? It presupposes the acceptance of one's dignity as a son of God in whatever environment he may be placed and the acknowledgement of binding moral law. It requires the free and deliberate acceptance of one's obligations in the position he occupies—in the family, in the church, in the corporation, in the labor union, in the nation, in the family of nations. It demands the rule of conscience, not self-satisfaction. It recognizes that every deliberate action of the human person has a relationship with his Creator and His purpose in creating the world. It affirms that every human action a man performs derives its significance from that relationship and makes him a cooperator with his Creator in forwarding the Kingdom of God. It is a solemn profession that consequently every product of his mind and his hand, every bounty wrung from the earth is to serve that high purpose. As man, bearing the image of his Creator, is the brother of every other human person, his noblest work is to bring to his fellow man the blessings of the destiny intended for him by God.

10.   It must be emphasized, especially in these times, that the freedom innate in man, as well as the social nature he enjoys, demands as a correlative the fullest personal responsibility. "Therefore every one of us will render an account for himself to God" (Rom 14:12). The marvelous inventiveness of the human mind, conquering space and making each man a neighbor of every other human being on earth, gives urgency to this twofold need: to maintain one's freedom by using it according to the limits and norms of rightful authority; to use it also according to his social nature and the needs of his fellow man.

For you have been called to liberty, brethren; only do not use liberty
as an occasion for sensuality but by charity serve one another. For
the whole law is fulfilled in one word, "Thou shalt love thy neighbor
as thyself" (Gal 5:13-14).

The social pressures of today's complex life do not excuse from, but
rather create a demand for, a greater exercise of personal responsibility. No man can be neutral in a moral cause. By his creation he is
born to be committed to the cause of God. The more difficult the
situation the more imperative the need for such a commitment.

11. If we are to restore man to his sense of personal responsibility
and to the acceptance of life as a mission, we must understand more
clearly the moral causes which have undermined men's sense of
responsibility.

12. First among these causes has been the marked decline in the force
of religious convictions. Washington warned the American people
that they should indulge with caution the supposition that national
morality could exist without religion. In spite of the much discussed
increase of church membership it cannot be doubted that for a long
time religious influences have been losing their vigor among the
American people, with a debilitating effect in consequence on both
public and private life.

13. As a result of this decline of religious convictions the grasp on
moral principles has been greatly weakened. Through a faulty concept of morality, modern man has come to imagine that sudden and
drastic changes in situations change principles; that principles no
longer control situations, but rather that situations shape principles.
Inevitably this type of "situational ethics" denies all unchanging principles and makes futile all moral judgments on which the sense of
responsibility rests. The need which the world faces is the acceptance
of an objective norm of morality, and hence of conduct.

14. This decline in religious belief and moral conviction leaves modern
man blind to his immutable spiritual nature. Thus, wittingly or unwittingly, he aligns himself with the forces of materialism among whose
tenets there is no room for the concept of personal responsibility.

15. Finally, the social ideals and purposes of modern man, due to
the declining influence of religious and moral convictions and to the
triumph of the material, tend in many subtle ways to efface the sense
of responsibility. As a people we seem to be moving more deeply
into a sensate culture. There is an excessive preoccupation with material security at the expense of spiritual well-being. Uniformity of thought
and supine loyalty to the organization, whether it be the industrial
corporation, the labor union, or the political party, are too often
encouraged and rewarded. The organizational man, cloaked in a sort
of anonymity, rather than the responsible individual, is favored and
advanced. The preparation for this condition is found even in the
field of education, where emphasis is placed on adapting oneself to

the thinking of the group. The pattern is so prevalent that some psychologists consider juvenile delinquency as a revolt, just for the sake of rebellion, against a stifling uniformity that fails to challenge the individuality of the student.

16. The correction of these basically moral evils and the restoration of a vigorous sense of personal responsibility belong primarily to the field of religion. The development of a truly Christian character is primarily the task of religion, although its inculcation is of vital concern to the state. It is the function of religion to teach man his unique dignity as a son of God and brother of Christ. Pope Pius XII explicitly stated this in describing the function of the Church:

> Always and everywhere, by unceasingly adapting herself to the circumstances of time and place, she seeks to model persons, individuals, and, as far as possible, all individuals according to the laws of Christ, thus attaining the moral basis for social life. The object of the Church is man, naturally good, imbued, ennobled, and strengthened by the truth and grace of Christ (September 19, 1955).

Religion Promotes Responsibility

17. Deepened religious convictions will bolster and reactivate the sense of personal responsibility. We must seek to enlarge the area of personal autonomy to protect the human personality from a greater encroachment on its freedom and responsibility. The individual person must assume as his proud right the accomplishment of whatever he can for himself and for others, especially those of his family, and herein lies the importance of the Christian home. The same principle of responsibility must be consistently applied to every level of action. Pope Pius XI explicitly emphasized this principle of subsidiarity in the *Quadragesimo Anno* published in 1931:

> Just as one cannot take away from individuals and transfer to the community the tasks they are capable of accomplishing by themselves, thus it would also be an injustice—and at the same time a harmful disturbance of the social order—if one were to remove from groups of lower rank functions they can exercise themselves and entrust them to a wider collectivity of higher rank. The natural objective of any intervention in social matters is to assist the members of the social body and not to destroy or absorb them.

18. Even when man enters into associations, as he must to achieve the goals which lie beyond his individual capacity, he should remember their purpose is in relation to his freedom and responsibility. In this respect, the Holy Father stated:

> But this is to be done on the condition that each of these institutions remains within its own sphere of responsibility; that it be offered to, not imposed upon, the free choice of mankind. They must under

no circumstances look upon themselves as an end making their members an instrument of their activity (Letter of July 12, 1960, to "Semaine Sociale" in Grenoble).

19. A fresh evocation of the principle and practice of personal responsibility can revivify our society and help to stem the seemingly inexorable march toward the automation of human beings and the steady loss of that freedom which is man's distinctive attribute. It will cure the mental lethargy and inertia which permit organizations to usurp, mainly by default, the rights of their members. It will stimulate a self-reliance which will automatically restore the balance between freedom and security. It will reject unwarranted pressure from groups that seek unjustly to aggrandize their power and will restrict them to their lawful ends. It will see in all business ventures of whatever size a means of serving others as well as self. It will have an immediate effect in every sphere of life—in the home, in the office, as well as in the workshop, in the factory, in our schools, in our cultural groups.

Individual Responsibility

20. An effective response to a call for personal responsibility need not wait for a mass movement. The response belongs to the individual person, as our Holy Father indicated:

> Fully conscious of what is at stake, moved by his apostolic zeal, he then makes a personal engagement with these communities that surround him, the result of a free and justified choice of careful thought about himself, his destiny, and the world (Letter of July 12, 1960, to "Semaine Sociale" in Grenoble).

Such a response by a representative number, given only in the silent sanctuary of the heart, will begin to have its leavening effect. Our appeal for action is made directly to our Catholic fellow citizens, but it reaches out also to all Americans who face the same problems as ourselves.

21. Before it is too late, we must revive in our midst and present to the world the ideals that have been the real source of national greatness. For America will fulfill its destiny when we have achieved that spiritual maturity, described by Pope Pius XII, as men,

> established in their inviolable integrity as images of God; men proud of their personal dignity and of their wholesome freedom; men justly jealous of their equality with their fellow creatures in all that concerns the most intimate depths of human dignity; men solidly attached to their land and their tradition (Pope Pius XII, February 20, 1946).

Signed by members of the Administrative Board, National Catholic Welfare Conference, in the name of the bishops of the United States

Francis Cardinal Spellman, Archbishop of New York

James Francis Cardinal McIntyre, Archbishop of Los Angeles

Richard Cardinal Cushing, Archbishop of Boston

Aloisius Cardinal Muench, Roman Curia

Albert Cardinal Meyer, Archbishop of Chicago

Karl J. Alter, Archbishop of Cincinnati, Chairman

Joseph E. Ritter, Archbishop of St. Louis

Patrick A. O'Boyle, Archbishop of Washington

Leo Binz, Archbishop of Dubuque

William O. Brady, Archbishop of St. Paul

Joseph M. Gilmore, Bishop of Helena

Joseph T. McGucken, Bishop of Sacramento

Lawrence J. Shehan, Bishop of Bridgeport

Allen J. Babcock, Bishop of Grand Rapids

Albert R. Zuroweste, Bishop of Belleville

Unchanging Duty in a Changing World

*A Statement Issued by the Catholic Bishops of
the United States*

November 19, 1961

1. Few nations of the world can look back on their historic origins with such justifiable pride as the United States. That pride, in large measure, finds its justification in the high moral principles which guided our Founding Fathers in laying the foundations of our government and in launching this nation on its history. Our first legal documents, the Declaration of Independence and the Constitution with its first ten amendments, marked us from the beginning as a nation committed to the principles of the moral law.

2. Those principles and the religious beliefs that underlie them continued to guide our people in their national development. At a time when our country was emerging from infancy into vigorous youth, De Tocqueville, in his still widely read *Democracy in America*, said:

> Religion in America takes no direct part in the government of society, but it must be regarded as the first of their political institutions. I do not know whether all Americans have a sincere faith in their religion—but I am certain that they hold it to be an indispensable to the maintenance of republican institutions.[1]

Later at the end of the nineteenth century when our country was entering upon its maturity, another European observer, James Bryce, still could write:

> Religion and conscience have been a constantly active force in the American Commonwealth . . . not indeed strong enough to avert many moral and political evils, yet at the worst times inspiring a minority with a courage and ardor by which moral and political evils have been held at bay and, in the long run, overcome.[2]

In the present century it was not without a sense of moral duty that the United States became an arsenal of defense against totalitarian aggression, a storehouse to feed the hungry and starving world, a Samaritan helping defeated enemy nations to rehabilitate themselves

---

[1]De Tocqueville: *Democracy in America*, Vintage Books, Vol. I, p. 310.
[2]James Bryce: *The American Commonwealth*, Macmillan Company, Third Ed., Vol. II, p. 599.

in peace. The history of our country has been generally infused with an ideal based on moral principles.

Moral Laxity

3.   The time has come to confess, however, that our national ideal no longer rests upon a foundation of broad and solid popular morality. Ignorance of moral principles and the rejection of the very notion of morality are on the rise today and threaten to undermine our nation and its most sacred traditions. The evidences of our moral decline are everywhere to be seen: in the alarming increase in crime, particularly among the young; in the sensational treatment of violence and sexuality in literature, on the stage, screen, and television; in the disclosures of greed and cynicism in government, labor, and business; in the stubborn continuance of race prejudice and injustice; in the multiplication of divorce and in the rapid disintegration of the family; in a harsh and pagan disregard of the sacredness of human life concealed under the mantle of science.

4.   This present moral deterioration cannot be interpreted as a mere temporary relaxation of standards which will be followed by the sort of moral reform past experience would lead us to expect. The conditions we face are unique; for them, the past gives neither precedent nor guide. Many men are questioning and often denying the objective distinction between good and evil and the ability of human reason to know with certainty what is right and wrong. They are cutting themselves off completely from moral traditions. For the first time in history they find themselves without a moral law to break.

5.   The reasons for this moral revolution can be ascertained at least in part. Just as the high morality of our early history found its strength in religion, so now the rejection of morality finds its most basic cause in the denial of God. Here, too, is something quite new. In the past there have always been men who for various reasons have denied the existence of God. But the present atheism is different. Now not only do many act and live as if there were no God to Whom they are responsible, but a steadily increasing number—some individuals of great influence—proclaim the nonexistence of God to be a scientifically established fact. The consequences of such an attitude are inescapable. If there is no God, then the old morality based on God is not valid. The whole of human life has to be reorganized on a new basis. Many modern men find themselves without God and religion, on a lonely eminence of their own making, left to create their own moral values, forced to determine for themselves what is good and evil, right and wrong.

6.   In their newly proclaimed independence, modern men have tended to place their main reliance on physical science. While the enemies of religion and morality have attempted to make science the principal

weapon of their attack, actually science itself has no part in this warfare. "Science," says one of its most eminent scholars, Dr. Vannevar Bush, "does not exclude faith . . . science does not teach a harsh materialism. It does not teach anything beyond its boundaries and those boundaries have been severely limited by science itself."[3] But many who have taken science as their creed and their cult do not share the humility of the scientist. With invincible self-assurance and with an air of unchallenged authority, they teach a scientism that denies God and makes sport of the moral law. From positions many of them occupy in schools and universities, in literature and journalism, with all the modern media of communication at their command, they succeed in impressing their doctrine on great numbers of misled minds.

7.   Toward the present moral decline, the modern media have done more than supply instruments for the spread of unbelief and moral revolt. Although the communications industry through many sincere and admirable leaders has made valuable contributions to human welfare, yet it has also inflicted on the modern world a pernicious cult of the "image." Submerged beneath waves of publicity from "image-makers" and "hidden persuaders," modern man tends to become a victim of the image. Whether a thing is true is less important than the impression it creates. Man's moral focus is distorted. For nations as well as individuals the all-important thing is the image that is projected on the minds of others. The rosy deception is rated good if it succeeds—in selling more products, in winning more votes, in convincing more taxpayers.

Education and Morality

8.   Popular education also bears a measure of responsibility for the decline and rejection of moral principles. At first, there was no intention of excluding either religion or morality from the common tax-supported school. But the diversity of our religious patterns and the rising pressure of secularism have produced the school without religion, and it was idle to suppose that this school could long inculcate in American youth moral convictions which would be firmly held. The result is that our society is now faced with great numbers of young people almost completely devoid of religious belief and moral guidance—young people who are causing increasing concern at every level of the community and in all parts of our country.

9.   Beneath these present trends and pervading all modern society has been the influence of secularism—the banishment of God from public and private life and the enthronement of human nature in His

[3]Vannevar Bush: *Modern Arms and Free Men*, p. 78.

244 Pastoral Letters, 1941–1961

place. Born in the "Enlightenment" of the eighteenth century, deriving its great impetus from the French Revolution, adopted and fostered by nineteenth century liberalism, it became and still remains the principal characteristic of modern society. Under its influence, men may not perhaps deny God; on the formal occasions, they may even mention His name. In practice, however, they simply ignore His existence. They do not openly reject moral principles; they may even pay them lip service. But they disregard them or reduce them to hazy generalities. In general, the only sanctions they recognize are those supplied by individual taste, public opinion, and the power of the state.

10. The result of these trends has been, even among those who have not rejected moral principles, a widespread moral apathy which touches practically every group: citizens who are not concerned enough to exercise the right to vote; elected officials who are interested only in their "public image," their personal power; union members, labor leaders, and industrialists who place their selfish interests above national security and the common good. Harmful as these weaknesses are, our acknowledgement of them can give no real comfort to our enemies. It is the American tradition to look at ourselves, to examine our conscience, to reappraise our moral position. In a dictatorship this is impossible. In a democracy it is a constant necessity.

11. Both apathy and amorality certainly run counter to the American tradition. Because we have been a moral people, it has been characteristic of Americans ultimately to be guided by moral considerations and, even in periods of laxity, to respond vigorously to moral appeals. Our best traditions have been based on moral principles and ideals. We must remain true to them. We of the household of the faith have a special obligation to promote them. What, then, are our particular duties in the face of present conditions?

12. In today's world, our most obvious duty is to speak out, to make open profession of religious beliefs and moral convictions, to reaffirm morality as the foundation of our nation's past greatness and of its future aspirations. We must indeed be prepared to demonstrate the falseness of the claims of scientism, the hollowness and futility of the cult of the image, the corrosive effect of secularism on both the individual and society. Especially we must recognize and affirm the essential place of religion and morality in the formation of the human personality if we are to survive as a moral people. But over and above all this, the temper of the times demands that, by our words and acts, we bear personal witness to the existence of moral principles grounded on religious belief. In a world in which individual obligation is being denied, we must show the reality of personal responsibility—transcendent responsibility to God for all acts and attitudes, personal accountability for self, for family, for community, for nation. In particular, our teaching, our influence, and our conduct must show that the soundness of society depends on the principles of family life: the unity and sanctity of marriage, parental duty and authority, filial reverence and obedience.

13. As God-fearing people we must not only bear witness to those principles governing personal and family life; we must also give testimony to the reality and importance of those moral principles which govern man's wider social relationships. Pope John has recently reminded all Catholics of this obligation. "The social teaching proclaimed by the Church," he tells us, "cannot be separated from her traditional teaching regarding man's life." The norms of justice contained in the great social encyclicals of the popes during the past seventy years are vital moral principles, just as are the principles of individual morality. We have the duty to know these principles through study and reading, through reflection and prayer. Nor can these principles be allowed to lie idle. "Social norms of whatever kind," says Our Holy Father, "are not only to be explained but also applied. This is especially true of the Church's teaching on social matters, which has truth as its guide, justice as its end, and love as its driving force."[4] The moral influence of these social principles must be made to permeate all of society and its institutions. The laborer must bring them to his union meetings; the industrialist, to the business world; the teacher, to his class; the parent, to his home—each to the sphere of life in which he moves. Only in this way will each religious person become involved with his fellow citizens in constructing a "public philosophy" based on a frank acceptance of God and the moral law.

14. In rebuilding a sound religious and moral foundation for America, a special difficulty arises from the varied character of our society. Since we are a people of many religious beliefs, of diverse racial and national origins, there will undoubtedly always be tensions and some misunderstandings. But these differences will not constitute insurmountable barriers to national peace and cooperation if we are faithful to the moral principles which are the foundation of our traditions— particularly if we complement justice with charity. This is true of the racial issue which continues to rise and plague our country; it is true of other issues which divide us.

Our Moral Responsibility

15. Our moral responsibility, however, transcends the limited circle of our individual lives and the confining borders of our country. Our interests and our obligations are worldwide—indeed our horizons are no longer confined to this earth, they have been projected into the uncharted seas of space. In its earlier years, our nation—young in its

---

[4]*Mater et Magistra*, NCWC edition, Nos. 222 and 226.

freedom and confident in the nobility of its democratic ideals—stood as an inspiration to all those who suffered in bondage and hoped for freedom. Country after country, encouraged by the success of our endeavors, threw off their shackles and asserted their independence. Millions flocked to our shores as to the haven of freedom and hope. Now, in our more mature years, the newer nations and some of the older impoverished ones have looked to us for material help and for the most part they have received from us a ready response. But they— particularly the emerging peoples—have needs that go deeper than the requirements for mere material help. They want more positive evidence of our understanding. They seek a recognition of their dignity, both individual and national. They crave the knowledge and technical skill which will enable them to help themselves. They need the vision which comes from faith, and the encouragement that comes from hope. They must have spiritual ideals and spiritual leadership. Our own freedom sprang in large measure from religious and moral sources. We must inspire these nations wherever possible to build on a religious and moral foundation if we are to contribute significantly to the achievement of their national aspirations. Meanwhile, we must be willing to open our hearts and our homes to those who come to our shores; to make room for them in our schools and universities; even to send our own sons to their lands to assist them. All these things we must do, not as mere countermoves against Communism, but for their essential rightness, as expressions of our highest principles: love of God and love of neighbor.

16. Because we have so often faltered in our course and because the Communist nations have profited by our mistakes to inspire false ideals and to awaken glittering but barren hopes, we must not be discouraged, imagining that our hour of opportunity has passed. It has not passed. The hour of greatest opportunity is striking now, as the forces of freedom and of tyranny gird for a decision. America's strength, bestowed by Divine Providence, has been given for this hour—that freedom may not fail. The exercise of our national strength, in order to achieve its true purpose, must be guided by those principles on which our strength was built. We must apply those principles in both national and international affairs. We shall be worthy of world leadership only if we are willing to pledge "our lives, our fortunes, and our sacred honor" in behalf of the right.

17. At present, when America is beset by so many frustrations, when there are so many temptations to despair, all who believe in God have the special duty of keeping alive within their own hearts and within the hearts of all free men a true and undying hope. Our hope will not be for a utopia of material well-being, although we do look forward to a world in which science and technology will be used to the full in eliminating needless poverty, hunger, and disease. Nor do we expect a world in which all will be morally and socially perfect. Our hope is for a world in which men, imperfect though they be, will accept the reign of God—a world in which the principles of the natural law and of the Christian dispensation will be recognized as the norm of moral judgment and the basis of the social order. Should such an order take hold on the world of today, there is not a single problem, no matter what its magnitude, which would not admit of a reasonable and, on the whole, a satisfactory solution.

18. Above all, the Christian today must have a profound sense of mission, which will cause him to bear witness to his religious faith and his moral convictions as the early Christians did—by deed and affirmation, even by death. Such was St. Paul's program of action; such, too, was St. Augustine's. Like Paul, we face a world largely paganized. Like Augustine, we see the encroachment of barbarism. Like both, we must be dauntless in proclaiming Christ.

19. In this way, we shall be true to our Christian duty in preserving God's moral order as man's standard of action. Only in this way shall we preserve the religious and moral traditions in which our country was born, and without which our country cannot survive.

Signed by members of the Administrative Board, National Catholic Welfare Conference, in the name of the bishops of the United States

Francis Cardinal Spellman, Archbishop of New York

James Francis Cardinal McIntyre, Archbishop of Los Angeles

Richard Cardinal Cushing, Archbishop of Boston

Aloisius Cardinal Muench, member of the Vatican Administrative Staff

Albert Cardinal Meyer, Archbishop of Chicago

Joseph Cardinal Ritter, Archbishop of St. Louis

Archbishop Karl J. Alter, of Cincinnati, Chairman

Archbishop John F. Dearden, of Detroit

Archbishop William E. Cousins, of Milwaukee

Coadjutor Archbishop Lawrence J. Shehan, of Baltimore

Bishop Emmet M. Walsh, of Youngstown, Ohio

Bishop Joseph M. Gilmore, of Helena, Mont.

Bishop Joseph T. McGucken, of Sacramento, Calif.

Bishop Allen J. Babcock, of Grand Rapids, Mich.

Bishop Albert R. Zuroweste, of Belleville, Ill.

Appendix

Chronological Table of Important Events in the History of the Church in the United States from 1941 to 1961

1941: Archbishop Mooney of Detroit in the name of the American hierarchy pledged to President Roosevelt all "the spiritual forces at our command to secure our God-given blessings of freedom." The New York *Catholic Worker* sponsored a Catholic conscientious objector camp at Stoddard, New Hampshire. Robert E. Lucey, outspoken defender of labor unions and the CIO, became archbishop of San Antonio.

1942: The War Relief Services of the NCWC was established.

1944: William Cardinal O'Connell of Boston died. President Franklin Roosevelt signed "G.I. Bill of Rights," which opened the doors of college to thousands of veterans.

1945: Four American churchmen named to College of Cardinals.

1947: Supreme Court decision in *Everson v. Board of Education*, which upheld a New Jersey statute authorizing municipalities to reimburse parents for costs in using regular bus lines to transport children to nonpublic schools, made constitutional history.

1948: Protestants and Other Americans for Separation of Church and State (POAU) formed with the aim of opposing federal aid to private religious schools. In *McCollum v. Board of Education*, Supreme Court disallowed religious education in public school buildings. Fulton Sheen's *Communism and the Conscience of the West* published. Thomas Merton's *The Seven Storey Mountain* introduced many Americans to an exceptional religious writer.

1949: Paul Blanshard's anti-Catholic volume, *American Freedom and Catholic Power*, published.

1950: Famed radio orator and TV personality, Fulton J. Sheen, later archbishop, became the national director of the Society for Propagation of the Faith.

1951: Dennis Cardinal Dougherty, Archbishop of Philadelphia, and senior Cardinal of the United States, died. *Orate Fratres*, a leading liturgical periodical, became *Worship*. The Supreme Court in *Zorach v. Clauson* upheld "released-time" religious education programs outside public school buildings. President Truman nominated General Mark Clark as American ambassador to Vatican City; nomination withdrawn at Clark's request because of widespread opposition to any American representation at Vatican City.

1953: Archbishop James McIntyre of Los Angeles named a cardinal.

1955: Death of Mother Katherine Drexel, whose cause for canonization has been introduced. Catholic Relief Services organized and in its first twenty years distributed more than $1.25 billion in relief supplies throughout the world.

1956: Holy See erected the new Dioceses of Atlanta, Jefferson City, and Springfield-Cape Girardeau to bring the total dioceses in United States to 134. Thomas E. Murray of the Atomic Energy Commission denounced the "totalization of war."

1957: Highest award of Department of Health, Education and Welfare presented to Daughters of Charity of Saint Vincent de Paul "for devoted services to the patients . . . and contributions to the success of the unique program at this hospital" (United States Public Health Service Hospital, Carvil, Louisiana, for lepers); Joseph Harris became first Negro elected President of the National Federation of Catholic College Students.

1958: Cardinal Samuel Stritch, Archbishop of Chicago, named Pro-Prefect of Congregation de Propaganda Fide; Christopher Dawson named first occupant of the Chauncey Stillman Chair of Roman Catholic Studies in the Divinity School of Harvard. Archbishop Richard Cushing of Boston and Archbishop John O'Hara of Philadelphia named cardinals.

1959: Aloisius Muench, Apostolic Nuncio to Germany, became an American cardinal in the Roman Curia; Catholics became the largest religious group in the United States Congress with twelve senators and ninety-one representatives, followed by Methodists with ninety-one in Congress. The number of students in Catholic elementary and Catholic high schools more than doubled in the last decade to over 5,600,000. Eleven percent of the school population was in private schools; 90 percent of them Catholic schools. Archbishop Albert Meyer of Chicago named cardinal.

1960: John F. Kennedy became the first Catholic elected to the presidency. Catholic population had doubled to forty-two million members from twenty-one million in 1940.

1961: Archbishop Joseph Ritter of St. Louis named a cardinal.

Growth of the Church in the United States

1941–1950[1]

Categories	1941	1950
Population	22,556,242	27,766,141
Dioceses	120	125
Priests	36,580	42,790
Seminarians	17,545	25,622
Parishes	18,985	15,292

1951–1961[1]

Categories	1951	1961
Population	28,634,878	42,104,899
Dioceses	125	140
Priests	43,889	54,682
Seminarians	28,798	41,871
Parishes	15,533	16,996

[1]These statistics are taken from the 1942, 1951, 1952, and 1962 editions of *The Official Catholic Directory* published by P. J. Kenedy and Sons, New York, N.Y. The Catholic population figures for these and succeeding years are most likely too low. Cf. George A. Kelly and Thomas Coogan, "What Is Our Real Catholic Population?" *American Ecclesiastical Review*, CX (May 1944), 367-377.

Organization and Purpose of NCCB/USCC

The National Conference of Catholic Bishops (NCCB) and the United States Catholic Conference (USCC) are the organizations of the American Catholic hierarchy. Through these distinct but closely related organizations—one a canonical entity, the other a civil corporation—the bishops fulfill their responsibilities of leadership and service to Church and nation.

The membership of NCCB consists in approximately 375 Catholic bishops of the United States. NCCB enables the bishops to exchange ideas and information, deliberate on the Church's broad concerns, and respond as a body. The conference functions through a general assembly, an administrative committee of 48 members, several executive-level committees, and some 40 standing and ad hoc committees. NCCB committees deal with pastoral matters important to the Church as a whole.

The United States Catholic Conference is the public policy agency of the Catholic bishops of America. Unlike NCCB, whose members are bishops exclusively, USCC's policy-making structures include priests, religious, and lay people. USCC shares several structures with NCCB. Its Administrative Board is the same body as NCCB's Administrative Committee, and the same executive-level committees serve both conferences. The General Secretariat in Washington, D.C., handles both NCCB and USCC business. Indeed, while most staff are assigned to one conference or the other, a significant number work for NCCB/USCC. The USCC provides an organizational structure and the resources needed to ensure coordination, cooperation, and assistance in the public, educational, and social concerns of the Church at the national or interdiocesan level.

Index

O'Hara, John F. (cardinal), 14, 133
Opportunity, equality of
opportunity, 15
Orate Fratres. see *Worship.*
"Oregon Case" (Pierce vs. Society
of Sisters, 268 U.S. 510), 118,
181
Organizations, 235, 237, 239
Orphans, 99
"Outlaw Nations" (phrase), 59
"Over-populated" (word), 223
Ownership. see Property rights.

Paganism, 5, 34, 47, 120
Parents and children, 4, 47, 83, 93,
94: *The Child: Citizen of Two
Worlds,* 97-105; *The Christian
Family,* 91-92, 93; displaced
persons, 70; *God's Law: The
Measure of Man's Conduct,* 142-
43; *Private and Church-Related
Schools in American Education,*
181-82; *Religion: Our Most Vital
National Asset,* 153; *Statement on
Censorship,* 197; *Statement on
Man's Dignity,* 166
Parishes, "Golden Age of American
Catholicism," 7
Parochial schools. see Catholic
schools.
Pastoral letters, 7, 134-35
Pathfinder (magazine), 111
Paul, Saint, apostle, 5, 159, 169,
209-10, 247
"Peace" (word), 214
Peace and Unity: The Hope of Mankind
(1956), 121, 186-89
Peace and war, 3, 11, 15, 16, 22, 28,
33, 38, 39-40, 42-43, 44-49, 56-61,
67-73, 80, 95, 113, 186-89, 214-20
Peace treaties, 69
Pearl Harbor attack (1941), 11
Pearson, Drew, 116
Peron, Juan Domingo, 119
Persecution: displaced persons, 70;
of Jews, 41; of religion, 14, 31-
32, 52, 64, 107, 119, 125;
*Persecution behind the Iron
Curtain,* 2-3, 146-47; *Religious
Persecution and Prayer Plan,* 3,
185; *Statement on Persecuted
Peoples* (1956), 190-91; *Statement
on Persecuted Peoples* (1957), 199;
Statement on Secularism, 79. see
also Repression.

Persecution behind the Iron Curtain
(1952), 2-3, 146-47
Persecution in Poland (1953), 160
Personal responsibility, 4, 134, 135,
234-40
Personality, 164
Pessimism, 148
Peter, Saint, pope, 158, 162-63, 185
Peter's Chains (1953), 113, 125, 161-
63
Philosophy, 162. see also Social
Philosophy.
Philosophy of education, 24, 57, 77
Piasecki, Boleslaw, 120
Pittsburgh Press (newspaper), 111
Pius IX, Pope, 11, 29
Pius XI, Pope, 12, 28, 29, 34, 54,
84, 238-39
Pius XII, Pope, 1, 11, 12, 14, 29, 30,
30-31, 41, 42, 54, 113, 114, 127,
163, 186, 187, 188, 194-95, 202-3,
204, 213, 227, 236, 238, 239-40
Planned parenthood. see
Contraception.
Planned Parenthood Association,
128, 223
Planning, 205
A Plea for Justice (1954), 3, 114-15,
178
Plenary Councils of Baltimore, 183
Pluralism, 126, 129-30, 153, 181,
183, 210
POAU. see Protestants and Other
Americans United.
Poland, 14, 18, 41, 52, 63, 113, 120,
146, 160
Police state. see Totalitarianism.
Politics and religion, 111, 143, 167
Poor, the poor. see Poverty.
Popes and papacy, 15, 111, 213
Population. see Transfer of
populations.
"Population explosion" (phrase),
221, 223
Potsdam Conferences (1945), 18
Poverty, 129, 168: *Between War and
Peace,* 64-65; Catholic Relief
Services, 21-22; *The Christian
Family,* 94; displaced persons,
70-72; *Statement on Freedom and
Peace,* 216, 217; *World Refugee
Year and Migration,* 226, 228, 230
Power politics, 57, 63
Prayer: *The Child: Citizen of Two
Worlds,* 98; *God's Law: The*

About the Editor

Reverend Hugh J. Nolan, Professor Emeritus of Immaculata College, was ordained a priest of the Archdiocese of Philadelphia in 1941 and procured his doctorate in American Church History with distinction in 1944. He established the Master's Program in American Church History at St. Paul Seminary, St. Paul, Minnesota and has taught at La Salle, Rosemont, and Cabrini colleges, Villanova University, and The Catholic University of America. He was head of the Theology Department at Immaculata College for twenty-one years and was elected a member of the Academy of American Franciscan History.

Father Nolan is the author of *Francis Patrick Kenrick, Third Bishop of Philadelphia, 1830–1851*. He edited the *Pastoral Letters of the American Hierarchy, 1792–1970* and contributed to the *New Catholic Encyclopedia*, *Minnesota History*, *America*, *Ave Maria*, and the *Catholic Historical Review*. He was Editor in Chief of the *Records of the American Catholic Historical Society* for twelve years and for ten years a writer of editorials for Philadelphia's diocesan newspaper, *The Catholic Standard and Times*. He wrote "Francis Patrick Kenrick, 1830–1851" and "Dennis Cardinal Dougherty, 1918–1951" for the recent *History of the Archdiocese of Philadelphia*. Father Nolan is presently pastor of St. Isaac Jogues Parish, Valley Forge, Pennsylvania.

Credits

Design: Mack Rowe Visual Communications, Ltd.; Alexandria, Va.

Cover Photo: Detail of a bishop's crosier from the ruins of the Cistercian Abbey, Boyle, County Roscommon, Ireland by Dan Juday

Production

Typeface: Palatino and Palatino Semi-bold

Typography: VIP Systems, Inc.; Alexandria, Va.

Printing: Banta Company; Harrisonburg, Va.